Reconstructing American Education

Reconstructing American Education

MICHAEL B. KATZ

Harvard University Press
Cambridge, Massachusetts
and London, England

Library of Congress Cataloging-in-Publication Data

Katz, Michael B.
  Reconstructing American education.

  Includes index.
   1. Education—United States—History.   2. Education,
Urban—United States—History.   3. Educational sociology
—United States.   I. Title.
LA212.K275   1987   370'.973   87–196
ISBN 0–674–75092–6 (alk. paper) (cloth)
ISBN 0–674–75093–4 (paper)

For David Tyack

Acknowledgments

The chapters in this book draw on material formulated during the last twenty years. To acknowledge all the people who contributed to them would require a very long list of colleagues, students, and friends. I have been unusually fortunate with all three, and many of them will recognize their contributions here. Others will be reminded of how stubbornly I resisted their advice, and many, I suspect, will not realize how profoundly they have helped and influenced me. For all this stimulation and counsel I shall always remain grateful. One colleague and friend, however, should be singled out. David Tyack not only has been generous with his time, insight, and friendship for many years. He also persuaded me to try to transform the diverse essays with which I began this project into a book, and he offered excellent advice about how to do it.

Michael Aronson and Maria Ascher of Harvard University Press were helpful and supportive in the conception and revision of the book. As always, my friends, neighbors, and family at Clioquossia, in Oquossoc, Maine, where this manuscript was revised, edited, and shaped, made sure my summer was enjoyable as well as productive.

Earlier versions of the following chapters appeared in my book *Class, Bureaucracy, and Schools* (Praeger); in *Eductional Theory, Harvard Educational Review, Harvard Graduate School of Education Bulletin, History of Education Quarterly,* and *Reviews in*

American History; and in William A. W. Neilson and Chad Gaffield, eds., *Universities in Crisis: A Mediaeval Institution in the Twenty-first Century* (Institute for Research on Public Policy). I thank the editors of these publications for permission to use the material.

Contents

	Introduction	1
1.	The Origins of Public Education	5
2.	Alternative Models for American Education	24
3.	How Urban School Systems Became Bureaucracies: The Boston Case, 1850–1884	58
4.	History and Reform	111
5.	The Politics of Educational History	136
6.	The Moral Crisis of the University	160
	Notes	185
	Index	209

Reconstructing American Education

Introduction

This book is about reconstructing American education in three senses. The first is as history: how did American education take shape? The second is as reform: what can a historian say about recent criticisms and proposals for improvement? The third is as historiography: what drives the politics of educational history? I show how the reconstruction of America's educational past can be used as a framework for thinking about the reconstruction of its present and argue that contemporary concepts, such as public education, modern organizational forms, especially bureaucracy, and institutional structures such as the multiversity originated as choices among alternative solutions to problems of public policy. They reflected circumstances at the time of their origin and the priorities of their founders. Nonetheless, the reification of these historical products has become one of the great obstacles to change. For it casts them as inexorable, transcending history, even natural, and, as a result, it limits the terms of debate. However, these historical products are neither inevitable nor immutable. They may no longer even be appropriate.

The role of history in interpreting the present, the understanding of history as a choice among alternative possibilities, and the realization of the contingent nature of ideas and institutions are the three central themes of this book. Others also are important. One, implicit in my argument about alternatives, is that organizational structures such as educational bureaucracy are not neutral shells in which an almost unlimited range of values can find expression. To the contrary: their structural details and operational rules reflect priorities, limit possibilities, and shape outcomes.

This book is also about the relations among democracy, capitalism, and bureaucracy. It sets the origins of education in the spread of capitalism and the formation of a working class as well as in the emergence of a political system reflecting republican ideas and democratic practices. It locates bureaucracy in the responses to a series of new social and institutional problems; it sees bureaucracy as guided by some of the priorities of both capitalism and democracy and, ironically, as ultimately at war with the latter.

These themes raise a variety of questions which are as much ethical and political as practical. How do we assess the relative importance of efficiency and responsiveness in institutions? Whom do we really want institutions to serve? If institutions and policies contradict fundamental political principles, are we prepared to change them? Why have some reform strategies failed consistently? How do we discard the intellectual blinders that have resulted from the reification of concepts and forms? On what models should institutions be based? Are we prepared to sanction the further assimilation of schools and universities to the marketplace and the state?

Chapter 1 examines the contexts in which public educational systems emerged and the purposes they were supposed to serve. The original version, written some years ago as a presidential address to the History of Education Society, has been substantially revised to reflect my current thinking and to take account of the recent important scholarship on the formation of a working class in antebellum America and the role of republican ideas and democratic political institutions in the same period.

Chapter 2 (also extensively revised since its earlier publication) continues the discussion of the origins of public education by delineating the four major models of institutional development that coexisted early in the nineteenth century. It explores the different priorities of each and the link between organizations and social structure.

The model that triumphed I call incipient bureaucracy. Chapter 3 traces bureaucracy from its beginnings through its full realization in one school system, Boston, between 1850 and 1884. It shows in detail how bureaucracy developed as a series of responses to specific problems and how its victory represented its grafting onto the career aspirations of educators. The story also highlights some of the essential internal politics of large educational systems and their implications for reform.

I often have been asked about the implications of educational history for contemporary reform. Chapter 4 is one answer. It relates the historical themes of Chapters 1–3 to current questions of educational politics and reform. Roughly chronological in order, the chapter spans the transition from equity to excellence as a focus of educational change.

Historians' attempts to reconstruct the educational past, including my own, have not been universally popular. Some educators closely identified with public schools have been defensive about criticisms, either implied or explicit. Others, with different agendas, have objected to the politics of much recent writing on educational history. Their counterattack took two forms. One was a polemical, distorted, ad hominem assault; the other was a serious attempt to prove the new histories wrong. Chapter 5 discusses the recent politics of writing about educational history. It shows how the new conservative history tries to minimize the importance of social class in America's past and how it tries to cover its own politics with an illusory mantle of objectivity.

Although Chapters 1–5 focus on public elementary and secondary education, their most important themes apply to higher education as well. Higher education retained the institutional model of corporate voluntarism, which was rejected by public education in the antebellum period. In the late nineteenth and early twentieth centuries, university expansion grafted bureaucracy onto corporate voluntarism; the form that emerged was the multiversity. Without a core of consistent principles, the multiversity has been unable to resolve the great moral issues confronting it in recent decades. Instead, it drifts, pulled by the tensions between democracy and bureaucracy, community and marketplace. Increasingly, bureaucracy and the market are winning. Chapter 6, which recounts this story, was occasioned by a searing incident that forced me to try to account for the contradictions in modern universities: the modification of their bureaucratic structure by faculty decision making, the limitation of their assimilation to the marketplace by the existence of tenure, their combination of intellectual strength and freedom with moral flabbiness. The corruption of both the universities and the schools leaves me convinced that there are no tasks as urgent as defining the limits of a market model for institutions and social policy and of reasserting the importance of moral criteria in our public and institutional life.

1

The Origins of
Public Education

Starting in the 1960s, a modest revolution took place in historical writing about education. Historians rejected both the metaphor and the method that had characterized most reconstructions of the educational past. The method had divorced inquiry into the development of educational practices and institutions from the mainstream of historical scholarship and left it narrow, antiquated, and uninteresting. The metaphor had portrayed education as a flower of democracy planted in a rich loam that its seeds replenished.[1]

The recent historians of education have incorporated current trends in historical scholarship to reconstruct the past, and their findings are largely critical. Despite major differences, all share the view ascribed by Hayden White to the "exponents of historical realism," namely that the historian's task is "less to remind men of their obligation to the past than to force upon them an awareness of how the past could be used to effect an ethically responsible transition from present to future." By contrast, the old metaphor and its supporters "remind men of their obligation to the past" rather than attempting to liberate them for a new educational future.[2]

The critical historians of education have dealt a devastating blow to the form in which the old metaphor was cast: a simple narrative of the triumph of benevolence and democracy can no longer be offered or taken seriously by any scholar even marginally aware of their work. Nonetheless, continuing disagreement among historians of education and the segmental nature of much of their work—such as the necessary concentration on detailed case studies—has thwarted the emergence of a new and satisfying synthesis. This chapter outlines the results of recent research on the origins of public education: why people established systems of public education, including the purposes they hoped such systems would serve. Chapters 3 and 4 address two major related questions: how the systems were established, and what results these efforts had.

The Contexts of Public Education

At the outset it is important to clarify exactly what I wish to explain: the emergence of *systems* of public education. Here the word *systems* is crucial. For schools in the nineteenth century were not unusual or novel creations, and they customarily received some public support, although in most places the line between public and private lacked even the rough precision it acquired later in the century. But although schools existed and frequently received some public support, the seventeenth, eighteenth, and early nineteenth centuries cannot be considered true progenitors of the school systems we know today. For by the latter part of the nineteenth century the organization, scope, and role of schooling had been transformed. In place of a few casual schools dotted about town and country, in most cities there existed true educational systems: carefully articulated, age graded, hierarchically structured groupings of schools, primarily free and often compulsory, administered by full-time experts and progressively taught by specially trained staff. No longer casual adjuncts to the home or apprenticeship, schools had become formal institutions designed to play a critical role in the socialization of the young, the maintenance of social order, and the promotion of economic development. Within forty or fifty years a new social institution had been invented, and it is this startling and momentous development that we must seek to understand.[3]

The origins of public educational systems coincided with five critical developments that reshaped American society during the first three quarters of the nineteenth century: the emergence of a democratic politics; industrialization, urbanization, and the formation of a working class; the state's assumption of direct responsibility for some aspects of social welfare; the invention of institutions as means for solving social problems; and the redefinition of family.

In the first half of the nineteenth century a distinctive form of democratic politics emerged in America. Four of its features are especially important: early universal white male suffrage; the formation of a party system through which political activity was channeled; the mobilization of political activity in cities by local machines; and widespread participation in politics, especially evident in high rates of voter turnout. American public education assumed its unique form partly because of the coincidence of its birth with the origins of this system of democratic politics.[4]

In the same period, urbanization, industrialization, and immigration reshaped the economy and society. One consequence was the formation of a working class. The pace and timing of social development varied, of course, from region to region, but everywhere a close temporal connection existed between social development and the creation of public educational systems. The date of the opening of the first high school provides a rough but convenient index of educational development, which, across the country, retained a strong association with social and economic complexity.[5] Although much remains to be explained about the connection between the creation of public education and the transformation of social and economic relations, the *temporal* association between them is clear and critical.

Systems of public education did not constitute the sole thrust of governments into the area of social welfare during the early and mid-nineteenth century. In these years the state governments (and most others in the Western world) generally began to exchange their haphazard and minimal concern with social problems for a systematic approach to questions of welfare. At the start of the period problems of poverty, public health, crime, insanity, disease, and the condition of labor remained more or less untended, subject to ancient legislation, custom, sporadic regulation, and public and private charity. By the end of the third quarter of the nineteenth century each had become the subject of public debate, legislative activity, and the supervision of newly created state administrative bodies with full-time, expert staffs.[6]

The state did not extend its role in public welfare without serious opposition. Its activity began at a time when the very distinction between public and private had not emerged clearly, and in this situation the definition of public responsibility remained especially elusive. Usually, voluntary activity preceded state action. Philanthropic associations, most of them composed primarily of women and associated with the spread of evangelical religion, first undertook the alleviation of social distress. In part their efforts reflected the inadequacy of the public apparatus for coping with the increased misery in the growing cities of the late eighteenth and early nineteenth centuries; in part, too, it reflected the belief that social distress represented a temporary, if recurring, problem that charitable activity could alleviate. The activities of voluntary associations, however, usually convinced their members that problems were far more widespread and intractable than they had believed, and voluntarists consequently turned to the public for assistance, first usually in the form of grants, later in the assumption of formal and permanent responsibility.[7]

No very clear models for action, however, existed, and people concerned with social policy debated not only the legitimacy of public activity but also its organizational form. On the issue of education, their disagreements over the nature of public organizations reflected fundamental value conflicts and alternative visions of social development. The shape that modern society eventually assumed may appear inevitable today, but it did not appear at all clear to the people of the time, which is why debates about social institutions and policies aroused so much passion. In fact, four distinct models for the organization of formal education (described in Chapter 2) coexisted and competed in the early and mid-nineteenth century. The one that triumphed can be called incipient bureaucracy. Although its advocates generally supported the extension of a competitive and laissez-faire approach to economic issues, they encouraged a strong regulatory role for the state in the areas of social welfare and morality. Their model organizations were controlled by relatively large bodies responsible to legislatures, financed directly through taxation, and administered by experts. They were, in short, public *institutions* in a novel and dramatic sense.[8]

The victory of incipient bureaucracy reflected a new faith in the power of formal institutions to alleviate social and individual distress, which was a radical departure in social policy. Before the nineteenth century, institutions played a far smaller and much less significant social role: the mentally ill generally lived with other members of the community or in an undifferentiated poorhouse; criminals remained for relatively brief periods in jails awaiting trial and punishment by fine, whipping, or execution; the poor were given outdoor relief or, if they were a nuisance, driven from the community. By the middle or third quarter of the nineteenth century all this had changed. In place of the few, undifferentiated almshouses, jails, and schools there now existed in most cities and states a series of new inventions: mental hospitals, penitentiaries, reformatories, and public schools. Shapers of social policy had embodied in concrete form the notion that rehabilitation, therapy, medical treatment, and education should take place within large, formal, and often residential institutions. In the process, they created the institutional state that governs and regulates our lives today.[9]

Responsible people at the time did see alternatives to an institutional state. In New York, for instance, Charles Loring Brace proposed the shipment of city urchins to the West as an alternative to their institutionalization, and elsewhere opponents and skeptics critically, perceptively, and, in retrospect, in an eerily modern way, pointed to the dangers and limits of institutions.[10]

One of their common arguments centered on families. Both proponents and critics of institutions found in their ideal family a paradigm for social policy. Proponents believed that, rather than supplying an alternative to families, institutions would literally become surrogate families for the mentally ill, the criminal, the delinquent, and the schoolchild. Institutions, according to their sponsors, were supposed to perform their rehabilitative, therapeutic, or educational work precisely through their recreation of a familial environment. The difficulty, as critics astutely pointed out, was that no institution could imitate a real family.[11]

Nonetheless, in the early and mid-nineteenth century both critics and supporters of institutions shared a widespread sense that families were in trouble, though about the exact nature of the difficulty they remained more vague. In fact, they probably mistook change for deterioration. The fragments of historical evidence about families in this period point not to breakdown but to important shifts in domestic structure and relations. Until recently, social theories held that the nuclear family replaced the extended family during industrialization. The work of Peter Laslett and of many later historians has shown that, as it usually was argued, this proposition was false for British, American, and Canadian society. The majority of families—or, to use Laslett's term, co-resident domestic groups—at any time appears to have been nuclear in structure. That is not to say, however, that their role and other aspects of their organization did not change, for they did, and historians have begun to appreciate these more subtle, but real and consequential, alterations. The most dramatic family change during industrialization was, of course, the separation of home and workplace. In both rural and urban areas the gradual separation between place of residence and place of work fundamentally altered the day-to-day pattern of family experience, the relationships among family members, and (sociologists would argue) the very influence of families themselves. The separation of home and workplace formed one part of the process through which the boundaries between families and communities became more sharply drawn. As part of the increased specialization of institutions, families shed their productive functions as well as their role in the treatment of deviance and dependence. (This, of course, is a bald summary statement about a complex, uneven, and lengthy process.) Rather than diminishing in importance, however, families gained stature through their heightened role in the socialization of their children, which earlier had been shared more widely with the community. This tightening and emotional intensification of families fundamentally reshaped the process of growing up.[12]

For centuries it had been customary for parents of various social ranks to send their children away from home to live as surrogate members of another household for several years between puberty and marriage. Young people in this stage of their lives, which I call semiautonomy, exchanged the complete control of their parents for a supervised yet more autonomous situation in another household. Semiautonomy as a phase in the life course virtually disappeared by the third quarter of the nineteenth century. By then (and, of course, the exact timing of the transition varied from region to region with the different pace of economic and social development), young people started to remain in their parents' home after they had found work, staying there roughly until marriage. At the same time, many remained in school much longer, and young men began to enter their fathers' occupations far less frequently. Admittedly, I am foreshortening a complex process to emphasize families' increasingly important and specialized role in the socialization of their children as part of a general tightening of the boundaries between social institutions and between families and community.[13]

Fertility trends highlight the heightened attention people paid to their children. In the United States, marital fertility among native-born whites fell sharply during the first half of the nineteenth century. Large numbers of people began consciously to limit the size of their families. The reasons are controversial. Some have argued that their decision reflected the decline in infant and childhood mortality: women needed to bear fewer children to assure that a reasonable number would survive. At the same time, decreased early childhood mortality gave parents more incentive to invest emotionally in each of their offspring. From a different viewpoint, parents had greater difficulty in providing for their children. As it became necessary to keep children at home and in school, large families became heavy economic burdens to people of middling means. Whatever its explanation, the fertility decline underscores a sharpened concern with shaping and controlling families and implies an intensification of emotional bonds between parent and child. Indeed, as Viviana Zelizer has shown, the late nineteenth and early twentieth centuries were the era of the transition from the economically useful to the economically useless but emotionally priceless child.[14]

Popular ideas about domesticity and the role of women reflected the redefinition of family. The "cult of true womanhood," as it has been called, urged women to create within the home a haven from the harsh world of commerce and a nest in which children could be reared with close attention and affection. Without doubt, the ideal of domesticity justified a not very subtle attempt to keep women at home subservient to their husbands. However, it also elevated the importance of women as the moral guardians and spiritual saviors of an increasingly corrupt and irreligious society. Despite this tension in its meaning, popular ideology reinforced the structural changes in families. In both social thought and reality, families—and I suspect eventually working-class as well as middle-class families—became increasingly private, intense, and sharply defined agencies for the nurture of the young.[15]

One key educational innovation—the feminization of teaching, which happened with remarkable speed around the middle of the nineteenth century—illustrates the complex connections between the history of schools and the contextual factors outlined above. By and large, women took over from men the education of young children in primary schools. As the ideology of domesticity implied, the moral and spiritual role assigned to women not only justified but also mandated their entrance into classrooms as surrogate mothers. If schools, like other contemporary institutions, were to resemble homes, they should be presided over by wise and loving mothers. This shift from men to women in the schoolroom paralleled the shift in primary moral responsibility from husbands to wives in the ideal middle-class home. As men increasingly left home to work, they left the schoolroom as well.[16]

Cultural imperatives were not the only forces pushing women into classrooms. States forced local communities to make schooling more accessible and to lengthen the school year while urban growth and the massive mid-century immigration swelled the number of eligible schoolchildren. The result was a severe strain on local finances. Women provided a ready solution to this problem, because towns paid them about half as much as men, who, in an era of expanding commercial and industrial opportunity, increasingly had before them job prospects more attractive than teaching. By feminizing its teaching force, a town could double its school places or extend the length of the school year and hold its expenses for salary roughly constant.[17]

Paying women half as much as men was a form of exploitation, to be sure, but it did not deter women from seeking jobs as teachers. Surviving contemporary accounts of hiring usually show that many women applicants competed for every job. The reason is not hard to understand. In this period women had essentially only four other major occupational alternatives: domestic service, dressmaking, work in a mill, or prostitution. To many young women, teaching, despite its low wages, must have appeared a welcome and genteel opportunity. The feminization of teaching thus illustrates how contextual elements intertwined with the origins of systems of public education in the nineteenth century. A closer look at two key contextual elements, capitalism and democracy, makes those connections clearer.[18]

Capitalism, Democracy, and the Expansion of Schooling

Most histories of the period from colonial times to about 1875 rest on a two-stage model: a shift from a preindustrial to an industrial society, or from a rural to an urban one.[19] This model does not clarify the relation between institutions and social change very well, because the chronological fit between industrialism and institutions is imperfect, and attempts to construct causal models or develop tight and coherent explanations are usually too mechanistic and vague. Consider the chronology of institutional development. In New York State dissatisfaction with the existing system of poor relief led to the passage of a law creating specialized county poorhouses in 1825; the first special institution for juvenile vagrants and delinquents opened in 1827; the New York Public School Society emerged out of the Free School Society in 1824. In Massachusetts the first state hospital for the mentally ill opened in 1833; poor relief underwent fundamental shifts in the 1820s; agitation for educational reform began in the same decade. These examples show that the drive toward institutional innovation *preceded* the industrial takeoff in the Northeast.[20]

With the addition of a third stage, the fit becomes tighter. The three-stage model inserts a merchant capitalist phase between the earlier mercantile-peasant and the later industrial capitalist stages. Although the pace of change varied from region to region and stages overlapped, the most important development in the late eighteenth and early nineteenth centuries was not industry or urbanism but the spread of capitalism, defined by Dobb as "not simply a system of production for the market . . . but a system under which labour-power had 'itself become a commodity' and was bought and sold on the market like any other object of exchange."[21] In New York City's occupational structure, to take an important example, the most striking change between 1796 and 1855, according to Carl Kaestle's figures, was the increase in the proportion of men who listed themselves simply as laborers, from

5.5 percent to 27.4 percent. Apprenticeship, whose emphasis on bound labor is incompatible with capitalism, ceased to function with anything like its customary character during the same years. As another example, Douglas Lamar Jones has pointed to an unmistakable increase in the wandering of the poor from place to place in late eighteenth-century Massachusetts. The expansion in commerce in this period has been documented extensively, and state governments abandoned their mercantilist economic regulations. Indeed, many historians in recent years have pointed to the formation of a working class in this era and to its ideological and political significance.[22]

Institutions originated during this massive social transformation, especially as a response to the pressures in cities and regions experiencing the emergence of capitalism. Capitalism fostered the creation of new institutions, including public school systems, most directly through its dependence on wage labor and the consequent need for a mobile, unbound labor force. The shift in social organization that accompanied the emergence of a class of wage laborers, rather than industrialization or urbanization, fueled the development of public institutions. Public education emerged along with the working class, whose formation is one of the central themes in antebellum American history.

Consider these circumstances: the seasonality and irregularity of work posed problems as great as the meager subsistence wages paid to laborers. At the same time that chronic underemployment became permanent, the creation of a mobile labor force and increasing transiency sundered the ties of individuals to communities. In crises or periods of difficulty, people decreasingly found themselves within a community of familiar neighbors and kin to whom they could turn for help. In this situation, state and local authorities had to innovate to cope with the dislocation, distress, and destitution of landless wage workers.[23]

Institutions reflected the drive toward order, rationality, discipline, and specialization inherent in capitalism. There is a parallel between the way a capitalist society processes its business and the way it processes its problems. For instance, one major problem was time: the transformation of casual, episodic, and flexible work patterns into steady, punctual, and predictable labor. Wasted time cost employers extra money, raised the cost of finished goods, and lowered their competitive position in the market. For these reasons, time was crucial, and within every institution order, predictability, and work also were central preoccupations. Another obstacle was the personalistic, ascriptive basis of much public life, which reformers hoped to replace with universal standards based on achievement and merit, defined as productive capacity, the ability to do a job better than anyone else or to meet a bureaucratic standard, like an examination. All this reflected the culture of capitalism, what Christopher Lasch has called the appearance of a "single standard of honor." The corollary, as Harry Braverman has pointed out, was disposing of those who did not or could not produce as cheaply and conveniently as possible (even if the reason was their youth) through the creation of institutions that cleared the marketplace of all but the economically active and productive.[24]

Capitalism and a working class emerged everywhere in the Western world in the same historical period. But education in America assumed a distinctive shape. Clearly, other factors also influenced its early history. Certainly the idiosyncratic character and peculiar intensity of American evangelical Protestantism played a pivotal role; it helped transform education into a crusade and to shape its pan-Protestant tone. In individual states, as Carl Kaestle has shown, party political configurations also helped mold educational controversy and development.[25]

Everywhere, democracy—or, more precisely, the links between class formation and political structure—also played a key role in shaping American public education. As Ira Katznelson and Margaret Weir have observed, the American working class had a distinctive relation to the state. Unlike their European counterparts, American workers did not have to struggle for the franchise. Consequently, they viewed the state as a potential if not immediate ally and channeled their protests through votes and the political process rather than through direct action. "Mass common schooling under public auspices" came into being in antebellum America in part because "working people...joined a coalition favoring such schools while at the same time many of their counterparts in Europe were resisting state schooling because, unlike European workers, white male working-class Americans were voting citizens." Democracy affected schooling in another way, too. In the early nineteenth century, the United States was the only capitalist society to commit itself to "a civic culture of democratic participation (albeit one restricted by race and sex) irrespective of property and class relations." Not only were schools assigned key roles in the diffusion of democratic culture; they also had to mediate the contradictions between democratic ideals and the continuance of class and inequality. According to Katznelson and Weir, "The inescapable tensions between the public and private realms, and battles at this boundary about the extensiveness of equal citizenship and popular sovereignty, took place in and were moderated in part by the system of schooling for all." The result was a "commitment to educate all children in primary schools paid for by the government . . . the most distinctive American public policy of the early nineteenth century."[26]

Two examples (discussed in detail in Chapter 2) illustrate the impact of democratic ideas about educational reform. In the 1830s and 1840s democratic ideology influenced successful attacks on the monitorial system that had dominated urban schooling for two or three decades. For the monitorial system had become associated with both the devolution of responsibility for popular education on private associations and a dual structure of education in which "public," as in "public education," signified "pauper." Democratic ideas also rippled through early criticisms of attempts to centralize education under the authority of state boards of education and to train teachers in state normal schools. In fact, early and mid-nineteenth century school promoters argued that public educational systems mediated the tensions associated with the spread of capitalism and democracy by attacking five major problems: urban crime and poverty, increased cultural heterogeneity, the necessity to train and discipline an urban and industrial workforce, the crisis of youth in the nineteenth-century city, and parental anxiety about adolescent children.

The Purposes of Early Public Education

A massive increase in both crime and poverty, argued many nineteenth-century writers, accompanied the growth of cities and the development of modern industry. Although they exaggerated, what matters is the widespread belief among the respectable classes that an epidemic of lawlessness and pauperism threatened the foundations of morality and the maintenance of social order. Crime and poverty, in discussions of the time, did not constitute two distinct problems. Rather, the terms *criminal* and *pauper* overlapped and merged into synonyms for deviant and antisocial behavior that stemmed from individual moral failure. How urbanization worked its mischief remained vague in mid-nineteenth-century social thought. Nonetheless, neither crime nor poverty was now regarded as the result of misfortune or deviance among an otherwise stable and orderly population. To the contrary, the emergence of fundamentally new classes, social critics and reformers argued, had accompanied social transformation. Criminals and paupers were not merely individuals but representatives of a dangerous and growing criminal and pauper class.[27]

Although explanations of crime and poverty often relied on environmental rather than genetic factors, they failed to take into account the relations between social structure and social deviance. Ultimately blame fell on the lower classes. Crime and poverty became moral problems that arose because the lower-class urban family failed to implant earnestness and restraint in the character of its children. Raised amid intemperance, indulgence, and neglect, the lower-class urban child began life predisposed to criminality and unprepared for honest work. By definition, the lower-class family was the breeding place of paupers and criminals.

Given these premises, schooling held an obvious attraction. Exposure to public education, school promoters argued, would provide the lower-class child with an alternative environment and a superior set of adult models. Through its effect on the still pliable and emergent personalities of its students, a school system would prove a cheap and superior substitute for the jail and the poorhouse. As some acute commentators at the time observed, the school was to become a form of police. Thus, although spending on schools might seem high, it would ultimately lessen the burden imposed on society by adult crime and poverty.

Mid-nineteenth-century social policy blurred more than the distinction between poverty and crime; it also equated cultural diversity with immorality and deviance. Thus the ethnic composition of expanding cities became a source of special anxiety, one exacerbated by the first massive immigration of the famine Irish. To

the respectable classes, poor Irish Catholics appeared alien, un-
couth, and menacing. Most contemporary research shows that the
Irish were not intemperate, shiftless, and ignorant, as nativists
portrayed them. To the contrary: the immigrants, it now is reasonable to suppose, may have represented a select, highly motivated, and unusually literate sector of Irish society. The instability
in their lives in America stemmed (as with ex-slaves later in the
century) from the harsh and discriminatory urban social structure
they encountered rather than from any moral slackness in their
culture.[28]

Nonetheless, as with crime and poverty, observers proved unable
or unwilling to connect the problem they thought they saw around
them with its structural basis, and consequently they again traced
the source of a social problem to moral failure, in this case embedded in a set of foreign and inferior cultural patterns. As with most
instances of nativism, the shrill exaggeration with which observers
dwelt on the subversive potential of the immigrants' alleged sensual
indulgence reveals more about the critics themselves than about
their targets. It is tempting to argue that nativists projected onto
the Irish the sensuality they consciously repressed in their own
lives and hated them for acting out the fantasies they denied themselves. Certainly, the key concepts in contemporary prescriptions
of the good life were restraint and the substitution of higher for
lower pleasures, attributes precisely the opposite of those many
thought they saw in the lives of the Irish immigrant poor. Whether
this speculation is correct or not, it is quite clear that the brittle
and hostile response to Irish immigrants revealed an underlying
fear and distrust of cultural diversity.[29]

Widespread anxiety about cultural diversity had clear implications for the role of schooling. Although the personalities and
behaviors of adult immigrants might prove intractable, the impending rot of Anglo-American civilization could be averted
through a concerted effort to shape the still-pliable characters of
their children into a native mold. This massive task of assimilation
required weakening the connection between the immigrant child
and its family, which in turn called for the capture of the child by
an outpost of native culture. In short, fears about cultural heterogeneity propelled the establishment of systems of public educa-

tion; from the beginning, public schools were agents of cultural standardization.

The need to discipline an urban workforce intersected with the fear of crime and poverty and the anxiety about cultural diversity to hasten the establishment of public educational systems. The problem of work discipline, which persists in developing societies today, arose first in its modern form during the early industrialization of Britain, as E. P. Thompson has described so eloquently. It reflected the incongruity between customary rhythms of life and the requirements of urban and industrial work settings. In contrast to the punctuality, regularity, docility, and deferral of gratification demanded in a modern workforce, both peasant and urban populations usually had governed their activities more by the sun than by the clock, more by the season and customary festivities than by an externally imposed production schedule, more by the relationships within small work groups than by the regimentation of the factory.[30]

Rewards customarily had been distributed on the basis of ascribed rather than achieved qualities. Social position devolved on successive generations mainly as a result of heredity; it was correct, not corrupt, to favor a kinsman over a more qualified stranger in the award of jobs or favors. Although modern custom has not totally reversed this practice, democratic ideology, with its emphasis on merit and concepts such as equality of educational opportunity, has advocated the substitution of achievement for ascription as the ideal basis for the distribution of rewards in contemporary society.

Their promoters expected public school systems to bring about precisely this substitution of achievement for ascription and to inculcate modern work habits. These disciplinary goals appear in the reports of local school committees across the country. Everywhere, the major obsessions—and difficulties—were punctuality and regularity of attendance, while the villains were parents uneducated to the importance of schooling who allowed or encouraged their children to remain at home for what, to school promoters, appeared whimsical reasons or who took the side of their child against the teacher. For good reason the mass production of clocks and watches began at about the same time as the mass production of public schools. In the same years, state authorities continually complained about the refusal of local school committees to base the hiring of teachers on universalistic criteria. Too often, they simply hired kin or friends. By contrast, school promoters intended new school systems to be object lessons in the organization of modern society, forces radiating their influence outward through entire communities and transforming the habits of their people.[31]

Contemporary complaints about urban problems included denunciations of the masses of idle and vagrant youths roaming city streets. Despite their moralistic tenor, these complaints did reflect actual social behavior, because observers saw in nineteenth-century cities a very real crisis of youth. In earlier times, long-standing customs had defined with reasonable precision the expectations and duties of people throughout their life course: young people had left home, perhaps around the age of fourteen, to work as servants or apprentices, almost always dwelling in another household. Never had it been unclear where young people should live or how they should spend their time. Idleness on a large scale had been an unimaginable social problem.[32]

However, during the rapid growth of cities in the eighteenth and nineteenth centuries, the population of young people increased enormously while apprenticeship gradually decayed as an effective social institution. Indeed, the disappearance of prolonged, highly regulated apprenticeships accompanied the first phase of capitalism and preceded industrialization. The practice of keeping male servants apparently had declined even earlier. Whether young women found fewer opportunities for work as domestic servants remains unclear, but large numbers were neither in school nor employed outside their family.[33]

Customary practices declined not only before industrialization but also before the creation of any institutional network to contain and manage young people, who now literally had almost nothing to do. Before industrialization, little work existed for young men in commercial cities. Their labor was scarcely more necessary than adolescents' today. Without schools or jobs, large numbers of youths undoubtedly remained unwillingly idle until the males became old enough to find work and the females married.

The crisis of youth was similar in Canadian and American cities. In Hamilton, Ontario, during the 1840s, when population growth made the youth problem most acute, about half the young people over the age of thirteen or fourteen were neither in work nor at school, and exactly how they spent their time remains a puzzle. Not a puzzle, though, is the timing of the creation of a school system in the following decade. The establishment of a school system with special provisions for young people over the age of eleven or twelve quickly and dramatically reduced the proportion of idle youth. It is clear, though, that many youngsters entered school simply because they could not find work, for when jobs in factories first became available during the next decade, large numbers of working-class young men left the schools while their more affluent contemporaries—and young women—remained behind. A similar process characterized the relations among young people, work, and schooling in Philadelphia.[34]

All but the poorest parents probably supported the expansion of schooling because of anxiety about their children's future. The poorest parents did not share that anxiety—downward mobility—because they had already hit the bottom. Anxiety about slipping down the economic ladder permeated both social commentary and fiction and related in a complex way to experience. Nineteenth-century cities revealed at once a curious combination of rigidity and fluidity. Within them sharply entrenched patterns of inequality persisted, while the experience of individual people and the very identity of the population itself changed with dazzling rapidity. Imagine them as railroad stations with waiting rooms for different classes. Although the population of the station constantly changed, those who departed were replaced by people with remarkably similar features. Although their populations constantly increased, the proportions in the various waiting rooms remained about the same. Studies of individual social mobility in nineteenth-century cities reveal this combination of stability and transience. They show a high rate of status transmission from father to son; the image of a continent of opportunity wide open to talent simply cannot be sustained, although many men made modest gains that undoubtedly were critical to their lives. Few laborers, that is, replicated the rags-to-riches version of success, but many managed eventually to buy a small house. At the same time, businessmen failed extraordinarily often. Indeed, entrepreneurial activity entailed enormous risks, which kept the threat of catastrophe ever present. For example, almost half of one small sample of mid-nineteenth-century businessmen whose histories I followed failed in their businesses.[35]

For different reasons, the position of artisans became increasingly insecure as technological development eroded the association of skill and reward that had been the hallmark of many crafts. In the 1850s, for instance, the introduction of the sewing machine suddenly brought about a deterioration in the position of shoemakers and tailors as manufacturers flooded the market with cheap goods. In this situation, artisans could no longer assure the comfort and prosperity of their sons by passing on their skills. Indeed, it is poignant to observe the extent to which sons of shoemakers ceased to follow their fathers' crafts during only one decade. In practical terms, for an artisan to assure his son a position commensurate with his own he had to help him enter a different occupation, particularly one in commerce or the expanding public bureaucracies.[36]

A generalized uneasiness about adolescence itself accompanied this widespread anxiety about the transmission of status. This showed clearly in controversies between supporters of high schools and supporters of private academies. Their debate revealed a growing reluctance to send youths away from home. No school, opponents of residential academies argued, could replicate a family, and increasingly a family environment appeared critical for adolescents. Heightened anxiety about young people partly reflected their newly ambiguous and uneasy position in families and communities and partly uncertainty about their economic prospects. One of the outcomes of the *intensity* with which people began to worry about what we have since come to call adolescence was a search for a form of schooling that would allow young people to live at home while they acquired the education increasingly necessary for economic success. Despite a good deal of egalitarian rhetoric, I suspect that parental anxiety—especially in moderately affluent families who otherwise would have strained to pay tuition at private schools—about their adolescent children formed the driving force behind the creation of public secondary schools and solidified the commitment of the middle classes to public education.[37]

The cultivation and the transmission of cognitive skills and intellectual abilities as ends in themselves had far less importance for early school promoters than the problems outlined above. Public school systems existed to shape behavior and attitudes, alleviate social and family problems, and reinforce a social structure under stress. The character of pupils was a much greater concern than their minds.

The process by which school promoters translated their aspirations into institutions is nearly as important a topic as the purposes they hoped to achieve. The style of educational development had lasting consequences for the relations between school systems and the communities they served and for the quality of educational experience. More case studies such as the one in Chapter 3 are needed to account for the way in which institutions embodying a passionate commitment to social reform turned relatively quickly into large, rigid, and unresponsive bureaucracies. More research should focus, too, as David Tyack, Ira Katznelson, and Margaret Weir have done, on the way ethnicity, class, and politics have intertwined to fashion and refashion school systems. The relations between education and social class also remain an especially intricate and important topic (and cannot, as Chapter 5 shows, be simply minimized, as the new conservative historians of education try to do). We know least about what working-class parents and spokesmen (and we should not assume an identity of interest between the two) wanted from public education. Education, clearly, was "contested terrain," but the goals and aspirations of one party to the contest still are much clearer than those of the others.[38]

Underlying these issues is the problem of American faith in public education. Nineteenth-century educational promoters not only erected school systems; they also helped engineer a lasting popular conversion to public education as both the cornerstone of democracy and the key agency for the solution of virtually every major social problem. Their success reflected the resonance of the American theory of public education with the premises of democratic capitalism in the same era. It reflected, too, the usefulness of public education for displacing family problems and substituting for redistributive reform. In both their strengths and their limits, school systems, with their emphasis on equal access and unequal rewards, their fictive meritocracy, and their bureaucratic organization of experience, became miniature versions of America's social and political order.

2

Alternative Models for American Education

The early institutional history of public education is not the story of an inexorable march toward bureaucracy. Rather, it is a more complex and more interesting tale of competition among alternatives, each passionately believed to be singularly appropriate to America's polity and social structure. This chapter delineates the four major organizational models that competed in the first half of the nineteenth century. I call them paternalistic voluntarism, democratic localism, corporate voluntarism, and incipient bureaucracy. Real and fully developed examples of each existed, but most organizations had features of more than one model, although usually one feature dominated and defined them.

The creation of institutions preoccupied early nineteenth-century Americans. Whether they were building banks or railroads, political parties or factories, hospitals or schools, Americans confronted the inappropriateness of traditional organizational arrangements, and their attempts to find a suitable fit between the form and context of social life stimulated a prolonged national debate. For the most part the public record of the controversy resides in massively tedious proposals for the introduction or alteration of particular organizational details, and in the prosaic and even trivial record of practical men solving everyday problems. Yet the arguments of these practical men over the external features of institutions frequently represented a fundamental clash of social values. The task of appropriately arranging public activities formed an intimate part of the larger task of building a nation, and alternative proposals embodied different priorities and aspirations for the shape of American society.[1]

Most of the early nineteenth-century American debate centered on objective questions, that is, definite structural characteristics on which organizations may be said to differ. The primary factors in controversy were scale (or size), control, professionalism, and finance. Each proposal concerning one of these organizational characteristics rested on social values which, though often remaining implicit, had enormous emotional significance. (We have only to recall the decentralization controversy in New York in the late 1960s to realize the emotionally laden content of issues of control and professionalism in education.) At the same time, values often explicitly enveloped the debate, especially when proponents raised questions of organizational purpose. And here the issue most frequently contested became the degree of standardization desirable in American institutional forms, behavior, and cultural values.[2]

Paternalistic Voluntarism

The New York Public School Society represents the paradigm case of paternalistic voluntarism in educational organization. Established as the New York Free School Society in 1805, its purpose was "extending the means of education to such poor children as do not belong to, or are not provided for, by any religious society." The Society offered poor children training in the rudiments of literacy and in morality as it unabashedly tried "to counteract the disadvantages resulting from the situation of their parents." By its use of the term "free school," it should be noted, the Society did not advocate free tax-supported education in our contemporary sense. Rather, it promoted free schooling only for the very poor.[3]

For almost twenty years the Society's members aimed only to be "humble gleaners in the wide field of benevolence," touching only the unchurched poor, "such objects . . . as are left by those who have gone before." However, by 1825 the Society had reversed its goal and now argued that "it is totally incompatible with our republican institutions, and a dangerous precedent" to allow any portion of the public money to be spent "by the clergy or church trustees for the support of sectarian education." One reason for this change of position was the Society's involvement in an acrimonious controversy concerning the alleged misappropriation of educational funds by the Bethel Baptists, who allegedly had used their yearly share of the state education grant to build a church rather than a school. The interdenominational bickering that resulted convinced the Society that only the establishment of one nonsectarian educational agency for the entire city could "prevent strife and jealousy and preserve the harmony which has heretofore so happily existed between the several religious societies in this place."[4]

The generally low quality of small private schools and the evident dissatisfaction of many parents with existing school facilities combined to bolster the Society's claim that a major reorganization of education within New York City had become imperative. Never modest, the Society claimed to be the most appropriate agency to assume the task of educating all the city's children, by virtue of "an experience of nineteen years, during which period it has educated more than twenty thousand of our poor children." With the legislature's acceptance of this claim, the Society became the New York Public School Society (NYPSS) and began to disburse virtually the entire public grant for elementary education in New York City.[5]

Throughout both phases of its history, voluntarism underlay the organization of the Society, which was administered by an unpaid self-perpetuating board of first citizens, "who having a desire to serve mankind, associate together" and "offer themselves to the public as agents to carry out certain benevolent purposes without money and without price" as "servants" of the people. The Society's champions considered that the unrewarded and disinterested dedication of "that class of men" found in "large cities... having leisure and... benevolent feelings, who may not wish to mingle in the contest of politics... but who desire to devote themselves to some good and benevolent objective... and in a quiet way accomplish something for the benefit of mankind" and who would not stoop to practice democratic politics, gave this form of organization its distinctive virtues. "All experience *will* demonstrate, that public objects are better accomplished by these voluntary servants, than they are usually accomplished by persons chosen directly by the people."[6]

Voluntarism in practice embodied honesty and zeal. Between 1813 and 1840 the Society had spent over one million dollars and "like faithful servants . . . accounted for every cent." In distributing funds the Society's members had revealed an enthusiastic interest in the cause of education that no paid agent could ever match; during a representative year they "themselves visited the schools *eleven thousand times.*" "Point out to me," challenged a Society champion, "your school commissioners who, receiving pay, have done such service," and, he asked a basically hostile audience, "Will you, as wise men, say we shall avail ourselves of these voluntary services, or shall we mingle every thing in the turmoil of politics?"[7]

To the supporters of the Society voluntarism remained a variety of noblesse oblige; it rested on faith in the individual talented amateur. At an overall administrative level, voluntarists scorned the need for elaborate organization, state control, or professional staff. As its defenders pointed out, from one perspective paternalistic voluntarism worked extremely well. With a minimum of administrative expense and scrupulous financial integrity, with commendable efficiency and unpaid administrators, the Society maintained an extensive network of schools that for decades annually taught thousands of children.

Voluntarism was without question a class system of education. It provided a means for one class to civilize another and thereby ensure that society would remain tolerable, orderly, and safe. To the Society the alarmingly low level of school attendance represented "either . . . the extreme indigence of the parents . . . or their intemperance or vice; or . . . a blind indifference to the best interests of their offspring." Thus nurtured in "ignorance and amidst the contagion of bad example," these urchins, "instead of being useful members of the community, will become the burdens and pests of society." One of the Society's means of class civilization was the instruction of parents through public addresses, in which the poor were admonished to "use all endeavors to preserve" their children in "innocency" and to practice temperance, industry, piety, frugality, and, of course, "cleanliness," without which "your enjoyments as well as your reputation will be impaired."[8]

The schools themselves formed the other, and major, agency of class civilization. Their particular form of pedagogy clearly reflected the Society's goals and perception of its clients. The Society offered mass education on the cheapest possible plan, the monitorial or Lancasterian system, which counterbalanced the lack of central organization with rigid internal arrangements for each school. As DeWitt Clinton put the case enthusiastically in 1809, the Lancasterian system "is, in education, what the neat and finished machines for abridging labor and expense are in the mechanic arts." This system arrived "at its object with the least possible trouble and at the least possible expense." Aside from its minuscule per-pupil cost, this mechanistic form of pedagogy, which reduced education to drill, seemed appropriate because the schools served lower-class children who could without offense be likened to unfinished products needing polishing with middle-class virtues.[9]

Within Lancasterian schools "solitary study" did not exist; children were "taught in companies." Teachers and monitors formed "constant habits of attention and vigilance . . . and an ardent spirit of emulation" was "kept continually alive . . . The discipline of the school is enforced by shame, rather than inflicted by pain."[10] A very specific ideal of an urban working class was implicit in these pedagogical arrangements. The working class would be alert, obedient, and so thoroughly attuned to discipline through group sanctions that a minimum of policing would ensure the preservation of social order. On the other hand, programmed from an early age to compete with each other, working-class children would not grow up to form a cohesive and threatening class force. The zealous amateurs of the NYPSS did not design their system for their own children or for the children of their friends. Rather, they attempted to ensure social order through the socialization of the poor in cheap, mass schooling factories.

Critics of paternalistic voluntarism stressed three defects. First, it delegated to "a private corporation the discharge of an important function of government, without a direct and immediate responsibility to the people." As such it was undemocratic and violated the basis of the democratic theory of public organizations by exemplifying "a principle . . . hostile to the whole spirit of our institutions." That principle asserted the "competency" of the people "to manage all the affairs of government"; thus, to deny them the ability to "determine on the mode, manner, and extent of instruction to be given to their offspring" amounted to overturning "the foundation of our whole system."[11]

More than that, according to critics, the New York Public School Society perverted the notion of voluntarism; "it is not a *voluntary system*, in the fullest and broadest meaning of the term." The Society's plan violated the criteria of a voluntarist system because it assumed "exclusive control" of children without permitting their parents any participation in "the direction of the course of studies, the management of the schools or ... the selection of teachers." The Society ordered parents with "no action or cooperation" to submit their children to the "government and guidance of others, probably strangers, who are in no way accountable to those parents."[12] This attack on the Society signaled a shift in the meaning of voluntarism, which by the 1840s in America no longer found favorable expression through noblesse oblige but through willingly offered participation in the conduct of institutions owned and managed by elected public representatives. (In this way the repudiation of paternalistic voluntarism reflected the general attack on monopolies that characterized public discourse in Jacksonian America.)

Finally, in the view of its critics, paternalistic voluntarism ignored the variety of American life and reflected an unacceptable cultural bias by imposing uniform services upon a diverse clientele. Though often couched in religious terms, this criticism revealed a perception of important cultural differences of which religious doctrines served as symptoms. To the opponents of the Society, religious differences represented one form of cultural variation, toward which a democratic state had to remain neutral. Herein rested a dilemma: schools were culturally sensitive institutions; by definition they touched the areas of irreconcilable difference between denominations. The result was an inverse relation between the size of the school system and the degree of satisfaction it could offer its clientele. This was why, argued critics, country school districts had the advantage; in them, small and relatively homogeneous groups controlled and shaped local schools to suit their own preferences. Here, too, lay the defect of the NYPSS; simply because of the scale of its operation it could never satisfy the various publics of New York City. The defect, critics made clear, rested less in the Society's peculiar insensitivity than in faults endemic to large organizations. "The defect is one which, so far from being peculiar to the Public School Society, is necessarily inherent in every form of organization which places under one control large masses of discordant materials, which from the nature of things, cannot submit to any control."[13] From this point of view, an educational agency that could not adapt to the variation of urban life clearly violated the criteria for free and democratic institutions.

Animosity to upper-class benevolence underscored both religious and political denunciations of paternalistic voluntarism. The Catholic spokesman, Bishop Hughes, argued that the class bias inherent in the NYPSS alienated poor Catholic children and their parents. To the assertion that the schools had the confidence of all classes, Hughes countered that the Society had been so unable to overcome the reluctance of poor parents to send their children to its schools that it had applied for "a legal enactment ... to compel an attendance." Class, as well as religious, resentment underlay Hughes's bitter observation that the Society had obtained "two enactments from the Common Council, depriving the parents, in time of need—even when cold and starvation have set in upon them—of public relief, unless the children were sent to those or some other schools." So concerned with the problem of attendance had the Society become that it urged "ladies ... to obtain" the "confidence" of the poor "by soothing words" and "employers to make" school attendance "the condition of employment." Still, Hughes scoffed, the Society pretended to have "the confidence of the poor."[14]

Middle-class hostility to paternalistic voluntarism was related to working-class antagonism. Through the existence of organizations such as the NYPSS free education, public education, and the monitorial system had all become identified with lower-class education. Thus when a New Jersey teacher first observed the monitorial system in the 1820s, he supposed that it was "particularly appropriate to large schools for the poor." However, after studying its operation for a time, he changed his mind and returned to New Jersey to open a monitorial school for children of all classes. "But I found the rich sent poor children to me, and with-

held their own. They had the common ideas about the system."
His school lasted only twelve weeks.[15]

The attempt to dissociate public and pauper underlay the free-
school movement. Pennsylvania provides a case in point: the constitution of 1790 provided free education only for the poor, and
free education had thus come to be associated with charity. In the
1830s the state legislature passed permissive legislation allowing
local school districts to introduce free schools for all children.
When representatives to the state's constitutional convention of
1837–38 tried to enshrine the free school principle in their revised
constitution, a full-scale debate, in which the free-school forces
lost, ensued. Both sides to the debate professed their allegiance to
the idea of universal education and to the provision of education
without cost to those too poor to pay. But the opponents of free-
school legislation had two misgivings about the proposed constitutional provision. They disliked the style of imposed social change
which it represented (a point to which I shall return), and some
simply could not see why the necessity of a public declaration of
poverty would deter anybody from taking advantage of a free
education. It was the insensitivity of this point of view to which
the free-school proponents addressed most of their arguments. One
tried to describe for his colleagues how "a feeling of repugnance"
accompanied a public declaration of poverty and "prevented many
persons from accepting the means of education." If the people
"should be educated at the public expense, only on condition that
they are certified and recorded as pauper," then they would surely
refuse to avail themselves of the offer."[16]

Thaddeus Stevens, the state's leading advocate for free schools,
connected the question with middle-class pride and status anxiety,
touching what may have been many a very raw nerve in the dis-
locations of 1837. Many people with children to be educated, he
pointed out, "may have seen better days—may have been unfortunate in life, and, by reason of their reduced situation and circumstances, may be unable to educate their families. Shall we,"
he asked the delegates, "do nothing to allay the prejudice which
persons in this condition, will almost surely entertain, against allowing their children to be educated in public schools?" By his
very terminology Stevens reached the heart of the problem; only

a radical reorganization could expunge the legacy of paternalistic voluntarism and divorce the concepts of public and pauper, thereby providing institutions acceptable to proud and enterprising parents of limited means.[17]

Democratic Localism

The first alternative proposed was democratic localism. Its sponsors sought to adapt to the city an organizational form current in rural areas, the district or community school. The thorough triumph of a centralized and bureaucratic form of educational organization has detracted from the historical significance of the democratic localists and obscured the seriousness with which men propounded an alternative course for American education. Therefore, it is worth dwelling on a few examples.

One is the plan offered by New York Secretary of State John C. Spencer in his attack on the New York Public School Society. The problems within New York City, he argued, arose from a "violation" of the "principle" underlying education elsewhere in the state, namely, the operation of the schools by local districts in which the "whole control" of education remained "to the free and unrestricted action of the people themselves."[18] Thus the New York situation could be remedied simply by making each ward of the city an independent school district with exactly the same powers as the districts in country towns, watched by a board of commissioners with strictly limited powers. Nothing in Spencer's plan would prevent a Catholic majority in a district from hiring Catholic teachers or from choosing textbooks sympathetic to their religion. Democratic localism, like all other ideologies, served many functions. One was to rationalize the drive for Catholic power in much the same fashion that democratic localism today has sometimes served as a theoretical justification for black power.

The democratic localists were active in Massachusetts as well, most audibly in the report of a legislative committee that in 1840 favored the abolition of the Board of Education, founded in 1837 and presided over by Horace Mann as secretary. (The Board of Education was primarily a creation of Whigs; its critics and most of the committee were Democrats.) Although the Board of Education had powers of recommendation only, the committee warned it would soon be "converted into a power of regulation" through its close association with the legislature. Even if the Board were limited to collecting and diffusing information, it should be abolished because of its inefficiency compared with the "voluntary associations of teachers, which preceded" its existence. "In these voluntary associations a vast number of persons are interested, a spirit of emulation exists."[19] This spirit, and with it all educational progress, would be crushed by teacher conventions called by the state.

In fact a central Board of Education, argued the committee, characterized European countries, where governments had to compensate for "the ignorance and incapacity of the administrators of local affairs." There, especially in France and Prussia, the schools were all modeled "upon one plan, as uniform and exact as the discipline of an army." This of course represented the antithesis of the American idea, which assumed the competence of the people to manage their own business. Thus the Board of Education appeared to be "the commencement of a system of centralization and of monopoly of power in a few hands, contrary, in every respect, to the true spirit of our democratical institutions." The bureaucratic regulations of the Board, moreover, formed an unnecessary nuisance, forcing teachers to fill out forms when they should be teaching children. In short, the Board could only fatally damage Massachusetts education by removing its mainspring, the enthusiasm generated by participatory democracy on a local level: "any attempt to form all our schools and all our teachers, upon one model, would destroy all competition,—all emulation, and even the spirit of improvement itself."[20]

Orestes Brownson formalized the democratic localist point of view into a theory of governance for American society. According to Brownson, the "individual State, as well as the Union, should be a confederacy of distinct communities," in which each vital interest remained within the smallest possible unit. The smallest of these units would be the district, "which should always be of a size sufficient to maintain a Grammar School." In education the district should remain always "paramount to the state," and each individual school should be "under the control of a community composed merely of the number of families having children in it." Although Brownson pointed out that education, like other governmental affairs, would be "more efficient" in proportion to the degree of "control" by "families specially interested in it," efficiency was not his primary objective.[21] Nor was it the paramount concern of other democratic localists who subordinated both efficiency and organizational rationality to an emphasis on responsiveness, close public control, and local involvement.

Democratic localists fought on two fronts: against paternalistic voluntarism, as in their opposition to the NYPSS; and against bureaucracy or centralization, as in the attack on the Massachusetts Board of Education. Their stress on variety, local adaptability, and the symbiotic relation of school and community permeated both conflicts. In the resistance to bureaucracy, however, two other aspects of the democratic localist viewpoint emerged most strongly. One was antiprofessionalism. They were not, as the sponsors of the NYPSS had been, vaguely indifferent to the concept of the professional educator; instead, they were hostile and suspicious. Brownson played on the theme that normal schools were a Prussian importation in order to raise the specter of a cadre of Whiggish teachers learning and then imposing state-defined doctrines. "As soon as they can get their Normal Schools into successful operation," he warned, "they will so arrange it, if they can, that no public school shall be permitted to employ a teacher" not trained in one. Then, good-bye to "all liberty of instruction"; "Adieu then to republicanism, to social progress."[22]

Like Brownson, the legislative committee recommending the abolition of the Board of Education dismissed normal schools as European institutions unsuited to a free society and destructive of the progress that came from academies and high schools rivaling each other to produce the best teachers for common schools. To this the committee added scorn of the whole idea of professional instruction for teachers; "every person, who has himself undergone a process of instruction, must acquire, by that very process, the art of instructing others," and teachers needed special schools no more than mechanics. Nor was it desirable to raise the job of school teaching into a "distinct and separate profession," given that schools were open only three or four months a year. "We may as well have a religion established by law," wrote Brownson, "as a system of education [so established], and the government educate and appoint the pastors of our churches, as well as the instructors of our children."[23]

To the democrats the threat of a state educational apparatus represented the essential fault in the centralizing viewpoint: the willingness to impose social change and to force attitudes onto the people. An advocate of a local option system for education in Pennsylvania stressed that even more important than the existence of free schools was to "adapt the system, as nearly as possible, to the *wishes*, as well as the *wants* of the people. No project, however beneficial may be its anticipated operation, should be forced upon the community by other inducements, than those arising from its own merits." Ultimately, this point of view rested on a subtle theory of the process of successful institutional innovation: "any system perfectly fitted to the wants of society, cannot long remain unpopular," whereas to force innovation upon the community prematurely "can only produce evil, as it may be the means of preventing the general spread and adoption of a system intrinsically beneficial." A delegate to the constitutional convention pinpointed the desire to compel the maintenance of free schools on "gentlemen" who believed that "the mass of the people are not intelligent enough to act upon the subject themselves."[24]

Thus, the democratic localists' case rested on a combination of faith in the people and a point of view about the source of social change. "If we ever expect to root deeply this system in the affection of the people," warned a delegate to the Pennsylvania convention, "we must make the system voluntary,—entirely so. But if we force it upon the people, it will be taken with an ill grace, and will be made use of, if used at all, with reluctance and suspicion." Legislatures should enact, and not lead, the public will. If a large minority happened to oppose an issue, however desirable the outcome might seem, it would be folly to legislate until the people had changed their minds. In Pennsylvania, in the last analysis, the most important legislative consideration remained the fact that "the prejudices against this system of education are very strong."[25] The imposition of social change would never work; changes in society, in habits, and in attitudes came only from people themselves as they slowly, haltingly, but surely exercised their innate common sense and intelligence. By being left to their own devices, by perhaps being encouraged, cajoled, and softly educated, but not by being forced, would the people become roused to the importance of universal education and of the regular school attendance of their children.

As a proposal for the organization of urban education democratic localism flourished for only a short time. Its failure was predictable from the start, for it rested on a distinctly rural point of view. The proponents of democratic localism did not adapt their viewpoint to the city and hence ignored critical differences between rural and urban contexts and the particular problems that the latter posed for the conduct of education (points to which I shall return). Nor did its sponsors, for instance Berkshire Congregationalists in Massachusetts, see the ironically undemocratic possibilities inherent in giving free rein to local majorities.

Democratic localism referred at once to an intellectual construct and to a real situation. Its problem was the lack of congruence between the two. As an intellectual construct it offered a simple explanation and a simple cure for feelings of powerlessness and dislocation induced by the rapid social changes of the 1830s and 1840s. But unfortunately it rested on a nostalgic memory whose relationship to reality was at best problematical. For was the small rural town truly a warm, enlightened, coherent exemplar of democracy? Certainly, at its worst democratic localism in action was the tyrannical local majority whose ambition was control and the dominance of their own narrow sectarian or political bias in the schoolroom. Orestes Brownson notwithstanding, the people of the Berkshires probably concerned themselves more with the problem of putting orthodox texts in the classroom than with the theory of federalism. Whatever John C. Spencer believed, democratic localism at one level rationalized the Catholic desire to run Catholic schools with public money. The reality of democratic localism came closer, more often than its theoretical exponents would care to admit, to the Hoosier schoolmaster than to Brownson's portrait. Walking into Flat Crick, Indiana, in search of a teaching job, Ralph Hartsook confronted one of the local trustees, "old Jack Means":

> "Want to be a school-master, do you? You? Well, what would *you* do in Flat Crick deestrick, *I'd* like to know? Why, the boys have driv off the last two, and licked the one afore them like blazes...."

They'd pitch you out of doors, sonny, neck and heels, afore Christmas" ...

"You see," continued Mr. Means, spitting in a meditative sort of way, "you see, we a'n't none of your saft sort in these diggins. It takes a *man* to boss this deestrick. Howsudever, ef you think you kin trust your hide in Flat Crick school-house, I ha'n't got no 'bjection ... Any other trustees? Wal, yes. But as I pay the most taxes, t'others jist let me run the thing."[26]

Nevertheless, despite its intellectual softness, at its best democratic localism provided a compelling alternative vision; it embraced a broad and humanistic conception of education as uncharacteristic of nineteenth- as of twentieth-century schools and schoolmen.[27] Consider, for example, Brownson's exhortation, which eschewed the specially utilitarian in education in terms of a distinctively American social structure:

Here professions and pursuits are merely the accidents of individual life. Behind them we recognize Humanity, as paramount to them all. Here man, in theory at least, is professor. Professions and pursuits may be changed according to judgment, will, or caprice, as circumstances permit, or render necessary or advisable. Consequently, here we want an education for that which is permanent in man, which contemplates him as back of all the accidents of life, and which shall be equally valuable to him whatever be the mutations which go on around him, the means he may choose or be compelled to adopt to obtain a livelihood.

The education of importance thus was "general Education" or the "Education of Humanity," that education "which fits us for our destiny, to attain our end as simple human beings."[28]

Corporate Voluntarism

A third model was corporate voluntarism, or the conduct of single institutions as individual corporations operated by self-perpetuating boards of trustees and financed either wholly through endowment or through a combination of endowment and tuition (sometimes with help from the state). Corporate voluntarism was found primarily in secondary and higher education, academies and colleges (as well as mental hospitals, reformatories, and schools for special classes of dependents, such as the deaf or blind). It was the social-welfare counterpart to the business corporation, which, newly sanctioned by legislation and judicial opinion, began to dominate commercial activity in the same era. As with democratic localism, the victory of the public secondary school as we know it today obscures the seriousness with which many nineteenth-century educational promoters considered this alternative model. Indeed, it has remained the fundamental organizational form of higher education, combined, since early in the twentieth century, with bureaucracy (with consequences described in Chapter 6). For a time it appeared as though corporate voluntarism would become the general pattern for secondary education too, for, in the late eighteenth and early nineteenth centuries, state governments promoted it as public policy by giving legislative and financial assistance to academies, which were supposed to fill the evident need for secondary education. Not until after mid-century did the public's preference for high schools over academies—for public bureaucracies over corporate voluntarism—become unmistakably clear.[29]

Controversies between supporters of academies and supporters of public high schools provide the most explicit example of the debate over corporate voluntarism. One of the most interesting happened in 1856 and 1857 between the sponsors of the Norwich (Connecticut) Free Academy, especially Reverend J. P. Gulliver, and the editor of the *Massachusetts Teacher*, a vigorous champion of public high schools then most numerous in Massachusetts. According to Gulliver the movement for educational reform, which began in Norwich as elsewhere in New England in the 1830s, continually encountered frustration. Particularly strong hostility greeted the proposal to establish a public high school, which was defeated by the votes of the poor:

A few (but only a few) of the heavy tax-payers were the first to smell treason. They passed the word to a set of men, who flourish in their own esteem, by exhibiting their powers in thwarting what others attempt to do. The usual cry was raised, "a school for the rich!" The prejudices of poor men were appealed to. This very class who were to be most benefitted by the change, were excited to oppose it.[30]

Thus the measure failed and the cause of educational improvement languished in Norwich until a group of wealthy men determined to take the initiative by uniting to "establish a high school and endow it, which should be open, free of all charge, to all classes."[31] This they did, and the Norwich Free Academy, well financed, carefully planned, and educationally progressive, opened in 1856. It was the clearest example in the country, its sponsors well knew, of an alternative to the public high school.

The sponsors of the school did not hesitate to point out the implications of its successful establishment. "There is no subject," asserted Gulliver, "which more imperatively demands examination at the present moment than the expediency of endowments for literary and educational purposes. The attention of men of wealth all over the country is now directed with great interest to the subject."[32] Gulliver had no doubt that the Free Academy had answered this question by providing a practical demonstration of the virtues offered by endowment and essentially private management. As he made his case, Gulliver echoed in part the attributes of the New York Public School Society in the eyes of its champions.

Honesty: never had there been a case of misappropriated funds on the part of a self-perpetuating board of trustees. Enlightened management: the public simply lacked the competence to conduct secondary schools. Public discourse, said Gulliver, too often degenerated into "talk about 'popular sovereignty' and the rights of the people to manage everything that in any way affects their interests—which is nothing but miserable cant." After all, Gulliver asked, why not allow the people to manage banks or insurance companies? Or why not give to the town meeting the management of "manufacturing corporations, benevolent societies, philanthropic institutions, military organizations, and ships' crews?" Clearly, to do so would be absurd; thus it implied no denigration of the people to assert their incapacity to manage "a school for instruction in the ancient and modern languages, the higher mathematics, the sciences, and the fine arts."[33] In short, endowment lifted education out of politics and assured it competent direction.

Edward Hitchcock, president of Amherst College, stressed a related though distinct theme of corporate voluntarism, the congruence between the flexibility of essentially private institutions and the variability of American conditions. Much like the democratic localists, proponents of corporate voluntarism assumed that "systems of education ought to be wisely suited to the character and condition of the people among whom they are introduced." From this assumption, the argument for corporate voluntarism proceeded along two lines. According to the first, "Freedom from governmental interference with our literary institutions" as a basic principle underscored the right of the parent to select his child's education. This right in turn found expression in the establishment of academies of varying types and suited to varying tastes. To exchange this mild anarchy for a state system of secondary schools would produce a "treadmill system" that was nothing but a "wretched substitute." The other line, emanating from the original premise, related the individuality of the American character to the varied degree of civilization across the country. Both called for an educational system that could reflect sensitively and provide for personal and cultural idiosyncrasies. One of the "excellencies" of the academies, offered Hitchcock, is that "they can conform to all the irregular demands of society, without destroying their individuality."[34]

Hitchcock was not simply rationalizing low academic quality. Academies, especially smaller, unincorporated ones, were flexible institutions uniquely appropriate to nineteenth-century rural and small-town America. They accepted a wide age range of students, allowed them to enter and leave as seasonal or other work required, charged low tuitions, taught a broad array of subjects, and usually accepted women as well as men.[35]

Corporate voluntarism did seem to combine the virtues of the other two models. Without the stigma of lower-class affiliation, it offered disinterested, enlightened, and continuous management that kept the operation of education out of the rough and unpredictable play of politics. At the same time, by placing each institution under a different administrative authority it retained the limited scope essential to institutional variety, flexibility, and adaptation to local circumstances. Moreover, this corporate mode of control matched contemporary arrangements for managing other forms of public business. As states turned from mercantilist regulation of their economies, their new liberal stance identified public interest with unrestricted privileges of incorporation and the removal of regulations governing economic activity. The argument that autonomous, competing corporations, aided but not controlled by the state, best served the public interest extended easily from finance, transportation, and manufacturing to education. Academies, for instance (as Gulliver implied), were educational corporations.[36]

The emergence of a new definition of "public school" signaled the demise of corporate voluntarism as public policy in secondary education. George Boutwell, sometime governor of Massachusetts, secretary of the Board of Education, and eventually United States senator, stated the matter precisely. "A *public school* I understand to be a school established by the public,—supported chiefly or entirely by the public, controlled by the public, and accessible to the public upon terms of equality, without special charge for tuition." With great care he went on to specify why the Norwich Free Academy and similar schools could not be considered public. Although they were "sometimes, upon a superficial view, supposed to be public," schools of this sort were only "public in their use . . . not in their foundation or control, and are therefore not public schools."[37] Academies could not be considered public schools, and in the context of the times "public" had become a necessary label. Thus, as it became apparent that only institutions financed by the community or state and directly controlled by its officers merited that definition, both paternalistic and corporate voluntarism were doomed.

Incipient Bureaucracy

Among the competing organizational models, incipient bureaucracy triumphed. The promoters of bureaucracy, including the great figures of the "educational revival," concentrated on attacking democratic localism. They struck first at the notion that democratic localism was in fact democratic by pointing out that it would permit 51 percent of local parents to indicate the religious, moral, or political ideas taught to the children of the remainder. The proponents of democratic localism erred by assuming the widespread existence of homogeneous potential units of school administration. In actuality the variety within most communities, city wards, or neighborhoods would foster intensely political competition for control of the local school in order to ensure the propagation of particular points of view, or, at the least, the exclusion of rival ones. "If one man claimed to have his peculiar doctrines taught, why not another?" asked Horace Mann. "Why not all?—until you would have a Babel of creeds in the same school, which a heathen would be ashamed of."[38] "If religious societies are to be the only participators of the portion of the school fund for the city of New York," the Free School Society warned, "a spirit of rivalry will...be excited between different sects, which will go to disturb the harmony of society, and which will early infuse strong prejudices in the minds of children taught in the different schools."[39] Aside from the debilitating effect of political struggle upon education, the result could easily abridge the liberties of parents by forcing them to choose between submitting their children to alien points of view and expensive private schooling.

The second defect of democratic localism was a rural bias, which overlooked the special educational problems posed by cities. Population growth and heterogeneity made extremely decentralized administration inefficient in an urban setting because the existence of "two or more independent...half belligerent and jealous districts" and "a double or treble set of officers" represented a duplication of facilities and the maintenance of uneconomical units that squandered financial resources. Democratic localism within a city also encouraged an inequitable situation, for it allowed a lack of parity in educational facilities and standards within a relatively small geographic area. Thus the improvement of the "territorial and administrative agencies, and organization of our common schools so as to enable all the people of a city or borough to act on this great interest as they act on their other great interests"— an "immediate union of all the districts"—represented the "first great step" in urban school reform.[40]

The inefficiency of democratic localism prevented the schools from undertaking the distinctive tasks assigned them in urban settings. School reformers perceived the city through an ambivalent and nostalgic lens, which registered modern life as at best a problematical substitute for the pastoral setting of early New England. Once there were "no cities and but few large towns"; most people lived by "agriculture and the ruder forms of mechanical labor." By contrast the "attendants" of modern civilization were "populous cities, narrow streets, dark lanes, cellar habitations, crowded workshops, over-filled and over-heated factories, and...sedentary pursuits that tax and wear and destroy the physical powers, and undermine the moral and mental." With its "melancholy train of evils" civilization "is not an unmixed good; and we cannot offer to the city or the factory any adequate compensation" for the pure and healthful life "which may be enjoyed in the country villages and agricultural districts."[41]

Whether the compensation could or could not be adequate, it was to come primarily from one source. For many reasons (outlined in Chapter 1) schools came to be perceived as the key agencies for uplifting the quality of city life by stemming the diffusion of poverty, crime, and immorality that were thought to accompany urban and industrial development. As Henry Barnard phrased the problem: "The condition and improvement of her manufacturing population, in connection with the education of the whole people, is at this time the great problem for New England to work out." Schools had to stem the impending degeneracy of the New England character and to heal the developing class gulf within New England cities where there existed "poverty, ignorance, profligacy, and irreligion, and a classification of society as broad and deep as ever divided the plebeian and patrician of Ancient Rome."[42]

In this setting the first problem of the schools became, very simply, securing the regular attendance of all children for a prolonged, systematic, and carefully structured formal education. In the city "so unfavorable" were "surrounding circumstances," so "numerous . . . the temptations in the street, from the example and teaching of low-bred idleness" that school attendance should begin at the age of five. In fact, the incompetence of the urban poor as parents implied the need to exchange the natural for an artificial family setting:

> No one at all familiar with the deficient household arrangements and deranged machinery of domestic life, of the extreme poor, and ignorant, to say nothing of the intemperate,—of the examples of rude manners, impure and profane language, and all the vicious habits of low-bred idleness, which abound in certain sections of all populous districts—can doubt, that it is better for children to be removed as early and as long as possible from such scenes and examples . . . [43]

As might be expected from their image of the urban poor, school reformers held that "the primary object" in removing the child from the influence of the parent to the influence of the school was "not so much . . . intellectual culture, as the regulation of the feelings and dispositions, the extirpation of vicious propensities, the pre-occupation of the wilderness of the young heart with the seeds and germs of moral beauty, and the formation of a lovely and virtuous character by the habitual practice of cleanliness, delicacy, refinement, good temper, gentleness, kindness, justice and truth." Under the influence of a surrogate mother, a female teacher, this process should continue until the age of twelve, at which time working-class children might safely leave school to receive the rest of their character training amid the practical business of earning a living. This matter of school attendance, warned Barnard, was not to be taken lightly. Should its neglect continue, society would reap its "retribution" for the "crime of neglected childhood."[44]

Henry Barnard's complaint of the "want of system" in contemporary education followed from his perception of the importance of regular attendance. "What other business of society," he asked, "could escape utter wreck, if conducted with such want of system—with such constant disregard of the fundamental principle of the division of labor?"[45] Thus the first generation of urban schoolmen began with a rejection of democratic localism and argued for carefully structured systems of education. Fully developed plans for systems of schools and detailed discussions of architecture, curricula, and pedagogy mark the reports and appeals of Mann, Barnard, and their counterparts. Their goal was to uplift the quality of public education by standardizing and systematizing its structure and content.

All their plans had certain characteristics in common, the most important of which was centralization. This had two principal components. The first was the modification and eventual elimination of the bastion of democratic localism, the district system, whereby each section of a town or city managed its own schools with a great deal of autonomy. The case against this has been outlined above. The ultimate remedy was the replacement of the district by one central board of education. In most cases, however, this was politically impossible, and reformers consequently turned to an interim measure, the establishment of high schools. In Massachusetts, for instance, both the law and practical considerations required the high school to be a town school, administered by the town school committee and siphoning off students from all the districts into the one central institution. It was thus an administrative device for undercutting the power of the districts. In Philadelphia, for example, Central High School (founded in 1838) controlled the content of grammar school instruction and modified local autonomy through its entrance requirements.[46]

The grading of schools formed the second and related component of centralization. Within the district system children of all ages were taught in one room by one teacher. This is precisely what school reformers wanted to end. As Barnard put it, one of the principal "conditions of success" for "a system of public schools" was a "classification of scholars" that brought "a large number of similar age and attainments at all times, and in every state of their advancement" together within classrooms under the exclusive charge of the same teacher.[47] Reformers argued that graded schools yielded enormous increases in educational efficiency and effectiveness, and their blueprints featured carefully designed sequences of schools of which a high school formed the apex.

An emphasis on supervision accompanied centralization. The opponents of democratic localism argued eloquently for state boards of education with paid secretaries and, at the local level, for superintendents of schools. In Boston the Annual Visiting Committee in 1845 described a state of administrative anarchy— "twenty-four men, not paid for any labor, who share a responsibility, which, thus broken into fragments, presses no one"—and concluded that wholly lacking in the system were "permanence, personal responsibility, continued and systematic labor."[48] These could be introduced quite readily through the employment of a superintendent, an adequately paid, tenured, full-time administrator. Like the grading of schools, a superintendent would increase educational efficiency and the honesty of school operation to a degree that would more than compensate for his salary (see Chapter 3).

The stress on paid, full-time supervision spilled over into arguments for professional expertise. In this way the stress on teacher training and the development of normal schools became an intimate aspect of the bureaucratic strategy. With professional supervision, the normal schools case shared an important assumption: education had become a difficult and complex undertaking whose conduct and administration demanded the attention of individuals with specialized talents, knowledge, and experience. As one writer stated the matter: "The man who imagines himself a teacher, qualified for the responsible duties of an instructor, merely because he has seen others teach in a particular way, is just as much an empiric, as a pretender in medicine, who occasionally walks through the wards of a hospital." The "day for quack pedagogues is passed."[49]

The content of education presented a twofold problem: honoring minority sensibilities while inculcating the norms requisite for upright and orderly social living. The official response to the problem of minority sensibility proclaimed the school religiously and politically neutral. "The great ideal" of the common school system, pointed out Horace Mann, is "that those points of doctrine, or faith, upon which good, and great men differ, shall not be obtruded into this mutual ground of the schools." In practice the schools did not become neutral, as Catholic spokesmen all knew. Protestant ministers, as David Tyack has shown, played active and important roles in common-school promotion and management, and it is in fact impossible to disentangle Protestantism from the early history of the common school, which exuded an unmistakable chauvinistic pan-Protestant tone.[50]

The class bias of education, however, was as pervasive as its tepid Protestant tone. A configuration of moral and cultural values best described as mid-Victorian permeated school textbooks and, equally, such statements of educational objectives as "The Necessity of Restraint." Children, lamented the author (whose basic goal, like that of other reformers, might without too much distortion be termed the extirpation of sexuality), "have not learned that present self-denial is the price at which future good is often to be obtained, and that present suffering and toil are rewarded by subsequent enjoyment. These lessons the child *must* learn ... " Without restraint and direction, the child would become "the victim of passion, and having no rule over his own spirits, he would be exposed to fearful moral dangers." Untamed human nature, according to this frightened author, strove continually to break loose into an unbridled orgy of passionate, sensual indulgence. Without restraint, "without these counter-checks upon the passions," he exclaimed, "what would our race be!"[51]

Thus, sublimation became one goal of public education. In 1858, for instance, the Boston school committee admonished parents that "every pure and refined pleasure for which a child acquires a relish, is to that extent, a safeguard against a low and debasing one." A key function of the schools became to teach this substitution of higher for lower pleasures. "Passionate" and "sensual" became two of the most pejorative words in educational discourse. "Those, whose minds and whose hearts have been properly trained and disciplined by education, have control over their passions. Having cultivated a taste for simple and innocent pleasures, rather than a love for vicious excitement, their desires are awakened by objects higher than any gratification merely animal."[52]

In their objectives for education, schoolmen thus reflected the peculiarly Victorian combination of sexual and status anxiety that forms one of the least lovely aspects of nineteenth-century culture. Whether it was out of their own discomfort at suspecting mass indulgence of pleasures that they themselves had painfully renounced, or out of a desire for social control, it was apparent that the traits of character necessary to fit the working class for upright urban living represented an idealized self-portrait of a Victorian middle class.[53]

Herein lies an irony: schoolmen who thought they were promoting a neutral and classless, indeed a *common* school, education remained unwilling to perceive the extent of cultural particularity inherent in their own writing and activity. However, it was central and not incidental to the standardization and administrative rationalization of public education. For in the last analysis the rejection of democratic localism rested only partly on inefficiency and violation of parental prerogative. It stemmed equally from a visceral fear of the cultural divisiveness inherent in the increasing religious and ethnic variety of American life. Cultural homogenization played counterpoint to administrative rationality. Bureaucracy was intended to standardize far more than the conduct of public life.

An instructive instance of this point is a debate in Pennsylvania on the degree of official sanction to be given to the German language. Echoes of the contemporary debate over bilingualism are, of course, unmistakable. Said one speaker, "I think...that we ought no longer to be divided into separate races, and by distinct languages and habits." Another put the matter even more bluntly: "I think that the whole people of the state should be amalgamated as soon as that end can possibly be accomplished."[54] For many people, implicit in the "common" of "common school" was the assumption that education should forge social unity by eradicating cultural distinctiveness. Cultural difference implied inferiority, and this is how schoolmen perceived lower-class children. In 1845, for example, the Boston School Committee described its task as

> taking children at random from a great city, undisciplined, uninstructed, often with inveterate forwardness and obstinacy, and with the inherited stupidity of centuries of ignorant ancestors; forming them from animals into intellectual beings; and, so far as a school can do it, from intellectual beings into spiritual beings; giving to many their first appreciation of what is wise, what is true, what is lovely, and what is pure; and not merely their first impressions, but what may be their only impressions.[55]

This definition of its clients as inferior, so integral to bureaucracy, became entrenched even more deeply because quite early it acquired its functional utility as a defense of bureaucratic failure. In 1876 one commentator related an alleged decrease in the standard of educational attainment to the altered background of students. (See Chapter 3 for a more detailed discussion of this controversy.) No longer did they come from rural New England families where cultivated common sense and native intelligence ruled. The material the schools were "required to shape and polish" derived from different and inferior sources.

> A very large proportion of the pupils in our cities and populous towns come from homes utterly destitute of culture, and of the means and the spirit of culture, where a book is never seen, and reading is with the adult members a lost art, or one never acquired. There are schools in which four-fifths or more, of the children are of this class . . . In such minds a sunken foundation must be laid by months or years of unpromising toil, before any portion of the work begins to appear above the surface. It seems almost impossible to give them a conception of either the uses or the pleasures of knowledge, or to lead them to that primal exercise of judgment by which two ideas are compared or combined. Even the simplest object-lessons are often unintelligible to them. Instruction can hardly be

conveyed to them in terms which they can understand, and in what they attempt to learn, memory derives no assistance from association.[56]

What indeed? But to excuse his failure?

Incipient bureaucrats of the antebellum period did not advocate only order and rigid system. Their proposals for actual classroom conduct and a reformed pedagogy moved in precisely the other direction. In this they represented the opposite of paternalistic voluntarists, who accompanied a relative lack of external order with a rigid internal system of teaching. To the common-school revivalists "mechanical," as applied to pedagogy, was a thoroughly pejorative label. As they systematized the administration and grading of schools, these reformers argued for a softening of pedagogy. They wanted to reduce or eliminate interpersonal competition (or "emulation") and corporal punishment as sources of motivation and to substitute the arousal of interest, affection for the teacher, and the internalization of a desire to learn. As one writer stated their case, motivating children necessitated *"exciting their curiosity."* The model teacher connected "with his instruction, as far as possible, what is interesting and attractive so that the associations, formed in the minds of his pupils, will leave them in love with the subject of investigation, and, in proper time, bring them back to the pursuit with readiness and alacrity." The pupil of course "must be made to work; but he must work voluntarily, cheerfully, with hope." In this way the model for the teacher-pupil relation became the relation of parent and child at its finest, both firm and affectionate.[57]

In one other crucial way the leading figures of the educational revival did not behave like traditional bureaucrats; they did not adopt the bureaucratic ideal of personality. Neither was their ideal teacher or administrator to be a colorless public servant efficiently and quietly executing the public will. Quite the contrary; the model for the educational administrator came from neither business nor the military, but from evangelical religion. It was not by accident that the period of mid-century reform was called, even at the time, the educational revival. It was to be a secular evangelism. To Horace Mann educational reform was not a task or merely a necessity; it was—and this word permeates his published and unpublished writing—a "cause." Nowhere is the evangelical impulse at the heart of the educational revival more evident than in Mann's letters of encouragement to Henry Barnard. "I rejoice to learn that Connecticut is engaged in the work of education.... What cause can be nobler? What cause holds in its embrace so much of the well-being of the future millions?" "I welcome you," he wrote, "as a fellow laborer in the cause of education."[58] Of his strain amid the attempt to abolish the Massachusetts Board of Education in 1840, Mann told Barnard that he found his "consolation" in "laboring in a cause, which has my whole heart...I know it is the greatest of earthly causes. It is a part of my religion that it must prevail." Not only were the impulse and the language evangelical, so was the style. For these educational revivalists saw their mission as converting the populace, if need be town by town, to the cause of salvation through the common school. "When I took my circuit last year," reported Mann to Barnard, "I mounted *on top of a horse*, and went Paul Prying all along the way, and diverging off to the right or left, wherever I scented any improvement. I believe that was substantially the way that Peter the Hermit got up the Crusades."[59]

The educational revivalists retained from their religious counterparts the evangelical ideal of a moral and spiritual regeneration of American society through the moral and spiritual regeneration of individual personalities. This goal lay at the center of the new soft, child-centered pedagogy. It was to be a pedagogy that recognized the sterility and even the danger of purely cold and intellectual education. Warning that dire consequences would result "unless the heart be so influenced in the tenderness of its young growth, that goodness becomes part of its nature," one superintendent reminded his constituents that "heart-culture should be paramount to brain-culture, moral culture to intellectual culture."[60] Like evangelical religion, education had to awaken and shape the affective side of personality by delicately stimulating and cultivating the emotions. Likewise, too, it thus had to engage the interest and affections of the child if it was to engender a deep, personal commitment to a righteous life.

Compulsory education followed inexorably upon the demise of democratic localism. From one direction abridgment of the freedom of property owners by compulsory taxation for school support forecast the elimination of the freedom to be unschooled. "The power which compels the citizen to pay his annual tax for the support of schools," reasoned the state superintendent in Maine, "should, in like manner, fill the schools with all of those for whose benefit the contribution was made." Taxation represented a "solemn compact between the citizen and State"; the citizen contributed in order to protect his "person" and secure his "property." The "State compelling such contributions, is under reciprocal obligation" to compel attendance at schools. Thus compulsory education became "a duty to the taxpayer."[61]

Proponents of bureaucracy argued that the heightened importance of education in urban society required a vast increase in the proportion of community resources devoted to schooling and the attendance of all children. At first schoolmen neglected the logic of their perception of the poor, or they might have predicted a less than enthusiastic response to their reformed school systems. Instead, they expected that the poor along with everyone else would respond with alacrity to the excellence and transparent utility of new or refurbished institutions. Disappointed in their expectations, at first school promoters tried a number of expedients to promote attendance, the most notable of which was the creation of reform schools, special compulsory institutions to mop up the residue of the regular public schools. "For those who will avail themselves of our schools, open to every child, provision is already made," wrote a Massachusetts legislative commission in 1847, "but for those who, blind to their own interests, choose the school of vicious associates only, the State has yet to provide a compulsory school, as a substitute for the prison,—it may be for the gallows."[62] The Massachusetts reform school at Westboro, opened the following year, represented the first form of compulsory schooling in the United States.

It soon became apparent that the reform school was too small to accommodate all those reluctant to attend the common schools. Nor did the various truant schools in individual towns and cities solve the problem. Accordingly, in 1851 Massachusetts passed the first general compulsory education law. In this way a serious confrontation with the realities of nonattendance in that state and others forced school promoters to recognize the logic of their longstanding position. The Pennsylvania Board of State Charities, for example, came to the advocacy of compulsory education by uniting the traditional relation between ignorance and crime with equally familiar arguments about the nature of cities and city children: "The character of great cities exerts a powerful, and often a sadly controlling influence on the country, near and remote. They may be fountains of blessing to a State, or they may be sources of widespread corruption, nests of iniquity, festering sores upon the body politic. The children that grow up neglected in the city do not always remain there. They may carry the pestilential influence of their vices all over the State." Heightening this grave danger was the unmistakable fact that "it is precisely those children whose parents or guardians are unable or indisposed to provide them with an education: it is precisely those for whom the State is most interested to provide and secure it." It was, moreover, those children who preferred "the pleasures and license of vagabondage and truancy" for whom "education is most needed." "Clearly," reasoned the Board, "it is the duty, that is, it is the highest interest of the State, to secure the education of these 'neglected children,' " and the only way to accomplish this was through compulsion.[63]

Both compulsory education and bureaucratic reform rested on an assumption contrary to the one at the heart of democratic localism. This dependence became perfectly clear, for instance, when Thaddeus Stevens asked the delegates at the Pennsylvania constitutional convention of 1837: "when statesmen come into this hall, do they suppose that they come only for the purpose of acting out the ignorance of those who sent them?" If elected by men opposed to education, must a representative "therefore set his foot down against all education?" Similarly, argued another delegate, "We were told that it was dangerous to force this system upon the people, when they are not prepared to receive it; but he never heard in any state, of the people asking for provisions on the subject of education, until they were offered."[64] The assumption here is clear: social change flows from the top down—always and inevitably. The function of government is to lead and to educate, not to acquiesce in public whims. In the arguments of educational promoters this assumption unites a number of strands. If everyone was taxed for school support, if this was justified by the necessity of schooling for the preservation of urban social order, if the beneficial impact of schooling required the regular and prolonged attendance of *all* children, and, finally, if persuasion and a variety of experiments had failed to bring all the children into school, then, clearly, education had to be compulsory.

Bureaucracy retained a legacy from the organizational models that it superseded. It bowed in the direction of the democrats by accepting their redefinition of voluntarism and consequently placing educational institutions under boards that were publicly elected rather than self-perpetuating. It innovated in its rejection of a loose, personalistic style of operation for organizational rationality, impersonality, and professionalism. Nevertheless, in two respects the path from paternalistic voluntarism is direct. First, bureaucracy retained the notion of a central monopoly and systematized its operation through the creation of elaborately structured schools and school systems. Second, bureaucracy continued, and even strengthened, the notion that education was something the better part of the community did to the others to make them orderly, moral, and tractable. The embodiment of that idea in compulsory, bureaucratic monopolies has continued to characterize American education.[65]

A Comparison of the Models

Although the models presented above are distinct, in reality many organizations had features of more than one, although in most instances the characteristics of one model predominated. One example was the Boston Primary School Committee. Until 1818 Boston had only public grammar schools, entrance to which required literacy, usually acquired in small, private, fee-charging schools; this requirement of course proved a burden on the poor. In 1818, after prolonged agitation, the city established a network of very small primary schools in local neighborhoods. To manage these schools the city school committee itself appointed a Primary School Committee, which was composed of a separate trustee for each school. After its initial appointment, the committee filled vacancies in its own ranks and thus became virtually self-perpetuating. Although the committee operated under public auspices, it nevertheless represents paternalistic voluntarism because it considered *public* primary education as a charity offered to the poor through the benevolent spirit and labor of an upper class.[66]

Another sort of overlap has contaminated the bureaucratic model. This is the persistence of democratic localism in the form of locally elected school boards that have retained the ultimate authority over fully developed bureaucracies. Whether in fact a given locality is more democratic or more bureaucratic depends upon its size. In smaller communities direct board involvement with the schools is easier, whereas in large cities the very scale of the operation, by preventing intimate board involvement, fosters fuller bureaucratic control at all levels. It is one of the ironies of American education that democratic localism remains—even within cities—the official administrative ideology while bureaucracy remains the practice.

Not all advocates of democratic localism have accepted that model in entirety. The feature that has encouraged the most deviation has been antiprofessionalism. Democratic localists (such as Secretary of State Thomas Barrows of Pennsylvania) who had to confront the actual conditions prevailing in most localities recognized the appalling quality of teaching and, despite their ideological preference, realized the need to develop professional teacher training.[67]

Finally, proponents of bureaucracy promoted corporate voluntarism in the case of public institutions, such as reform schools and normal schools that served the entire state or a large segment of it rather than a single community. In Massachusetts, philanthropists offered money to the legislature for the establishment of reform and normal schools on the condition that the grant be matched from public funds. This act, essentially a form of endowment, stimulated the state to action in the areas of both teacher training and juvenile delinquency. The normal school and the reform school each began with its own board of trustees, appointed by the governor. The corporate voluntarist tone of state activity in these areas was underlined by the appointment of a separate board of trustees for each new reform and normal school created, rather than their governance by one central body.[68]

The precise differences between models will emerge in summary fashion if we briefly compare the position and role of the four objective dimensions—scale, control, professionalism, and finance—in each. With regard to scale, both the democrats and the corporate voluntarists advocated smallness and viewed the proper administrative unit as the individual institution or, at most, a section of a town. Both of the others recommended that the entire town or city at the least, the whole state desirably, and, in some cases, the nation serve as the administrative unit. On the other hand, paternalistic and corporate voluntarists united on the question of control and advocated essentially amateur self-management by boards removed from direct public control. On this dimension, at one level, the democrats and bureaucrats united in stressing the importance of assigning management to bodies directly responsible to and representative of the public. However, the bureaucrats extended this position to advocate that these public bodies delegate executive responsibility to public professionals, a proposal that democrats viewed with horror.

Neither sort of voluntarists concerned themselves particularly with the question of professionalism. Both assumed that as talented, educated amateurs they were fit to manage educational institutions. Thus, when they were in control, the question of professionalism simply did not arise.

The democrats, interestingly, were indifferent on the question of finance. They did not especially care whether schools were absolutely free and tax-supported or whether they were partly supported by rates. In fact, if free schools meant the imposition of state authority on community will, they were positively opposed (as the Pennsylvania constitutional convention clearly showed). On democratic localists' scale of priorities, free schools, though ultimately desirable, remained subordinate to community self-determination. The bureaucrats, with a few notable exceptions, ardently championed free schools, which were logically necessary to their ideal of universal education. The voluntarists supported tuition for those who could pay, free education for the poor and endowment where possible.[69]

On the social role of education, the corporate voluntarists and democrats retained a pluralistic vision. As one democrat put the matter, government had as a "right no control over our opinions, literary, moral, political, philosophical, or religious." On the contrary, its task was "to reflect, not to lead, nor to create the general will." Government thus "must not be installed as the educator of the people." The democrats could see no particular virtue in uniformity. It was, after all, the idiosyncratic character of community schools shaped by local parents that gave the common school its "charm."[70]

The paternalistic voluntarists and the bureaucrats, of course, saw education precisely *as* the educator of the people, as leading, not reflecting, the general will and at the least shaping moral opinions. The "charm" of the common school did not especially concern them, if indeed they ever noticed it. Rather, they hoped for an increasing standardization of institutions, practices, and culture in American society. Safety of property, upright behavior, a reduction in crime and welfare expenses—these values marked both voluntarists and bureaucrats as the advocates of law and order of their day. As Brownson, the acute critic of the Massachusetts Board of Education, pointed out with unmerciful clarity, the Board viewed education as "merely a branch of general police" and "schoolmasters" as only "a better sort of constables." The "respectable" members of the board promoted universal education "because they esteem it the most effectual means possible of checking pauperism and crime, and making the rich secure in their possession." Education thus had "a certain utility," measured by "solid cash saved to the Commonwealth."[71]

Organizational Form and Social Structure

Even if the specific models proposed in this chapter are rejected, the underlying argument should be persuasive: that the analysis of organizational models provides direct insight into the key value conflicts within nineteenth-century society. In their arguments over the details of organization, nineteenth-century Americans revealed most clearly both their aspirations and their anxieties concerning the society they would build and bequeath. Why has the nature of organization been of such primary importance? Was the nature of organization as passionate and value-laden a subject of controversy in other countries during the same period? I suspect that the answer, at least insofar as England and Canada are concerned, is no; Americans made organization uniquely their own national problem. They did so precisely because they lacked fixed traditions and the security of ancient forms. The search for the distinctively American in art, architecture, and government, to name but three aspects of American culture, is too well-known a point to belabor.

This nervous self-consciousness knew few boundaries; it made the creation of organizations—their forms and characteristics—an intellectual and even nationalistic issue. It thus assumed special importance in the American context.[72]

But the question can be put in a more general way. Even if not quite so emotionally charged, it nevertheless was important elsewhere during the nineteenth century. In both England and Canada, for instance, problems of devising or revising organizations to cope with poverty, ignorance, and other forms of social distress enlisted enormous amounts of thought and energy in precisely the same period. One reason is that organizations mediate between social structure and social change. They are the medium through which groups or classes give form to their response to social imperatives. Hence, men and women have brought to the design of organizations their values, ambivalences, fears, and, above all, their aspirations for the shape of their society.

It is clear that nineteenth-century Americans did see alternative ways of organizing public and private life. Although it may seem inevitable today that bureaucracy prevailed, it did not seem so to men and women at the time. Perhaps if they had been that much wiser—who can say? Their failure and their vision provide respectively enduring notes of both pessimism and hope, to which we cannot afford not to listen today.

3

How Urban School Systems Became Bureaucracies: The Boston Case, 1850–1884

As an organizational model, incipient bureaucracy offered only a rough guide for the detailed design of urban school systems, which in practice emerged from the accumulation of responses to specific problems, not from a master plan. Although a reasonably consistent set of assumptions underlay the solutions chosen, the process itself was uneven, conflictual, and imperfect. Despite its dreary and often parochial detail, the story of how bureaucracy came to dominate public education is instructive: it clarifies some of the internal politics of education, helps explain the uneasy relations between schools and communities, and points to the basis of enduring dilemmas for would-be reform. Of course, bureaucracies did not develop in identical ways in every city. Nonetheless, only case studies can provide the detail essential to an understanding of their story, and there is no better one than Boston's, which was among the earliest and most dramatic.[1]

"It is said," reported a very knowledgeable observer, that in 1880, when Francis Parker left Quincy after working a minor revolution in its schools, "he received this advice from Charles Francis Adams: get a new suit of clothes, a tall hat, and keep your mouth shut, if you wish to succeed."[2] The advice was excellent, for Parker was walking with his customary nonchalance into the hottest and most confused educational hassle that Boston had known since Horace Mann and the grammar school masters had engaged in a vitriolic clash in the 1840s. At first glance the con-

testants looked similar; lay reformers were openly attacking grammar school masters and striving to reorganize the school system.
However, unlike the situation in the 1840s there was now a superintendent, or rather three superintendents, before the fight was
over, and the roles of these varied successively from champion of
the masters to ally of the reformers to seeker of compromise and
truce. But this was not the only difference. In the earlier struggle
it was the lay reformers who were championing a centralized model
of educational administration while the beleaguered masters strug-
gled to retain their traditional autonomy and freedom from supervision.[3] By the 1870s, however, reformers had become disenchanted with the effects of a centralized educational system and
championed an ideal that confusedly tried to combine bureaucracy and charisma, and the schoolmen, more than they knew, had
accepted bureaucratic structure, to which they now looked, ironically, for autonomy and protection.[4] Other cities experienced a rash
of similar skirmishes between lay reformers disenchanted with
the rigid educational organizations that had emerged so quickly
out of the enthusiastic educational revival of mid-century and the
now more organized and powerful schoolmen.

The Emergence of Bureaucracy

Between 1850 and 1876 the Boston school system had become a
full-scale bureaucracy. Sociologists have proposed different definitions (though similar in main outline) of the exact nature of a
bureaucracy's features. Carl Friedrich's definition matched the Boston situation better than the more familiar one by Weber; Friedrich's is more clearly stated and stems from a comparison of
relatively modern political-administrative units. "The six elements
of a bureaucracy," writes Friedrich, "fall naturally into two
groups. Three of them order the relations of the members of the
organizations to each other, namely centralization of control and
supervision, differentiation of function, and qualification for office
(entry and career aspects), while three embody rules defining desirable habit or behavior patterns of all the members of such an
organization, namely, objectivity, precision and consistency, and
discretion."[5] All of these elements of bureaucracy emerged in Bos-

ton during the third quarter of the nineteenth century, as the following table partially reveals.

The first element of bureaucracy, "centralization of control and supervision," was reflected in the shift from a system of diffuse supervision by over one hundred lay officials to a small school board and full-time central administrators. In 1850 no professional supervised or administered the Boston schools. All administration and supervision were delegated to committees of lay citizens who watched over the schools in their spare time. Supervising the grammar and high schools was a school committee of twenty-four members elected by wards (two from each of the city's twelve), and guiding the primary schools was the Primary School Committee of seventy-three men appointed by the school committee but with authority to act independently. In 1854 the number of school committee members elected from each ward increased from two to six in preparation for the abolition of the Primary School Committee, effected the next year. Consequently, the size of the committee, augmented by the annexation of neighboring towns, eventually grew to 118.[6]

In 1851 the school committee hired the first full-time administrator, a superintendent. In 1866 the second superintendent, John Dudley Philbrick, persuaded the school committee to add another level to professional administration by appointing the grammar school masters principals of the primary schools in their districts. The school committee itself was altered fundamentally in 1875 when a legislative act transformed it into a school board of twenty-four elected at large from the city. The same law added to the system six paid full-time "supervisors" and a Board of Supervisors chaired by the superintendent. Thus, by 1876 lay control had been centralized and seven full-time administrators, assisted by forty-eight principals, had been added to the Boston school system.

"Differentiation of function," the second element in Friedrich's definition of bureaucracy, was also apparent in both ways he has used the term. First, technical differentiation occurred as administrative duties became fixed and defined by regulation and as departments, specialist teachers, specialized schools, and age-grading were introduced. In 1850 Boston had an English High School for boys and a Latin School, which took boys of grammar through high school age; that was all the secondary education the city provided. By 1876 it had added a high school for girls and five new high schools in the communities that had been annexed and established some entirely new kinds of schools: a normal school, a school for deaf mutes, a school for licensed minors, a kindergarten, and evening schools. Within the primary schools, the prevailing pattern in 1850 was one teacher for each small one-room school; 164 teachers taught in 161 primary schools. By 1876 the number of primary schools had actually decreased to 114 despite the rise in enrollment from 11,000 to 19,000; now there were nearly four teachers for each school.

Accompanying this consolidation and growth in size was the grading of the primary schools. The superintendent in 1857 recommended that each teacher take a different class rather than remain with the same group of pupils throughout its entire school career, and this change was gradually introduced wherever school size permitted. Within the grammar schools the system of age-grading had begun in 1847, and by 1876 the process apparently had been completed. Another sort of differentiation of considerable significance was the introduction of specialization within the teaching force. The practice of requiring all teachers to teach all subjects altered with the emergence of a whole corps of specialist instructors: these included teachers of music, art, drawing, physical culture, military drill, French, German, and sewing. Most of these special teachers traveled between two or more schools, teaching only their specialty.

The second sort of differentiation, the development of hierarchy, emerged as the number of ranks within the system expanded rapidly and the salary gap between the highest and lowest positions widened. Between 1850 and 1876 the four different "grades" or ranks of high school teacher, each carrying its own salary, had expanded to seven. New titles, likewise, appeared. One was headmaster in the high school; others included assistant principal and the four distinct grades of assistant in the grammar school. Each specialist teacher, too, occupied a different place in the hierarchy, and over these, of course, were the forty-eight principals of primary schools (also masters of grammar schools), six supervisors, and the superintendent. The latter earned large salaries. In 1850 the difference between the highest and lowest salaries paid to people in the school system was $2,100; in 1876, it was $3,900. The

Structure of Boston school system, 1850 and 1876

	1850			1876		
Lay supervision[a]						
School committee	24			school board	24	
Primary School Committee	73					
Total	107			24		
Professional supervision[b]						
None	—			superintendent	1	
				Board of Supervisors	6	
				principals	48	
Total	—			55		

Schools[c]

	Enrollment	No. of schools	No. of teachers	Enrollment	No. of schools	No. of teachers
Primary	11,000 (approx.)	161	164	19,221	114	423
Grammar	9,071	22	167	24,788	50	580
Latin School (1635)	96	1	3	355	1	18
English High School (1821)	165	1	5	483	1	20
Girls' High School (1872)	—	—	—	569	1	25
Suburban high schools[d]	—	—	—	516	5	51
Normal School (1852)	—	—	—	69	1	8
School for Deaf Mutes (1869)	—	—	—		1	8
School for Licensed Minors (1867)	—	—	—		1	2
Kindergarten (1870)	—	—	—		1	1
Evening schools (1857)	—	—	—		17	142
Evening drawing schools	—	—	—		4	16
Total		185	339		197	1,294

Hierarchy of teaching positions and salaries

	Rank	Salary[e]	Rank	Salary
High school teachers				
male	master; submaster Latin School, English High School; usher	$800–2,400 ($1,320–3,750)	first grade: headmaster, master, sub-master, usher	$1,700–4,000, including increments within each position
female	—	—	third grade: assistant principal; first, second, third assistants; normal school assistant	$1,000–2,000
Grammar school teachers				
male	grammar and writing master, usher	$300–1,500[f] ($490–2,960)	second grade: master, sub-master, usher	$1,700–3,200, including increments within each position
female	—	—	fourth grade: first, second, third assistants	$600–1,200, with increments only for third assistant

	1850		1876	
	Rank	Salary[e]	Rank	Salary

Hierarchy of teaching positions and salaries (cont.)

	Rank	Salary[e]	Rank	Salary
Primary school teachers	primary school teacher	$300 ($490)	fifth grade: fourth assistant	$600–800
Special teachers	—		special grade: 36 different positions, e.g., director of drawing	highest: $3,300
Supervisory personnel	—		superintendent supervisor principal	$4,500 $4,000 receives salary for teaching rank
Special instructors[g]	—		general supervisor of music	1
			director of music	6
			normal art instructor and general supervisor of drawing	1
			special instructor of drawing	6
			vocational and physical culture: high schools	1
			military drill: high schools	1
			French: high schools	5
			German: high schools	3
			sewing: grammar schools	26
			truant officers	14

School expenditures

	1850	1876
per pupil	$10.65	$29.88
tax rate[h]	0.92	1.86
total	$311,494.95	$15,252,199.73

Population

	1850	1876
Ages 5–15	24,275	66,720
Total	138,788	341,919

a. Two members of school committee elected from each of city's 12 wards in 1850, with mayor as *ex officio* chairman; changed to 6 elected from each ward in 1854; grew to 118 members. Primary School Committee appointed by, but with authority independent of, school committee; abolished in 1855 and jurisdiction transferred to school committee. School committee changed to school board 1875, with 24 members elected at large from city.

b. First superintendent appointed 1851. Position of supervisor created by legislation, 1875. Masters of grammar schools appointed principals both of their own schools and of primary schools in their districts, 1866.

c. Latin School took students of grammar as well as high school age; Girls' High School separated from Normal School. Evening high school estab. 1869; evening drawing school estab. 1870. Figures

d. Suburban high schools—including Brighton (estab. 1841), Charlestown (estab. 1848), West Roxbury (estab. 1849), Roxbury (estab. 1852), Dorchester (estab. 1852)—came into Boston system as result of annexation of respective towns. Figures mask an internal change: primary schools were not only consolidated and made larger; they were also graded, starting in 1857. The grading of grammar schools began in 1847.

e. Salary figures in parentheses indicate approximate value of 1850 salaries adjusted for changes in cost of living to 1876 equivalency.

f. Salary of grammar school teachers not differentiated by sex; most likely all those labeled assistant were female.

g. Special instructors are also included in enumeration of teachers in different schools. Authorization to teach sewing was given in 1854.

h. Tax rate represents mills per dollar of valuation raised by taxes for school support.

elaboration of hierarchy was very significant, for it made possible a career within the school system, a development that made education a far more appealing occupation than before.

The third element of bureaucracy is "qualification for office"; that is, appointment and promotion rest on objective qualifications. In 1850 the loose rules for the examination of teachers were applied casually, and the examinations themselves were conducted by amateurs with no necessary capacity for determining the fitness of a candidate for teaching. The teachers themselves, by and large, had had no specific pedagogical training. By 1876 the level of appointment of a teacher supposedly rested on predetermined, professionally derived and administered standards; examinations, now much more formal, were conducted by the supervisors, and candidates were awarded different classes of certificates according to their performance on the tests. Moreover, a sizable proportion of teachers now had been trained in normal schools, especially the one operated by the city.

The Boston school system for the most part reflected the behavioral as well as the organizational elements of bureaucracy. The first is "objectivity" or "expertise" in performance. Innovations and administrative decisions had traditionally been made by amateur lay officials without recourse to professional advice or opinion. By 1876 an increasing number of decisions were being left to the career administrators, and, with some notable exceptions, the career administrators (considered "experts") exerted more and more influence on the decisions of the school board itself.

"Precision and continuity" constitute the second behavioral aspect of bureaucracy. Only meager statistics were gathered in 1850; there was no set pattern for administrative routine; the whims and preferences of lay officials largely governed their administrative and supervisory actions, which consequently had little consistency. By 1876 the gathering of elaborate statistics to serve as a basis for analysis and decision making had become established custom; rules existed to routinize administrative decisions and introduce consistency. In one respect, however, the Boston school system did not reflect this element of bureaucracy, for despite the complaints of schoolmen and their supporters, there was no tenure system to assure continuity of personnel, and both administrators and teachers remained insecure about their jobs.

(5) The final element of bureaucratic behavior is "discretion." No secret or private information was gathered in Boston in 1850; in 1876, however, the supervisors introduced a "black book" in which they recorded judgments on individual teachers. The book, which became infamous among the teachers, was open only to the school board and superintendent.

The bureaucratization of the Boston school system between 1850 and 1876 illustrated a general process in American urban life and in places besides Boston. In Boston, for instance, the various functions originally associated with the police were gradually being assigned to new specialized agencies, and the police force itself was becoming professionalized and more elaborate in organization. Elsewhere, commentators who tried to describe American education in the 1870s and 1880s stressed the bureaucratization of urban education. An example is the critical description by B. A. Hinsdale, then president of Hiram College in Ohio:

> Our common schools constitute a highly complex and differentiated, a vast and powerful system. The machinery of this system is tens of thousands of school houses, thousands of libraries, vast illustrative apparatus, boards of directors and boards of examiners, Normal Schools and Institutes, reports and bureaus, commissioners and superintendents, and more than a quarter of a million of teachers. In the towns and cities, the system has taken on a form especially complex and costly. There are the primary, grammar and high schools, with their grades, A, B, C, and D, not to mention the minor divisions which a layman can hardly keep in his head while hearing them; each one of which divisions is supposed to represent some definable stage in the training of a man. There are the teachers of the various grades, from the primary teachers up by way of the principal to the Superintendent of Public Instruction and his staff of assistants. Behind these come trooping in the Kinder-garten teachers, the normal and training teachers, followed by the music- and drawing-masters—each one having his bundle of reports under his arm and his sheet of percentages in his hand. The whole body of public school teachers constitutes an intelligent, active and powerful profession; presenting in some respects the appearance of an hierarchy of education.[7]

From the timing of the various developments in Boston and elsewhere one important fact about the nature of bureaucratization becomes clear. It did not spring fully developed on the city or from some carefully drawn master blueprint. Although the structural features of the Boston school system were clearly interrelated, these features had developed singly and at different times. In this sense bureaucratization can be a misleading term, because it encompasses a number of distinct innovations and alterations (such as age-grading, the introduction of a superintendent, and the centralization of the school board). Clearly, bureaucratization was a piecemeal operation. Thus, in one sense, an account of the reasons for each structural change is necessary in order to explain the development of bureaucracy. However, a more general approach to the problem is still possible because underlying the different innovations were certain pressures and predicaments that forced educational development in the direction of bureaucracy.

Perhaps the most fundamental problem facing school systems was the increasing complexity of administering urban education. Boston is a useful example. In 1855 the city had only a superintendent and a school committee of seventy-six part-time lay members to supervise and coordinate over 160 primary schools, which fed nearly fifty grammar schools, which in turn led to the two high schools. A part-time interest of busy people, the school committee could not oversee the work of individual schools with any care. At least under the recently abolished Primary School Committee someone had been responsible for each school. In some cases this arrangement had undoubtedly led to a close if paternalistic supervision. Now, however, these schools, taught by largely untrained young women chosen through haphazard methods, were left without guidance. The superintendent, for all his remarkable energy, certainly could not regularly visit and advise over two hundred schools. Thus there was little coordination or direction in the school system, which staggered under a growing, increasingly dense, and heterogeneous population. Grammar school masters had no way of assuring that the children coming to them from the primary schools had received a reasonably systematic, competently taught primary education. Nor, on the other hand, could the high schools assure that their students had a reasonably common educational background. No reliable or systematic process existed for weeding out ineffectual teachers or for preventing their entry into the system at the primary level. In short, to function with any degree of efficiency and effectiveness the school system desperately needed some coordination and increased supervision.[8] In 1851 this argument had been effective in persuading the school committee to hire the first superintendent; it was convincing in 1876 in spurring the appointment of a board of supervisors and in streamlining the school committee. The argument had been effective, too, in making the grammar school masters principals of the primary schools in their districts.

The appointment of the grammar masters as primary principals was one of the most momentous of Philbrick's innovations. He first urged this change in 1865, and it took effect the next year after a subcommittee of the school committee unanimously recommended its adoption. The subcommittee, in recommending the change, offered a number of reasons, including the magnitude and increasing complexity of the administration of Boston's schools. As individual schools had grown from 200 to sometimes 600 or 800 pupils, they had been divided into classes taught by teachers with often little experience and of varying abilities. With no central direction teachers taught as they wished, and in passing from teacher to teacher, the child, buffeted between different approaches, received an inconsistent education. Because it lacked a "master mind" the school system was "unwieldy and inharmonious." Certainly neither the school committee nor the superintendent could remedy the problem by themselves; rather, the grammar school masters, men "of large culture and wide practical experience," were the ideal persons to undertake the upgrading and coordination of the primary system.[9]

Complexity of administration was an implicit assumption in the organizational model of urban superintendents, who argued that all large organizations from industry to the army depended for coordination on centralized professional direction by a superintending officer. The success of professional supervision, especially in the various branches of industry, indicated the need for this type of direction in education. Supervision was necessary because organizations should be based on a division of labor, which to these superintendents was the process underlying social development. The growth of civilization represented, according to the influential superintendent and professor of pedagogy William H. Payne, "a process of differentiation," whose stages of progress could be measured by the degree of functional separation between activities. Differentiation within school systems was thus an integral and progressive part of the development of a more civilized and complex society.[10]

Underlying this belief in the necessity of a division of labor in school management was the assumption that the growing size and expanded role of the schools had made their management a far more difficult and specialized task than ever before. The division of labor grew out of the increasing differentiation of institutions that marked social growth. By definition, it made society and its institutions more elaborate and complex and introduced a need for specialization and coordination not present in earlier periods. Thus, schoolmen saw such innovations as the superintendency, the elaboration of hierarchy, and increasing specialization as necessary ways of meeting their increasingly complicated tasks.[11]

As an idealized standard, schoolmen used the example of industry that over and over again formed the basis for their justifications of the superintendency. Quite often they described their school systems as factories and used metaphors based on the corporation and the machine. Modern industry, they could see, had developed its remarkable capacity through a rational organization that stressed hierarchy, the division of labor, and intensive professional supervision. If these methods worked in industries as diverse as textiles and railroads, why would they not work in education?[12] Still, it is unlikely that schoolmen attempted to model their systems directly on factories. They never advocated, for instance, as minute a division of labor nor the degree of passivity in their teachers that supervisors of factories required. An intensive comparative analysis of school and factory organization in this period has yet to be made, but it is likely that such an analysis would find that schoolmen used the industrial analogy loosely to justify the introduction and elaboration of certain general features of their school systems, such as supervision and departmentalization. This supposition is reinforced by the very vagueness with which they deployed analogies. No superintendent made a close analysis of the structure of industry or discriminated between service and production industries. Nor did any of them see any inconsistency in switching from an industrial analogy to a military one. Rather, the success of industry highlighted the relevance to schools of certain general features of organizations because both factory and school superintendent were faced with the same underlying problem: the coordination of large numbers of people in a complex enterprise. Because industry had seemingly conquered this problem of coordination, it offered valuable lessons for public education.

Schoolmen pointed out that a professionally supervised school system based on the division of labor should be based on an elaborate hierarchy and explicit chain of command necessary to keep each member working at his or her particular task in a responsible and coordinated fashion. At the head of the hierarchy should be one "vested with sufficient authority" to "devise plans in general and in detail" and to "keep all subordinates in their proper places and at their assigned tasks." Within the hierarchy itself, roles and duties should be defined clearly so as to avoid the possibility of conflict, and all members should give unquestioning, prompt obedience to the orders of their superiors. The great danger in a complicated organization, according to Payne, was "disintegration," whose chief cause was "non-conformity," something not to be tolerated in either pupils or teachers.[13]

To perfect their hierarchies, schoolmen argued, it was necessary to carry even further the development of career lines within school systems. To make education an attractive profession to men, "promotion from the ranks," tenure, and pensions were absolute prerequisites. Subject to annual election by a school board, superintendents and teachers were thoroughly insecure and forced into timidity in order to survive. Generally paid a meager salary, teachers were unable to save and had to teach until either total disability or death (or, in the case of women, marriage) forced them from the classroom. When teachers were uniformly offered a career, security, and protection, schoolmen asserted, their hierarchical systems would be nearly perfect.[14]

Added to the challenge of complexity were the problems of politics and personalities. Hardly anyone at the time would have quarreled with the sentiment that teachers should be chosen for their qualifications and not for reasons of personal favoritism or nepotism. But diffuse, lay-controlled school systems rendered objectivity a scarce commodity. Politics exacerbated the situation, for to anchor school boards to city wards was to put them in the midst of the most intense political pressure, with often predictable results. The introduction of those features of bureaucracy designed to provide impartial standards and to centralize control were erected as defenses against favoritism.[15] The introduction of the supervisors in Boston, for instance, was considered a means of lifting the appointment of teachers above the personal, amateur, and political level. The development of more elaborate and specific written regulations was intended to make the operation of the school system more routine, that is, more impartial and equitable; and the removal of the school board from ward politics was designed to raise the schools above partisanship as well as to foster increased coordination through centralization.[16]

One other reason for the development of bureaucracy is critical: it offered specific advantages to practicing schoolmen in their quest for "professionalism," and its development enlisted their whole-hearted and vigorous support. The first of these advantages we have noted already: the development of career lines within education. Superintendents fostering the elaboration of hierarchies were really creating careers for themselves and their contemporaries. Partly their motivation was altruistic: a desire to create those conditions that would attract more able men into schoolwork. Partly, too, they probably wanted to improve their own chance of advancement; those who had reached top positions could use hierarchy to augment their own power as armies of subordinates became increasingly subject to their control.

Bureaucratization also served schoolmen by mitigating an emerging problem: the regulation of behavior within the occupation itself. The concern of schoolmen with this issue was revealed, in one instance, by Thomas Bicknell in a presidential address to the National Council of Education. Bicknell noted that the alluring career prospects were tempting ambitious individuals and often introducing into school systems destructive careerist competition that generated hostility and tension throughout a staff. The division of educational opinion in the country offered "perpetual temptation" to "undignified intrigue" and "violent excitement." The existence of the newly formed Council, composed of the elite of practicing American educators, would serve as a "warning to ambitious young teachers" by offering authoritative pronouncements on the bewildering array of innovations being peddled around the country. Most likely schoolmen hoped the

Council would reinforce on a national level the sort of regulation of behavior that bureaucracies were trying to enforce on a local level.[17] Bureaucracies place a premium on acquiescent, rule-following behavior. Within them the individualist, the aggressively ambitious, is not only uncomfortable but unacceptable. The instruments that educational bureaucrats had for the task of regulating behavior were uniform rules and prescribed patterns of action (such as centrally defined courses of study) coupled with the sanctions of collegiality and promotion obtainable only for faithful service and quiet good behavior. Schoolmen undoubtedly hoped to reduce the tension and threat to themselves that arose from eccentric and innovative behavior on the part of individuals such as the reformer Francis Parker. Indeed, as I shall show, by the time Parker arrived in Boston, bureaucracy had so firmly established its grip that he stood out in an unfavorable light and ultimately was unable to adjust to the requirements of the system.

Thus, in the third quarter of the nineteenth century increasingly complex administrative problems reinforced by the nepotism and politics that afflicted school practice made the rationalization and coordination of urban school systems appear urgent. Faced with the need to rationalize and coordinate, schoolmen (and some laymen as well) justified their organizing principles with analogies from industry, which they believed had successfully solved the same basic problem: the management of large numbers of people performing different tasks. The process of bureaucratization within education was so thorough and so rapid because of the enthusiasm of the schoolmen themselves, who saw in the new organizational forms the opening up of careers and a partial solution to the problem of regulating behavior within the occupation.

Schoolmen were able to foster the development of bureaucracies as rapidly as they did because they encountered little opposition. One reason was that in the beginning influential laymen agreed with their goals. More than that, the years of the rapid spread of bureaucracy were precisely the years of withdrawal of lay interest in education. By the mid-1850s the first enthusiastic phase of the antebellum educational revival had begun to decline, and the lay interest that had sustained the movement dwindled. The antebellum reformers, however, had created incipient bureaucracies (see Chapter 2) by fostering an increase in the number of common schools and teachers, by urging grading, and by sponsoring the development of high schools and professional administrators. As lay interest dwindled, the new class of professional educators consolidated the systems they had inherited. For roughly two decades schoolmen were able to carry on this task of consolidation with a minimum of lay interference. In this process they introduced into the new school systems the classic features of bureaucracy. The withdrawal of lay zeal had left school systems open to capture by the professionals, who, quickly seeing the advantages of bureaucracy, had acted with dispatch. In the 1870s a new generation of lay reformers suddenly discovered with horror that these professionals had built large, hierarchical, differentiated, uniform, and rigid organizations.

Critics of Education: The New School Board in Boston and the Firing of John Dudley Philbrick

In the 1870s criticism of the public schools spread throughout the country. Critics attacked the results of public education, its bureaucratic structure, and, especially in the beginning, its costs. As citizens nationwide searched for ways to trim municipal expenses in the aftermath of the depression of 1873, they focused on the schools with an intensity unmatched for nearly two decades, and they noted with alarm that the expenses for public education had mounted enormously since the 1850s.[18] Indeed, although financing remained far from adequate, one of the successes of the new class of career administrators had been to persuade the public to spend steadily increasing amounts of money on their schools. This was evident, for instance, in Boston, where the expense per pupil had risen from $12.04 in 1855–56 to $36.54 in 1874–75, the year before the reform began. For many people this was an extravagantly large increase; Boston schools were already the most expensive in the country. To cries of extravagance Philbrick and his supporters replied that in Boston more children attended public and fewer private and parochial schools than in any other major urban center, and this they felt justified high expenditure on the schools. Nevertheless, lay reformers were not convinced, and one of the principal goals of the reformist movement that started in Boston in 1875 was to cut school expenses. By 1883–84 the per pupil cost had been cut by roughly one third, to $26.54. (In both social welfare and education, throughout modern American history reform has often been a euphemism for cutting costs.)[19]

When laymen turned to the schools with the hope of cutting costs, they discovered that the quality of education was not only low but had, they claimed, actually declined. In a study of the West Point entrance examination results, for example, Burke Hinsdale observed that whereas 8 of 175 had failed in 1840, 66 of 175 had failed in 1874. Although schoolmen offered solid evidence against the validity of these statistics, critics were not convinced. The West Point examination results, said Hinsdale, proved that "our common-school education is not what it ought to be."[20] The most widely acknowledged and bitterly resented critic of the public schools, minor New York littérateur Richard Grant White, similarly concluded that "According to independent and competent evidence from all quarters, the mass of the pupils of these public schools are unable to read intelligently, to spell correctly, to write legibly, to describe understandingly the geography of their own country, or to do anything that reasonably well-educated children should do with ease."[21] Likewise, with characteristic vigor and color, Gail Hamilton (the pen name of Mary Abigail Dodge), a journalist and novelist, joined critics of expense and poor results with special reference to Massachusetts:

> The school system of Massachusetts, with all its supervision and all its superintendence, and all its expensiveness, is so ineffective, it so magnifies and nourishes itself, and so neglects, not to say dwarfs, the pupils, that a child may go through the whole course from primary to high school inclusive without a single absence or tardiness and receive his diploma of graduation, and come out thoroughly illiterate, absolutely uneducated, absolutely untrained—with no accomplishment except slang, with no taste above dime novels, with neither brain nor nerve nor muscle braced for the battle of life ... The taxes of the people go to fatten "organization" and the children suffer.[22]

By 1875 the sentiment of community leaders in Boston, reflecting national criticism of public education, clearly favored a radical reform in the school system. The editor of the *Transcript*, for example, observed that "grave doubts are creeping about as to the absolute perfection claimed and conceded for the [school] system

...The system is, first, too costly, and next, too vital if it cost nothing, to escape criticism much longer."[23]

Aside from their desire to cut expenses, reformers, at the start of their campaign, would have found it hard to express precisely their goals, and the concrete aims of the reformist movement emerged in the course of its development. At the beginning reformers argued that children learned too little and that too poorly; the atmosphere of the schools was too rigid and mechanical; the key personnel of the system exerted too strong a hold on its operation and fresh thinking was imperative. The first actions of would-be reformers were in fact contradictory. Their initial achievement was to obtain from the state legislature a bill calling for the appointment of supervisors and reducing the school board from 118 members elected from wards to 24 elected at large. This action continued the centralization of power and increased the amount of expertise in administration, classic aspects of bureaucratization that had marked educational development in Boston for twenty-five years. But the reformers also wanted to change the operation of the system itself and to break the hold of its existing leaders. Because reformers felt considerable contempt for the career personnel of the schools, they sought to perfect the system in a way that deliberately undercut the authority of the superintendent, by failing to clearly define and demarcate the duties and spheres of influence of the supervisors, the new addition to the hierarchy. Thus reformers acted in a way that contradicted their alleged ideal of rational centralized organization. The immediate result was an ambiguity of role definition for administrators within the system, and the ensuing conflict effectively prevented the new administrative arrangements from accomplishing much good.

Opponents of the measure pointed out that the motivation of the legislation changing the nature of school administration appeared more complex than a simple effort to effect reform through centralization. Most of the opposition came from those Catholics who believed the maneuver aimed to exclude them from the management of school affairs. They asserted, too, that the bill had been pushed through the school committee in an illegal and clandestine manner. To the protestations of John E. Fitzgerald, a Catholic member of the committee, that the supporters of the bill had only the most benign intentions, the editor of the *Pilot* replied that he "knew—he was told by members of the Legislature, that the committee that framed the Bill had asked several members of the House and Senate to support it because '*it would exclude the foreign element from the School Board.*' "[24]

Fitzgerald had put the positive case for the reorganization in a way that was frequently echoed. "Because the present cumbrous School Board is a nuisance and a hindrance to education" it should be abolished. "Its tendency has been to lower rather than to raise the popular interest in the schools." Generally only the least able men were nominated for the board, because "any other position" in city government was "more sought for and honored than this."[25] Of course no supporters of the legislation ever openly admitted any anti-Catholic sentiment, although that may well have been part of their motivation. They based their case, and it was a good one, on the inefficiency of a large board, the preponderance of unqualified members, and the danger that partisan politics and even corruption might enter school affairs conducted at the ward level. Leading citizens in Boston, like their counterparts elsewhere, were searching for a way of overcoming the partisanship and corruption that had entered the political life of the expanding city, and they hoped to change the administration of city government as well as of school systems. They wanted to mitigate partisan politics in city affairs by increasing the power of intelligent and disinterested public executives and centralizing control. Both municipal and educational reforms were part of a program for overcoming the weaknesses of urban democracy.[26] This is why the *Pilot*'s charges had some validity. Mugwump reformers considered immigrants and their spokesmen responsible for the decline in the quality of municipal life. Consequently, attempts to reform civic conduct were, by definition, efforts to reduce their power.

Welcoming the first and newly elected school board, the editor of the *Transcript*, the semiofficial voice of respectable, native Boston, recognized the intent that had led to administrative reorganization. "The Community," he declared, "looks to the present School Board for reform. That body is not expected to run in old grooves." The new board was a "crystallized and condensed" body that had to "innovate" in order to succeed.[27] Through innovation the new board was to pose a deliberate challenge to the city's educational establishment, and when it began to flex its streamlined muscles, it came into conflict with the city's schoolmen, who were the objects of reform. This conflict between a reformist board and a conservative teaching force provided much of the dynamic for the controversy that rocked Boston over the next eight years.

The first important task of the new school board was to elect a superintendent; for in the middle of 1874 Philbrick, superintendent since 1856, had resigned. Philbrick was an important man in educational circles that extended beyond Boston. The editor of the *New England Journal of Education* called him "a representative American educator," and the label was quite accurate. At one time or another Philbrick was president of almost every important state and national educational association. He was far more than a local superintendent; he was one of the few recognized spokesmen for American schoolmen. One reason for Philbrick's resignation, given in retrospect, was ill health, but it is likely that Philbrick sensed the impending change in school organization and wanted to give the new board a chance to start afresh with a new superintendent. Indeed, his candidacy for a second term encountered serious trouble when a faction of the school board, in a surprise move, tried to elect someone else superintendent. Although Philbrick won the election, his position as superintendent with a large fraction of his aggressively reformist school board against him was shaky, to say the least.[28]

After choosing a superintendent, the board had to elect six people to fill the newly created, important, and highly paid ($4,000 per year) positions as supervisors. The act that had established the school board left the definition of the supervisors' duties to the board. The board specified five sets of duties:

1. To visit and examine the schools in detail twice in each year.
2. To visit all the schools as often as practicable, and inquire into the character of the discipline, the methods of instruction and other matters.
3. To collate and combine their reports.
4. To visit and examine the evening schools when designated to do so by the board of supervisors.
5. To perform such other duties as the school committee may require.[29]

Together with the superintendent as chairman the six supervisors formed the Board of Supervisors; they were left virtually free to develop examinations and to organize the way in which they would carry out their other assignments.

It is important to note that the line between the duties of the supervisors and those of the superintendent was far from clear. The school board had created an imperfect hierarchy whose top members had overlapping authority and duties. This was a situation bound to breed trouble. The potential for conflict was increased by the nature of the appointments themselves. A committee of the school board nominated twelve people as supervisors; of these, six were the committee's first choice. The important and distinguishing feature of these first choices was that all were practicing schoolmen: an urban superintendent, the principal of a state normal school, the president of the Massachusetts Teacher Association, an experienced teacher, and two popular grammar school masters.[30] Had this slate been elected much of the trouble that ensued would have been avoided, for these men and Philbrick would have shared common assumptions about their respective duties and authority and about the management of urban schools.

The reform faction within both school board and city was not satisfied, for reasons made clear in a letter to the *Transcript*. "Our schools," the writer justifiably claimed, "are now virtually forty or more baronies or lordships, each directed by a master who is independent of every other master, independent of the school committee," with the result "that we have the most expensive and probably the worst school system of any of the large cities of America." With difficulty a change had been made in the structure of the system, but this necessary alteration was being sabotaged. First had come "the election of Mr. Philbrick, an amiable man of the schoolmaster type who 'likes to be friends with everybody.' He is more responsible than any single being for the failure of the last fifteen years." His election meant that "the combination of 'barons,' who like to have things 'as they were,' have united to reelect him and have succeeded." Now the election of supervisors looked as if it would follow the same course; for the people who nominated supervisors, instead of seeking out the best men, had chosen only schoolmen who would agree with Philbrick.[31]

A majority of the school board must have felt the same way, for only two of the committee's first choices were elected. The remaining four supervisors had a minimum of practical experience in public education: a minister who had been chairman of the school committee in a small town, a young lawyer who was a part-time principal of an evening high school, a lady philanthropist-reformer who had had some marginal connection with public schools years before, and a man whose present occupation was unclear but who was definitely not a professional educator. The majority of the supervisors represented the lay reformist interest on the school board. Truly, the school board had asked for the trouble it received; it inconsistently had elected a schoolman of known views and temperament as superintendent and then chosen a majority of supervisors whose views would conflict with his. The result was predictable.[32]

Throughout the first year under the new arrangements the conflict between the Board of Supervisors and the superintendent simmered just barely below the surface. By the end of the year it had come into full and public view. Not only Philbrick regarded the new board with some suspicion; the grammar and high school masters liked it no better. Recalling the early days of the board, John Tetlow, at the time headmaster of the Girls' Latin School, wrote that "in the early days of school supervision . . . the Board of Supervisors was not, with the supervised, a popular feature of the educational system." The teachers "were accustomed to hear from official sources that the supervisors were the 'eyes and ears' of the school committee." The teachers knew of and resented the secrecy involved in the supervisors' operations; the supervisors rated them "according to a numerical scale in a book open not for our inspection but to the inspection of the committee"; their "work was reported on and . . . defects noted in another book, also open to the committee but not to us." Not surprisingly, the teachers regarded supervision as "a euphemistic term for espionage. There was a widespread prejudice against it." Though hostile to the supervisors, the teachers did not complain publicly, for their position was tenuous. Each year they faced reelection by the school board, and public criticism of school policy could easily cost an experienced teacher his or her job. Complained one commentator, "It is a notorious fact that the mouths of our teachers are closed."[33]

Philbrick acted forcefully to discredit the work of the supervisors. In his semiannual report he included a section, "The New Departure," that attacked the plan of work adopted by the supervisors. The incensed school board forced him to expurgate the report. Although the report published as the official school document did not contain Philbrick's accusations, he published the original version separately and reprinted the offensive section in the *New England Journal of Education*.[34]

The supervisors had made three mistakes. They had adopted a "radically wrong" theory for examining teachers; they had settled on a faulty plan of examining the schools; and, most offensively and frustratingly, they had given to the regulations governing their actions an interpretation that brought them into "direct conflict with the functions of the superintendent." Philbrick thought that the supervisors were, strictly speaking, examiners subordinate to the superintendent. The official regulations of the school board stated that the superintendent "shall advise the teachers on the best methods of instruction and discipline," yet the supervisors had written into their plan of work the provision " 'that the teachers' " should come to them for " '*assistance* or *counsel*.' " This was only one instance of serious conflict that was arising, claimed Philbrick, and he wished to refrain from detailing others. Part of the trouble he located in the regulations themselves, which were ambiguous and, in the interests of harmony, required alteration.[35]

The conflict of authority and function between superintendent and supervisors revealed the extent to which the administrative arrangements in Boston violated Philbrick's idea of educational organization. Like other urban superintendents, he saw as the only possible response to the complexity of school administration a rigidly hierarchical and centrally directed system. "The smooth and harmonious working of a great and complicated system requires that all its parts should be properly adapted to each other." Boston had a "defect in co-ordination," which could not be overcome if lines of authority were weak or unclear. The regulations of the school committee and city council had continually hampered the efficacy of the superintendent and contributed to the remaining sloppiness in the school system. "The regulations prescribing the duties of the office [the superintendency] seemed to be designed to prevent the incumbent from doing harm, rather than to invest him with the power to do good," complained Philbrick, adding that throughout his entire service he had "labored under the greatest disadvantages" in his attempts "to correct abuses and to introduce improvements." The only remedy, he asserted, echoing a common plea of frustrated superintendents, was to follow the lead of St. Louis, which he had visited on a recent tour of western cities, and invest the superintendent "with the requisite power and authority to render him in reality *the responsible head and chief executive officer of the system.*"[36]

To Philbrick's attack one supervisor replied in an article approved by the others. In attempting to counter Philbrick's most serious charge, the supervisor contended that he and his colleagues were giving only advice, not direction, to teachers who received advice from many other sources as well. Besides, the regulations of the school committee explicitly denied both the superintendent and supervisors the power to tell teachers what methods they should use. Therefore, he speciously concluded, no one was *directing* teachers how to teach. Surely Philbrick was confusing advice with direction, and this mistake undercut his whole argument concerning overlapping authority.[37] What the supervisor failed to analyze was the strong, informal source of coercion at his disposal. Teachers who failed to heed a supervisor's advice might be marked with a low score in the notorious "black book," which would be referred to when time came for their reelection. Armed with the power of secret evaluation and recommendation, the supervisors had no need for the legal authority to direct. They saw no overlap or chance for confusion. Despite the vagueness of the regulations, clearly noted by Philbrick, the supervisors could recognize no ambiguity. They failed to point out that although the superintendent was chairman of the Board of Supervisors and presided over their meetings, he had no power to issue them directives nor had they any responsibility to report to him or follow his advice.

The school board itself continually moved more and more toward the side of the supervisors. Because of the intense and now public controversy, two subcommittees were appointed to investigate the relationship between superintendent and supervisors. The first offered a vague, unconvincing elaboration of the supervisors' point of view and an exoneration of the regulations governing their actions. The second, instead of offering substantive motions, tried to analyze the source of the friction; its only contribution was the pious hope that both sides could settle their differences peacefully. Philbrick himself showed a desire to moderate the conflict.[38]

Philbrick's attempt to reach a compromise with the supervisors failed. As the reformist influence on the school board grew more dominant, his position worsened, and Philbrick lost the election. After twenty-two years of service as superintendent of schools he was unceremoniously fired. The harshness of the act was underscored by Philbrick's "expressed desire to be vindicated by a re-election, after which he was determined to resign." Ruthlessly bent on change, the school board would not allow Philbrick the dignity of an honorable retirement.[39]

It is hard not to sympathize with Philbrick in his quarrel with the school board. For twenty-two years he had labored energetically to construct and operate a school system. He had worked without any security in a city subject to all the stresses and frustrations that accompanied late nineteenth-century population growth and urban politics. In this trying setting he had managed not only to hang on to his job, a feat not to be taken lightly, but also to bring increasing order and system to the schools of Boston. True, he ran an expensive school system, but his plausible answer to this criticism was, first, that fewer children attended private and parochial schools in Boston than in any other large city and, second, that good schools were expensive. That the schools by the standards of the time were in fact good is a conclusion reinforced by the claims of many foreign observers, cited by Philbrick, that the Boston schools were the best in the nation. But the issue was not a simple one. Philbrick lacked imagination, vision, and the desire or instinct to innovate. His ideal of education was dull, mechanical, and rigid. Just what further progress education in Boston would have made under his direction, aside from a further systematization of administration, is unclear, and it is unlikely that he would have inspired the reforms in pedagogy and tone necessary to infuse vitality into the classrooms. Insofar as the reformers aimed at the kind of freeing of the curriculum and change in spirit that Francis Parker effected in nearby Quincy, they were urging innovations needed in urban schools. Their perception that the existing key people in the Boston schools, the superintendent and his lieutenants, the grammar masters, would not of their own accord introduce these reforms was undoubtedly accurate. But the reformers lacked sensitivity and a sense of strategy.

"In Boston," wrote the angry editor of the *New England Journal of Education*, "it is too well known that there has existed an educational war between Mr. Philbrick and a portion of the school committee and supervisors, and acting in concert, they have accomplished a purpose over which they are exceedingly exultant." The editor made it unmistakably clear where his journal would stand in the ensuing years: "In this issue we wish to hold no neutral ground." At the moment victory seemed in the hands of the reformist faction, but, the editor predicted, "the temporary victory has in it the elements of a most disastrous defeat; for the act is not only personal to Mr. Philbrick, but to every teacher in Boston." In fact it "touches every educator in America." From Philbrick's unceremonious ouster the editor drew an important moral: "Are professional educators, when study and experience fit them eminently for useful service, to be dropped unceremoniously from the ranks without due consideration for their own as well as the public interests and the rights of our profession?" If so, then the prerogatives of educators were "as worthless as a rope of sand."[40]

The school board undoubtedly hoped that Philbrick was sufficiently crushed to sink quietly into oblivion. But he was not to be silenced, and he added to the bitterness aroused by his firing with a long defensive letter to the *Transcript*[41]. The school board did not count on the possibility that Philbrick might rise to even greater eminence and thereby attain a position from which he could counterattack with increased prestige and authority. But in March 1878, Philbrick left the superintendency of the Boston schools to become United States Commissioner of Education at the Paris Exposition. He was gone temporarily from Boston, but, if the school committee breathed a sigh of relief, it was a sigh of false optimism. The submerged anger of the masters at Philbrick's firing made further trouble predictable. Philbrick had promoted the interests of the masters and increased their powers substantially. In turn he had won their loyalty. During his "long period of school service," noted the editor of the *New England Journal of Education*, "Mr. Philbrick has held the firm support of the best educators of the city... The best evidence of his success appears in the strong support received from the Boston Teachers." As evidence the editor cited a unanimous resolution of praise passed by the teachers of Boston and a testimonial written by Joshua Bates, one of the oldest and most influential of their number.[42] The school board had seriously underestimated both the popularity and strength of their opponent and the resistance of his supporters. By firing Philbrick it had not quieted but inflamed the controversy.

The removal of Philbrick ended the first phase of the controversy. This phase had revealed one of the problems inherent in the development of a bureaucracy, namely the definition of roles. When bureaucracy arises in a piecemeal fashion, as it did in Boston, the demarcation of duties and lines of authority becomes blurred and tensions arising from overlapping functions are almost inevitable. In Boston this problem was exacerbated by the school board's sloppy process of organization building. Hostile to Philbrick and his ideas, the school board had created a semiautonomous Board of Supervisors with powers so ambiguously defined that conflict with the superintendent was unavoidable. Had the school board wanted to perfect bureaucratic organization, it should have invested Philbrick with full executive authority, subordinated the supervisors to his direction, and filled the new positions with men who shared his point of view. Instead it tried to compromise by keeping Philbrick and appointing a hostile set of supervisors. Had the board clearly defined its goal as reformist and anti-Philbrick, it should not have elected him to begin with but have chosen a superintendent in sympathy with its wishes and with the sentiment represented by the supervisors. But the school board members in these few years proved to be both bad bureaucrats and ineffectual reformers. Instead of rejuvenating the schools, they merely caused trouble. Although they may have had a more lively idea of the possibilities of education than Philbrick, they did not share his understanding of organizations and their constraints. After disposing of Philbrick, the reformist faction attempted to go about its job in a more thorough, ruthless, and efficient manner. But, again, ultimately it failed through its insensitivity to the nature of organization. In this case the reformers failed to reckon with the power of entrenched informal groups within the system itself.

Critics of Bureaucracy: The Attack on the Grammar School Masters

The Boston school board added to its problems by its choice of a successor to Philbrick. The man elected, Samuel Eliot (a relative of Harvard's president), had little practical experience in the administration of public education. Born in Boston in 1821, Eliot had graduated first in his class from Harvard at the age of eighteen. Following graduation he toured Europe and wrote a series of history books, including *The History of Rome, The Early Christians,* and a *Manual of U.S. History.* In 1856 Eliot became professor of history and political science at Trinity College in Hartford, and from 1860 to 1866 he served as its president. In 1874 (the intervening eight years are vague) he became principal of the Girls' High and Normal School in Boston but resigned after only two years because of ill health and family bereavement. Eliot, a scholar and an amateur in public school affairs, appealed to the reformist element of the school board, and his reports quickly made it evident that he sympathized with the faction that had deposed Philbrick. Eliot's difficulties were compounded by his snobbish social darwinism and isolation from the schools. As a practical administrator he was generally inept. In contrast to Philbrick his reports were filled not with pragmatic discussions of practical subjects but with long and florid discourses more suitable to a late nineteenth-century literary magazine than to the report of an urban superintendent.[43]

Throughout 1878 the reformist faction continued to gain power. Despite heavy opposition, it managed to reelect one of the laymen who had been serving as a supervisor. This triumph was reinforced later in the year when fourteen of the twenty-four places on the school committee passed to new people at the annual election. Although one new member, ex–grammar school master George Hyde, was a solid schoolman, the new committee was heavily reformist in composition, and it was led by a brash young man who had a model for educational reform in the experience of his older brother. This young man was Brooks Adams.[44]

The diagnosis of educational ills offered by the new school board reflected the concerns of lay reformers throughout the country. Added to the national concern about the cost and quality of education was an often subtle perception of the effects of bureaucratic organization on teachers and students. One of the common themes in their criticisms of bureaucracy was its rigidity. "It cannot be denied," claimed Burke Hinsdale, "that the graded school system is exceedingly rigid and inelastic. Its tendency is to stretch all the pupils on the same beadspread." One consequence of this, he concluded, was that the schools recognized no differences among pupils and sacrificed the "brightest children to the dullards or to the mediocre" in an inevitably doomed attempt "to make equal the legs of the lame." Much the same held true for pedagogy within rigidly graded classrooms, and Hinsdale singled out for attack "the teacher's tendency to formalism and routine."[45] Similarly, Gail Hamilton remarked satirically, "The ideal of the [public school] system is to take a key and wind up at the centre and have the whole mechanism, to the very circumference, tick, and strike, and move with unchanged regularity." Shrewdly Hamilton singled out the metaphor offered by schoolmen in defense of supervision: the factory. "The fatal weakness which is fastening on our schools," she said, "is succinctly suggested in this figure."[46] Likewise, Charles Francis Adams, Jr., characterized the current phase of the super-intendency as "the drill-sergeant stage in education, or the school company-front." Children had become raw material moving down an assembly line: "they must receive the same mental nutriment in equal quantities and at fixed times." Public school systems were "huge, mechanical, educational machines, or mills," combining "the principal characteristics of the cotton-mill and the railroad with those of the model state's prison."[47]

The consequences of this rigidity particularly alarmed critics. Perceptively they recognized the effect that a bureaucracy has on the personality and behavior of its members. "Many minds," wrote Hinsdale, "are incapable of using forms without becoming their slaves." Equally unfortunate was that routine and ritual drove a wedge between teacher and pupil. The "personal force of the teacher," he lamented, "goes for much less," and the pupil received far less "inspiration" than before. The old "no-system" plan was, he felt, far more conducive "to developing individuality of char-acter." In the process of becoming slaves to the routine of formal requirements, teachers lost their perspective:"the teacher has a tendency to destroy school perspective—to exaggerate little things—to sink the important." One effect of bureaucracy on behavior was to turn means into ends. All the pressures on the teachers reinforced this effect. The city schoolteacher by an "acquired bias of mind" had become a "martinet" who liked "the machine better the stiffer and firmer it can be made." By stressing the meek acceptance of orders from superiors the system "narrows responsibility and stifles thought"; it thus became "death to all inventive minds."[48]

Gail Hamilton noted that bureaucracy confused means and ends. "The servants of the people are sonorously busy, here, there and everywhere, about the 'system,' but meanwhile the child for whom it is, was, or ought to be created, has escaped untaught." By harassing the teachers with petty, time-consuming duties supervisors destroyed their "individuality." The result was that "all active, original, independent and stimulating minds" were leaving the public schools, and their places were being filled by "only such as are obliged by poverty to teach, and such others as are so listless and sluggish and uninterested that they care not what they do or leave undone" as long as the term ended and they received their pay. Bureaucracy, Hamilton perceived, had created a structure that demanded a particular sort of personality.[49] Bureaucracy could accommodate only the bureaucrat.

The more perceptive critics, such as Hinsdale and Charles Francis Adams, Jr., saw the dilemma that faced would-be educational reformers. Hinsdale was too shrewd and realistic to believe that anyone could reverse the direction of development and return to the old no-system plan of public education, even if it had in its day produced better results. Organization was necessary. Still, organization crushed spontaneity and originality. Here was the organizational dilemma, and to his credit Hinsdale recognized it in all its complexity. "You cannot have the greatest personal intrepidity and the best organization—the most individuality of character and the best organization—the most individuality of character and the most imposing array of school children and schoolmasters." How, he asked, looking for a compromise, "shall we combine both elements most wisely?"[50]

For all his perceptiveness Hinsdale had little to offer as a solution; his only concrete suggestion was to prune and streamline the curriculum, which had become burdened with so many subjects that teachers, just to cover the ground, were forced into mechanical presentations. But this solution touched only the packed curriculum which made rigid, crowded timetables a necessity; it did not provide ways of lessening the effects of a centralized, hierarchical structure on the teachers and pupils. In short, it missed the underlying dimensions of the problem and offered only a very partial solution to the tough and troubling questions Hinsdale had asked. No one else, unfortunately, had a viable alternative to bureaucracy. Gail Hamilton could propose only a romantic importation into the city of the ungraded country schoolhouse she nostalgically remembered from her youth and the complete abolition of educational administration. Richard Grant White offered only the untenable solution of the virtual abandonment of public education and a return to a charity system inspired by his fond recollections of the New York Public School Society.[51] On the surface the most promising alternative was offered by Charles Francis Adams, Jr., but this, too, had serious deficiencies.

More than any other critic Adams accepted the need for a planned hierarchical educational structure. Adams's goal was to reduce the mechanical, formalistic tone of the structure by infusing it with new vigor and life. His proposal for accomplishing this was a revitalized superintending class trained scientifically in universities. But the weakness of this prescription lay in the fact that Adams was generalizing from his experience in Quincy, a town of only 10,000 people. He assumed that one man of magnetic personality, trained in educational science, could single-handedly rejuvenate, as had Francis Parker, an entire school system. Adams was relying on the hope that an intelligent charismatic leader placed in a bureaucracy would refine the necessary formal elements of that organization and simultaneously remove the deadening effect of systematizing on its spirit. Adams observed the effect that the structure of an organization could exert on the temper of its operations and the personality of its participants, but he did not consider these effects necessary and predicted that one inspired leader could remove them.[52] In a town of 10,000 charismatic bureaucracy might work, as Francis Parker had proved. But for a

school system in a city of hundreds of thousands charismatic bureaucracy was a very insubstantial model on which to place all
one's hopes.

In Boston the reformers, who agreed with the analyses of the
critics of educational bureaucracy, assumed that they could draw
up a new blueprint for the city's schools and simply put it into
effect. They realized that some resistance would come from teachers, especially grammar school masters, but they reasoned incorrectly that they could easily break the hold that the latter, through
their control over primary education, had on the system. They
would do this by substituting the supervisors, charismatic bureaucrats, for the masters. Through executive fiat they expected to alter
the conduct of an entire school system and all the relations within it.

On January 28, 1879, the new school board revealed its reformist aspirations when it appointed a committee on the revision
of the school system with the following order: "That a Special
Committee of five be appointed, with full authority, to examine
into every department of the school system of this city, to ascertain
what, if any, change or changes can be made in the organization
of the public schools, the courses of study, the furnishing of supplies, etc., by which the annual expenses may be lessened or the
efficiency of the schools increased." Between January and May the
committee, pursuing its twin objectives of economizing and improving, scrutinized virtually every facet of the school system and,
in a series of six reports, offered recommendations for sweeping
changes. The leading spirit of the revision committee, and the
author of its reports, was generally acknowledged to be Brooks
Adams. Reviewing the work of its special committee and its own
action at the end of the year, the school board asserted confidently,
"a new departure has been begun."[53]

Some of the revision committee's many recommendations were
designed, despite superfluous rationalizations, to save money.
Among these were the abolition of the kindergarten and inter-
mediate schools, the reorganization and centralization of the high
school system, a new scheme for furnishing supplies to students,
and the elimination of special instructors. Others were intended
to have a more directly educational effect. These included pruning
the curriculum (as recommended by Hinsdale), designing a new

grammar school course, and upgrading the Normal School by raising admission standards, adding a postgraduate year, and increasing the amount of practice teaching in the curriculum. By the end of the year one goal seemed clearly in sight, and the board reported with pleasure that it had already reduced per pupil spending in Boston, the highest in the nation, and expected the decrease to continue.[54]

The most controversial and consequential recommendation of the revision committee called for ending the supervision of the primary schools by the grammar school masters. Though once necessary, this plan had never been entirely satisfactory, argued the committee, because it made the masters both supervisors and teachers. To perform one duty well they had to neglect the other, and the improvement in the primaries was obtained at the expense of the grammar schools. Moreover, the masters diluted their influence by spreading it over a number of schools. "Teaching and supervising *in a school* are largely matters of personal magnetism, which, when extended to more schools than one, loses its power." For educational success, the committee was saying, charisma was as important as system, and it was charisma that the principalship of the masters had sacrificed.[55]

The committee also contended that in the modern world the "tendency . . . is to specialism." One person could not master two specialties (the committee conveniently forgot its proposed elimination of specialist teachers), and primary and grammar teaching were distinct fields. The principal who supervised both kinds of schools "must be master of two specialities," and this the committee felt was too much to expect of one man. In fact the grammar school masters, argued the committee, were "not fitted by a lively interest in the work, or by special study of the subject" for primary school supervision.[56]

As the committee analyzed the grammar school masters themselves, its real concerns began to emerge. Like other lay reformers throughout the country the committee believed that rigidity and formalism had stultified urban education, that reform required exchanging mechanistic models and procedures for ones infused with vitality and charismatic enthusiasm. "The tendency of our system in recent years has been to produce 'machine schools.'" Individuality in the teachers had not been "encouraged" and, indeed, had been stifled by "painfully minute details as to methods." The masters' principalship had brought improvement, but one purchased through a needless circumscription of the "independence and individuality . . . of the subordinate instructors . . . "[57]

The reformers in Boston recognized this effect of a hierarchical structure on personality quite as clearly as did their counterparts around the country. "The school-master," they wrote, "is proverbially dogmatic in his own sphere . . . One tendency of his calling is to make him arbitrary." The supervision of the principals had been "overdone," and a check upon the tendency to 'machine school-keeping' " was required "not in the Primary Schools only, but also in the Grammar Schools."[58] The effect of his position on his personality made the grammar school master peculiarly unfit for managing primary schools, the committee added, because the latter contained so many little girls. "However gentle the nature of a principal at the outset, the management of a large school for boys for a term of years would inevitably harden it." Likewise, management of a school for girls would soften a rough nature. "It is better," the committee sentimentally proclaimed, "that delicate and sensitive little girls should not be supervised by men who have not been subjected to all the softening rather than the hardening influences of the system."[59]

Because the recommendations of the revision committee were so critical and so sensitive, the school board referred them to another committee, which endorsed the conclusion that the grammar masters should be relieved of the primary principalships. Instead of turning the schools over to the supervisors, this committee recommended that the number of supervisors be reduced from six to four and a well-paid director of primary instruction be hired. However, the original plan, turning over the primary schools to the supervisors, was cautiously adopted. To see how well the new system would work the school board at the end of March placed one primary school under the care of a supervisor. Pleased with the results, the board decided to extend the experiment and designated three supervisors to take charge of the primary schools. Superintendent Samuel Eliot welcomed the change in primary school supervision and predicted its success in typically florid style.[60]

Caught up in its desire to free the primary schools, the revision committee had neglected to consider the real unity and strength of the grammar masters, whose close association and mutual bonds had welded them into an influential informal organization (the Boston Masters' Association) within the larger school system. For years the masters had met monthly for dinner and discussion of educational problems. Held together by ties of mutual interest and concern, they were in an effective position to undermine any educational reform they felt unwise or threatening. Their power and unity had been increased by Philbrick, whose granting of primary principalships revealed his shrewdness and real sense of the conditions that create loyalty within a large organization. Even their critics recognized just how much power the grammar masters had possessed, and how much they lost:

> Time was when each grammar school principal was also superintendent of the primary schools in his district. Within its limits he was a little king. With the consent of his district committee, a thing not hard to get in those days, when a shrewd master always expected to control his committee, rather than to be controlled by it, his power was well-nigh absolute. The appointment of teachers, not only in his school, but in the primary schools that were tributary to it, was practically in his hands ... The new system has changed all this.[61]

Between Philbrick and the masters had developed a mutual loyalty and respect that reinforced the cohesiveness of the career schoolmen in the Boston system. Philbrick's firing enraged the masters, who were in no mood to cooperate with the board that had caused his ouster. When the masters were in turn robbed of their power, Philbrick came vigorously to their defense. The reformers did not perceive the sense of unity, the tight informal organization within the Boston school system. Or, if they did perceive it, they failed to realize how impossible it was to ride roughshod over it.[62]

The Defense of Bureaucracy: The Masters Counterattack

Opposition to the change in primary supervision arose quickly. After the publication of the first of the revision committee's reports in April, the *New England Journal of Education* attacked the proposal as an attempt to disparage the ability of the masters. The separation between primary and grammar education made by the committee, commented a later editorial, was purely mythical, and to suppose that three supervisors could do the work performed previously by fifty-five experienced schoolmen was ridiculous. The ability of the masters as principals, claimed the editor, had been demonstrated by improvements in the schools and the satisfaction of the teachers, including allegedly harassed ones in the primaries, who "have almost unanimously petitioned the continuance of the [old] plan, and consequently expressed their opinion that a change is not called for." In short, asserted the editor, trying to mobilize the opposition of the entire teaching force, the uncalled-for and "indiscriminate attack" on the masters should touch all teachers deeply, for "whatever touches the reputation of the principals of our schools, affects every teacher in the city, and an attempt to disgrace the office is an assault upon the teaching-talent, experience, and reputation of all instructors similarly situated."[63]

Afraid to speak out because of possible reprisals at the annual election, the masters published almost no criticism of the new arrangements, but their cause was championed by others, including the *Journal* and the prominent and retired longtime Boston grammar master, Joshua Bates. The tendency of the new system was "to trespass on the prerogatives of the teacher"; this, not the masters, suppressed the individuality required in good teaching. Moreover, said Bates, it was the old system of primary supervision that had improved the primary schools radically and to an extent apparent only to one who had known them before the innovations of 1866. The plan introduced by the school board was bound to fail.[64]

By early 1880 Philbrick, now newly distinguished, had returned from Paris. Free of responsibility and the need to win reelection, he used his considerable influence to cause trouble for the school board and the supervisors. Philbrick bitterly resented the work of the revision committee, which had destroyed many of the administrative features he had labored to introduce into the Boston school system. To Philbrick the action of the revision committee was a repudiation of his many years as superintendent, and he did not intend to receive this insult in silence. Philbrick attended teachers' meetings, wrote letters to newspapers, meddled in the elections for school board and, most noticeably, between February and May

1880, published a series of scathing articles in the *Journal of Education* reviewing the "new departure" in Boston. Within the school board the masters had a few supporters, especially the retired master George Hyde. These tried unsuccessfully to persuade the board to reverse its earlier decision and return the primary schools to the grammar masters. At a school board meeting Hyde predicted correctly that "within two years the primary schools would be under the charge of the masters, as they should be."[65]

The implication of impending counterattack in Hyde's remarks reflected an unofficial mobilization of professional forces in Boston and other cities as well. Schoolmen throughout the country were under attack and for many of the same reasons as in Boston. The key men in the new urban school systems had to defend themselves against charges of contributing to a steady decline in the quality of public education by their rigid formalism, their exaltation of means over ends, their suppression of individuality, and their adoption of the personality and behavior of the drillmaster who reveled in the uniform, the petty, and the routine. To counter these serious accusations educators in Boston and elsewhere developed a number of strategies. The opposition of the Boston grammar school masters and their supporters to the revision committee was one aspect of a larger counterattack on lay reformers across the country.

Representative of the attitude of schoolmen was the response of Cleveland's superintendent and former National Education Association (NEA) president Andrew Rickoff to Hinsdale's assertion that the quality of education had declined because of the overdevelopment of highly differentiated, hierarchical, and rigid school systems. Rickoff rebutted Hinsdale on a number of points: he pointed out that Hinsdale's conception of a decline in educational quality rested on a faulty interpretation of the history of public education; he cited many observers who claimed educational improvement; he effectively demolished the validity of the West Point examination results as a source for judging the effectiveness of the schools; and he described the very real growth in the content of the curriculum. In the past, he proclaimed, the "pupil who made the utmost out of the opportunities afforded in the meager course of study provided, received an education which was little short of a burlesque compared with what may be received at present in almost any city or town of the North." Rickoff's central argument, however, was his open and unabashed defense of the bureaucracy. He argued that, instead of hindering, graded schools helped the brightest pupils as well as the dullest by increasing opportunities for individual attention. He gloried in the reorganization of school systems on the principle of the division of labor; and he championed a centrally defined, rigid curriculum. By introducing plan and direction into education, a centrally planned syllabus prevented the buffeting back and forth of the child between teachers with different ideas and approaches. "How," asked Rickoff, "shall unity of design in the fabric of education be guaranteed? We reply, in only one way, and that is by laying out our plans and specifications before the structure is commenced."[66]

To defend bureaucracy on grounds of efficiency, harmony, and rationality and to ignore its subtle effects on the temper of the schools was one of the most common strategies employed against critics of urban education. Another was to trim goals by bringing aspirations for public education into line with its actual achievements. Nowhere was this more evident than in the response of schoolmen to the accusations of Richard Grant White, the critic who aroused the most outrage and the most numerous counterattacks. White's point, boldly stated, was that there was no institution "in which the people of the country have placed more confidence, or felt greater pride, than its public school system. There is not one of them so unworthy of either confidence or pride; not one which has failed so completely to accomplish the end for which it was established. And the case is worse than that of mere failure; for the result has been deplorable, and threatens to be disastrous." White's attack included the charge that as "a mere imparter of useful knowledge the public-school system has utterly failed." But his principal and most clever argument was that the key assumption on which the case for public education had been advanced during the mid-century reform movement had been thoroughly disproved. The reformers had assumed that public education was necessary to the social and moral life of a community: education would cause a decrease in crime, immorality, and other social ills. In part, noted White perceptively, this argument rested on a confusion of correlation with causation; it assumed, from the frequent coexistence of ignorance and vice, that the former caused the latter. In reality, however, both were products of an underlying problem: poverty. Resting his case on more than theoretical grounds, White argued that if the theory was true, then the tremendous investment in public education over several decades had surely provided the most favorable conditions imaginable for its development and should have produced both a measurable and noticeable improvement in the quality of moral life and a decrease in crime. But everyone knew that the quality of society was steadily declining, that politics were ever more corrupt, and crime and vagrancy were on the increase. Despite massive attention and expenditure on public education, asked White, "Who needs to be told that in all these respects we have deteriorated?"[67]

White damaged his clever case by using faulty statistics from the 1860 census which seemed to show that school-laden Massachusetts had more crime, insanity, and suicide than did school-free Virginia. But he was careful to note that his argument should not be taken to imply that education had caused the rise in crime and the decrease in morals. Rather, he emphasized, his point was simply that it had done nothing to stop either trend.[68]

White's many attackers repeatedly stressed that his standing as an amateur made him incapable of judging the quality of education; that his attack revealed an antidemocratic animus (which in fact underlay the assaults of most of the critics of the time); and, perhaps the most justified, that his sources were faulty. But throughout these rebuttals White's professional critics refused to grasp his essential point that there was no necessary relation between ignorance and crime because both were products of poverty. In fact most of them, including Philbrick, totally distorted the point in their attempts to discredit White and claimed that he had asserted education caused crime. They rationalized the existence of crime and social problems by pointing out that in view of the obstacles they faced it was remarkable that the schools had accomplished so much. Indeed, they asserted, society would undoubtedly have been much worse without the moderating and uplifting influence of public education. As J. P. Wickersham, the eminent Pennsylvania public schoolman, wrote:

> There are hundreds of thousands of children throughout the nation that have never yet been . . . within their [the public schools'] reach. A very large proportion of those who do attend school remain . . .

but for a short time, scarcely long enough to acquire the merest elements of knowledge, much less to complete an even moderately liberal course of study, or to form a stable moral character... It frequently follows that the good influences of the school are neutralized by the bad influences of the street, and that vicious companions pull down quite as fast as the best of teachers can build up.[69]

Schoolmen explicitly denied that White's interpretation of the purpose of public education was accurate, although they did not generally state exactly what their version of the true theory was. One reason they felt no need to offer proof was that in 1873 a group of prominent educators (including Philbrick), under the leadership of William Torrey Harris, had published a credo widely taken as the official statement of the theory of education in the United States, and they considered reference to this statement sufficient to refute White's contentions about the social role of public schools, both past and present. Any reading of earlier theorists such as Horace Mann would show, they maintained, that public schools had never been viewed as social panaceas. Here White's critics were wrong, as a not untypical passage from Mann in 1848 reveals:

Without undervaluing any other human agency, it may be safely affirmed that the Common School, improved and energized, as it can easily be, may become the most effective and benignant of all the forces of civilization... when it shall be trained to wield its mighty energies for the protection of society against the giant vices which now invade and torment it; against intemperance, avarice, war, slavery, bigotry, the woes of want and the wickedness of waste—then, there will not be a height to which these enemies of the race can escape, which it will not scale, nor a Titan among them all, whom it will not slay.[70]

The *Statement of Theory of Education*, written by Harris and signed by prominent educators, had a very different tone. It contained no passionate metaphors and no predictions that the school would conquer social ills; in sober, unemotional language, thoroughly unlike Mann's, it merely stated that *one* function of the school in America was "to train the pupil into habits of prompt obedience to his teachers and the practice of self-control in its various forms, in order that he may be prepared for a life wherein there is little police-restraint on the part of the constituted authorities."[71]

The sober and modest 1873 document, lacking in boastful or extravagant claims, is typical of the period; parallels to Mann's emotional and optimistic rhetoric, quite common among those concerned with educational innovation and administration in the 1840s and 1850s, were hard indeed to find in the 1870s and 1880s. Thus both White and his attackers were simultaneously right and wrong. White was quite correct in stating that the quality of society was the test of the efficacy of popular education, which, he noted accurately, had originally been justified as a wonder-drug for social infection. He was wrong, though, when he implied that the same extravagantly high hopes were still held by schoolmen. The latter, on the other hand, were accurate when they faulted White for misinterpreting the goals of education in 1880. But they were quite wrong in their view of the original goals of popular education, started in fact by their immediate predecessors.

The disagreement between White and his professional critics about the role of education is particularly significant because of the process it reveals. In the 1840s education promoters had evangelically labored to convert the people to the cause of public schools, which they zealously described as necessary prerequisites to a secular millennium. Their successors, the second generation of public school leaders, inherited the school systems that had been established by the mid-century innovators. As it became more and more clear that these new systems were not reaching their original goals, the stated aims of education were gradually and quietly displaced by more limited and more realistic expectations. This displacement was necessary because to justify the massive and expensive organizations they operated and expanded, school administrators could no longer rely on the predictions of Horace Mann. The very survival of public education as a series of large bureaucratic school systems depended on the transformation of expectations.[72] It was a real question, though, whether the survival of their organizations became more important to schoolmen than the quality of education and the real needs of children.

Proclaiming the virtues of bureaucratic organizations, pointing out the enormous difficulties posed for the schools by their context, toning down the expectations for public education: these were the defensive strategies used by career educators. In Boston and else-where they added other activities, most notably the developmentof professional journals and organizations on a new scale. For by the1870s there existed a body of educators large enough and per-manently and seriously enough concerned with schools to sup-port national periodicals and to make regional and national orga-nizations more viable.

New publications and organizations fostered a sense of com-munity among administrators and teachers; in the pages of journals and at meetings they had the satisfaction of sharing their problems and anxieties and of knowing that they were not alone in their difficulties. The publications also gave them a forum in which to express criticism with relative safety. For instance, in its articles and editorial columns the *New England Journal of Education* (which in 1881 became the national *Journal of Education*) offered a strong and articulate defense of the career educators against lay critics as well as a national platform from which to launch a counterattack. The editor, Thomas Bicknell, was in an ideal po-sition to defend the schoolmen, for it was on their support, not on that of school boards or any other segment of the lay public, that the success of his journal depended. Bicknell thus could say what many others, circumscribed by insecure political situations, could only think. Through Bicknell the Boston grammar school masters were able to mount their strong and ultimately successful counteroffensive against their reforming critics. That schoolmen saw potential in professional organization is illustrated clearly by the establishment in 1881 of the National Council of Education as a part of the NEA. Most fittingly, its first president was Bicknell, who called the council "an association composed of our best think-ers and workers, who should hold stated meetings of several days' duration to consider with one another some of the more important questions of the day, and who should give to the public from time to time such conclusions as might be arrived at." The council considered itself a forum for mediating the claims of the many new and conflicting ideas for educational innovation and hoped its authoritative judgments would influence educational practice. The council, argued Bicknell, "will help to soften pedagogic as-perities and possibly check the growth of hostile schools and parties contending with the bitterness and bigotry that are the certain accompaniment of intense earnestness and narrow views." Bicknell believed that, divided among themselves, the professional educators would stand no chance against their opponents. Through softening enmity within the occupation and offering authoritative pronouncements the council would enable schoolmen to present to the world a united and strong front.[73]

The experience of the Boston grammar school masters reinforced Bicknell's contentions, for their internal unity and lack of contention were precisely their source of strength. In Boston, opposition to reform took the form not only of protests by supporters of the masters but also of covert and hard-to-prove resistance by the masters themselves. As one commentator noted, the masters did not like the new arrangements and "therefore, have tried, or many of them combined to ridicule the new system and throw obstacles in its way." The masters, it was widely—and probably correctly—believed, were doing all they could to subvert the new supervisory arrangements. Without writing in the journals or otherwise opening themselves to demonstrable charges of insubordination, the masters were doing what they could to ensure that the administration of the primary schools by the supervisors just would not work. The masters used their strategic position, their combination of prestige, influence, and informal organization, and their cohesiveness to plan and execute tactics that would harass and so destroy the "new departure."[74]

The Triumph of Informal Organization: The Victory of the Masters

The hostility of the masters and the controversy within the system were too much for Samuel Eliot. He could not, indeed he did not even try to, do anything to reduce it. He resigned in the middle of 1880, ostensibly because of ill health, but probably also because of the strained and tense atmosphere that he was unable to moderate. Even the school board had to recognize the urgency of finding a superintendent who could resolve the debilitating quarrel. The *Transcript*, which had been supporting the board, called for the election of a moderate man who would not press innovation. "We are now under the tension of several experiments," wrote the editor, "and a critical investigation would develop pretty deep water. A new superintendent, with new recommendations that are sure to come, would prove a shock too severe even for the schools of the 'Hub' to bear."[75]

Apparently the attitude of the grammar masters influenced the choice of the new superintendent, Edwin Seaver, for he was welcomed by them and by the *New England Journal of Education*. However, he had not been welcomed by all members of the school board. Seaver's election represented the important principle of promotion from the ranks that schoolmen were trying to build more firmly into their organizations. A native of Massachusetts, Seaver was a country boy who had attended Bridgewater Normal School and graduated with honors from Harvard College. After a brief tour of foreign schools he became a professor of mathematics at Harvard, whence "he was *elevated* [italics added] to the mastership of the English High School in Boston." Seaver, the *Journal* remarked happily, had maintained "cordial and fraternal relations" with the other Boston masters, "and none rejoice more heartily over his promotion than do the masters of Boston, and none will unite in giving to his administration a more intelligent ... support."[76] To top off his admirable qualities Seaver was a "conservative." Seaver was an ideal choice, not only because of his ability but also because he had qualities that appealed to both factions. The reformist faction could rest content with his Harvard education and professorship; the schoolmaster faction could glory in the fact that he was a successful and experienced teacher in the Boston system.

Like Philbrick, Seaver quickly showed that he understood the need for the loyalty and support of his teachers. At the first monthly meeting of the masters after his election Seaver outlined "the motives which would govern his action." The editor of the *Journal* remarked slyly, "It was very fitting, too, that he should thank the teachers for the sympathy extended to him as well as for the congratulations." Seaver suggested to the masters that when a policy they had criticized was adopted by the school board, "it would be the part of wisdom to 'let it run its race and be glorified,' or condemned." After the meeting Seaver "took his usual place at the monthly dinner of the masters, and that body ... seemed indeed to justify the remark of one of the most eminent of their number, that they were 'very, very, happy again.' "[77] With the appointment of Seaver and the consequent reunion of superintendent and masters, the weight of strength in the controversy shifted markedly to the side of the schoolmen. The dénouement became simply a matter of time. But before the final actions had been taken, Boston passed through more trials that revealed the inability of its bureaucracy to accommodate charismatic and individualistic personalities. For Francis Parker came to Boston.

Ebullient, charismatic, and a thoroughgoing individualist, Francis Parker, described by one influential school observer as the "poet of the new elementary education," had on his return from studying educational theory and practice in Europe so captivated the solid school board of Quincy (including Charles Francis Adams, Jr., and his brother John Quincy Adams) that they had given him virtually complete control of school policy, with the exception of finances, and a mandate to revolutionize the town's schools. Parker justified their expectations by radically altering the curriculum, pedagogy, and tone of the Quincy schools. Through his own infectious zeal and love of children he had inspired the town's teachers to make their schools places where children's happiness was of paramount concern. Many of the thousands of observers who annually trooped to Quincy to view Parker's work, loudly advertised by the Adamses and other school board members, testified to his success. But he changed more than the tone of the school. A comparative analysis of educational achievement in Quincy and elsewhere showed that where Parker's influence had been strongest, children had actually learned to read, write, and cipher much better. At the same time Parker doubled the enrollment of the high school, eliminated the problem of irregular attendance, and almost ended truancy, feats that other Massachusetts towns and cities had been striving unsuccessfully to achieve for decades. It was, then, not surprising that school reformers in Boston were anxious to lure Parker to their city, and in 1881 the combination of a salary double the one he received in Quincy and the parsimoniousness of the Quincy school board, which left him unable to retain its best teachers, prompted Parker to accept the offer of a supervisorship in the Hub. One quarter of the town's teachers went with him.[78]

In 1881 the appointment of Parker as a supervisor with special responsibility for primary schools underlined one goal of the reformist faction, the introduction of the Quincy system into the Boston primary schools. Most likely their desire to introduce the Quincy system was one reason the school board had removed the masters from the primary schools, for the masters were skeptical of the sort of innovation Parker represented. Stern traditionalists, they looked with skepticism on the introduction of oral instruction, the relaxation of discipline, and the attempt to introduce "sunshine in the schoolroom." The school board had never voted for the director of primary instruction that its subcommittee had once recommended, but this was, undoubtedly, de facto the role that Francis Parker was supposed to assume. One knowledgeable commentator observed that before retiring Eliot had selected Parker "to supervise the primary schools, but the school authorities placed him on a par with the five other supervisors." Shrewdly noting the lack of fit between Parker's style and that of the Boston school system, this observer continued: "As it was, instead of putting him in a round hole, they placed him in a square one; and, in consequence, he strikes a ragged edge every time he turns."[79]

There is a rumor that when Parker came to Boston he remarked, "I am going to have a hard fight here, and I am going to be beaten; but I shall make it easier for the next man."[80] His forecast was only partly accurate, for within a year he had a long row, and he lost. But his defeat, instead of strengthening, weakened the cause of reform. Parker apparently decided that he would run his section of the city as he had run the schools of Quincy, personally and as he saw fit, and with little reference to established procedures or even to the school board itself. A hostile editorial in the *Globe* proclaimed that "by sheer arrogance and assumption" Parker had "attained the position of 'boss' of the third division committee, and through that of the school committee in all matters relating to the schools under his control." Parker, the editor reported caustically, "came to think, and with apparent good reason, that 'he couldn't never be beat.' "[81]

Parker, so the story went, determined to prove the superiority of his system to all others by introducing it into the Prince School in the Back Bay, where the rivalry from excellent and prestigious private schools was keenest. A success gained in this school "would be relatively of greater importance than successes scored in two, or three of our public schools elsewhere." To create his demonstration Parker wanted to put a particular teacher from Quincy into the Prince School. Because no vacancies existed there, he determined to make one and executed a complex maneuver, described by his subsequent accusers as a game of checkers. The victim of Parker's game was Mrs. Lydia A. Isbell, fourth assistant in the Blossom Street School. Mrs. Isbell, a widow who had been raised in the district in which she taught, had served in the Blossom Street School for seventeen consecutive years. Her total service had been nearly thirty years. After marriage she had moved West with her husband and returned when he died. A popular and morally faultless woman who had taught many of the children and adults of the district, she had previously received a rating of "second" or "good" from the supervisors. Parker rated her sixth or "bad, very bad." His district committee, allegedly now completely under his sway, agreed to fire Mrs. Isbell summarily. Then the series of moves Parker had planned became clear. Miss Freeman of the Poplar Street School was to take Mrs. Isbell's place; that of Miss Freeman was to be filled by Miss Kendrick of the Prince School; and into the now vacant position in the demonstration school was to go Parker's favorite from Quincy. One additional complication was Parker's assertion that his Quincy teacher "could not compete with girls from the high and normal schools" in the standard teacher's examination, but he overcame this problem by bullying the committee to waive the test.[82]

The firing of Mrs. Isbell was too much for both the opponents of Parker and the residents of the Blossom Street district. They tried to persuade the school committee to reinstate Mrs. Isbell, but all attempts were "frustrated by Colonel Parker, who insisted that 'it was too late.' " A number of "the most worthy citizens of West Boston protested, and a petition, signed by Reverend C. A. Bartol, Alderman Slade, Thomas Gaffield [a retired merchant], F. T. Connell and others was sent to the School Board for a hearing." Under such pressure the board had little alternative, and at its hearing on the dismissal of Mrs. Isbell the full facts of the case emerged for the first time.[83]

Leading the violent attack on Parker during the hearing, Gaffield pointed out that Parker's opinion ran counter to testimony from all the competent educators who had observed Mrs. Isbell at work over the years. Parker had claimed that in his five short visits to

Mrs. Isbell's classroom, spanning eleven months, he had been unable to teach her anything, but Mrs. Isbell's plaintive reply was "How could it be so when he did not try to teach me?" Gaffield was particularly outraged by Parker's arrogance in the whole matter. Parker, he said (and Parker apparently did not deny the charge), had boasted, "I have laid my plans. I have beaten. When I lay my plans I am not turned aside by every whiff of wind." Alderman Slade also spoke for Mrs. Isbell. As for the Quincy system, he said: "We have had enough of it." Reverend Bartol defended Mrs. Isbell's character, and a number of former pupils "bore further testimony to her qualifications, and to the love which children have for her, and to the esteem in which she is generally held at the West End." The hearing was a thorough, public condemnation of Parker. He had gone too far. Amid the bureaucratic uniformity of the Boston school system his individualistic style, his contempt for regulations and standard operating procedures, emerged in a harsh and glaring light. After the facts became public at the hearing, the school board had little choice, and only Brooks Adams supported Parker. The board officially reinstated Mrs. Isbell in her school.[84]

Parker was not a man to take defeat lightly. When Gaffield decided to run for the school board the following November, he found the supervisors, no doubt mobilized by Parker, arrayed against him. But Gaffield won, and in early 1882, when it was time for a new election of supervisors, members of the school board remembered Parker's behavior and were no more forgiving than Parker himself had been; he squeaked into office with a majority of two votes. The reason for the hostility to Parker, claimed an inside observer, was his "intense egotism . . . His individuality has been plucked of some of its feathers, and should he accept gracefully the situation, he will have the satisfaction of assisting in the good work of the general pacification which is to come."[85] These critics, sympathetic to the grammar school masters, realized that it was precisely Parker's individuality, his inability to accept the system and its constraints, that made him unacceptable in Boston. That he had talent they admitted, but they wanted to curb his style and hone him down until he fit nicely into their machine.

It is not surprising that Parker soon left Boston. When he decided to take a job in Chicago, even hostile sources expressed regret, for no one could deny his magnetism and ability in a classroom. His new position suited Parker's personality far better than the supervisorship in Boston, for as principal of a normal school he enjoyed complete autonomy and authority.[86] Parker's experience in Boston revealed the incompatibility of charisma and bureaucracy; it showed the utopianism of those who proclaimed that one enlightened and magnetic man could transform a large urban school system. Boston reformers had placed their hopes on charismatic authority: able outsiders hired as supervisors were to break the grip of the masters and, by their personal influence, reform the temper of the schools. One reason the reformers failed was their reliance on this implausible dream.

By the end of 1881 it was clear that events in the Boston school system were still moving in favor of the masters and their supporters. For one thing, prosperity had returned and the need for economy was no longer urgent. Thus, noted the *Journal of Education*, the force motivating reform for the last five years had finally disappeared. Very possibly Parker's gaffe accelerated the reversal of the "new departure" by discrediting the supervisors and the revisionist faction on the board, especially Brooks Adams. At the city Democratic convention in 1881 only the chairman's tie-breaking vote renominated Adams for school board, and, with this evidence of dissatisfaction, he withdrew. The withdrawal of Adams and the election of Gaffield, the retired merchant who was Mrs. Isbell's knight, symbolized the shifting of educational opinion, reflected too in the letters to newspapers calling for a return to the old system. Some of these letters came from Philbrick, who, sensing that the city was ripe for change, vitriolically denounced the school board and called on the voters to turn them out of office en masse.[87]

Although only four of its twelve recently elected members were new, the school board of 1882 gave indications from the beginning of the year that change was imminent. The ex-master who wrote the anonymous column "Boston Gossip" for the *Journal of Education* noted with satisfaction that the board was now conservative, and he reported that even Brooks Adams had become convinced that the reforms imposed three years earlier by his committee had been unwise. Even the *Transcript* changed its position and favored a return of the primaries to the grammar masters.

Reports filtered into public, too, that the grammar school masters found the children coming from the reformed primaries less well prepared than those who came before the change. Predictably, then, in early February members of the school board offered two motions, one to return the principalship of the primary schools to the grammar masters and the other to subordinate the supervisors to the superintendent by making them assistant superintendents. Opponents of the measures tried delaying tactics, but eventually the board voted to consider the motions and held a special hearing at which, reportedly, four of the supervisors and all the masters summoned recommended the restoration of the primaries to the grammar masters.[88]

Until this hearing Seaver had remained silent as he tried to learn what sort of compromise could be achieved. In his first year of office he had made the study of primary supervision his major task and had visited each primary schoolroom at least once and many two or three times—no mean feat given that the city had between 500 and 600 primary school classrooms. His quiet diligence reaped dividends, for early in 1882 the school board reelected him unanimously. One supporter of the schoolmasters, welcoming his reelection, noted that although Seaver had developed no settled policy as yet, he had been remarkably successful in maintaining the existing balance and increasing harmony within the school system. Armed with a unanimous vote of confidence and now obviously far more secure, Seaver finally offered his opinion on primary school supervision to the school board's committee investigating the issue. His speech, published in his annual report in March, revealed that Seaver had formulated a masterful compromise.[89]

Careful to offend as few as possible, Seaver remarked that the removal of the grammar masters from the primary principalships had been beneficial in some respects. Methods of instruction in the primary schools had been changed, and for the better. But the new system had overburdened the supervisors. Here Seaver introduced the new distinction that formed the basis of his compromise. Supervisors, he said, had been forced to take on the duties of principals, and the appropriate line between supervision and principalship had been blurred. Consequently the supervisors had had to neglect a number of their proper functions, and the three supervisors who had charge of the primary schools had had to act as a separate board independent of their other three colleagues. Thus the Board of Supervisors, which was supposed to be a council considering policy for the school system as a whole, had been unable to act in a unified way.[90]

The remedy for the situation was to recognize the proper line between the duties of supervisors and the duties of principals. In practice this involved once again making the grammar masters principals of the primary schools, except where numbers were so large that a separate primary principal might be justified. The supervisors, on the other hand, would not be removed from all duties connected with primary instruction. They would still oversee general policy and would assume the important responsibility of devising the examinations for promotion from primary to grammar school. This arrangement would prevent the premature promotions that critics, Seaver disingenuously stated, had considered the main fault of principalship by the masters. After all, there were so many details involved in actual day-to-day school administration and discipline that the supervisors should feel relieved to be freed from this onerous routine, clearly beyond the capacity of any three men.[91]

Seaver's distinction between the supervisor and the principal was not entirely clear, and probing analysis certainly could have located serious theoretical weaknesses. But that was not the point. It was a compromise with something in it to appeal to each side. The supervisors and their supporters could find praise of the work of the past three years and a continued role for the supervisors in the primary schools; the grammar masters, though not finding quite the condemnation of the old system they had hoped for, were to be restored to the principalships they had so resented losing. Seaver's compromise was not analyzed deeply because both sides were anxious for a resolution of the debilitating three-year conflict.

The supporters of the schoolmen were quick to point out the significance of the vote. One called it a clear vindication of John Dudley Philbrick and proof that he had been right all the time. The editor of the *Journal of Education* termed the restoration a vindication of the "old regime" and proclaimed that the teachers of the city found it a "famous victory." Despite their weak untenured position, the masters had shown their real strength; the struggle and their eventual victory demonstrated that the days had passed when a school committee could impose reform without the support of its teaching staff. Alienated by the reform movement, the masters, with the support of the *Journal of Education,* had effectively prevented the successful operation of the "new departure."[92] An influential, cohesive, yet unofficial group within the larger school system, the masters had proved that without their approval no school policy could succeed. The reformers, blind to the constraints that impede changes within complex organizations, had failed to realize the potency of the masters and had blithely proceeded to innovate with full confidence that, as the legal masters of the system, they could work changes at will. They learned otherwise.

Although no substantive changes were introduced during the next year, 1883, restoration of harmony continued. Some masters had even been elected supervisors, as Philbrick had urged so vigorously in 1876, and the course of study in the primary schools had been revised in consultation with all the principals. In accord with the wishes of the principals a number of Parkeresque innovations were dropped. Within the primary school, remarked the board, the good effects of the restoration were already evident. The board had even unofficially adopted the notion of the superintendency that the schoolmen had been urging for so long. It called the supervisors "assistant superintendents" and referred to the superintendent as the "supreme executive" of the system. Pleased with the results of its recent actions, the board proclaimed that an "era of good feelings" had commenced in the Boston schools.[93]

The good feelings persisted between formerly hostile parties. All that remained for the counterrevolution was to pass regulations officially making the superintendent the sole head of the school system. The school board discussed this issue in the spring of 1884 and appointed a committee which recommended the move, and in November the recommendation passed by a very close vote. Now the superintendent was clearly superior to the supervisors. The new section added to the regulations stated in part, "The superintendent shall be responsible to the school board as the executive in the department of instruction over all supervisors, principals and other instructors." He was to "divide among the several supervisors, as equally as practicable, the working of inspecting and examining the schools" and to "assign each supervisor one or more departments of study through all the schools of the city."[94]

The *Journal of Education* welcomed this change with enthusiasm, for it was "in the line of what the *Journal* has urged for years."[95] It was also the policy that John Dudley Philbrick had urged vigorously in 1876 and had in effect cost him his job. The Boston bureaucracy was now complete. The centralization and addition of supervisory personnel effected by the 1876 reorganization had run counter to the principles underlying bureaucracies in some critical ways, for they had left the definition of roles unclear and assigned the same administrative duties to different individuals. Instead of a smoothly efficient hierarchy the changes had introduced confusion and controversy into the school system. Moreover, reformers had violated bureaucratic canons by appointing laymen to high office instead of promoting from the ranks. Now at least these problems had been solved. The supervisors had been given a definite place in the hierarchy; functions had been differentiated more clearly; control had been centralized more firmly; some Boston masters had even been elected supervisors. In fact as well as on paper the Boston school system had become a proper bureaucracy.

One consequence of bureaucracy, Amitai Etzioni has pointed out, is the separation of consumption from control, that is, the increasing divorce of those who are served by an institution from those who control it.[96] In education, this has meant the separation of school and community, signaled by the increasing ability of school officials to ignore parents, reformers, and others outside the system. Certainly, career educators needed autonomy from uninformed political meddling, but ironically the protection they won contributed to the sterility of urban education. Their isolation lessened their sensitivity to the communities whose children they instructed, to their students, and to the informed, constructive criticism that makes progress possible. In fact the reaction of schoolmen to lay criticism became a defensive reflex as the traditions of resistance forming in the nineteenth century calcified into the responses that often set urban schools and their communities against each other in the 1960s.

Bureaucracy's success has also been intellectual, for its triumph has foreclosed the serious consideration of alternatives. Bureau-cracy has transcended its mid-nineteenth-century standing as one choice among organizational possibilities. Its contingent, historical origins remain buried in the past as its reification has cast the progress of bureaucracy as inexorable, inevitable, and even natural.

4

History and Reform

In the 1960s, dissatisfaction with the schools surfaced from many sources. Academic critics worried about basic skills; urban reformers complained about blackboard jungles and dull, repressive classrooms; social scientists documented the schools' inability to promote equality; and civil rights activists found the schools not only segregated but racist. Standard histories could not explain the current state of American education. Clearly, a historiography that portrayed public education as the capstone of democracy and the guarantor of equal opportunity made no sense when confronted with the disaster mercilessly described by critics throughout the country. Provoked by the disparity between standard interpretations and actual conditions, historians began to reconstruct education's past to account for its present. Even though the new history of education has not provided administrators, policymakers, or reformers with concrete recommendations—indeed, no policy conclusions follow automatically or inexorably from any historical interpretation—its findings illuminate nearly all the major topics debated during the last two decades. Despite the recent shift in the focus of reform from equity to excellence, the new critical history of education remains vital to attempts to chart the schools' future. In this chapter, I attempt to show why. What follows is neither a history of reform nor a comprehensive examination of any proposed innovation. Rather, it is a series of perspectives intended to show how history helps frame some of the major questions of our time.

The Causes of Educational Failure

Consider, first, the question of why American education was in such serious trouble. One of the first distinguished voices to diagnose American education as dangerously sick was Charles Silberman, whose widely read and much-acclaimed book *Crisis in the Classroom* also attempted to account for the origins of the illness and to prescribe for its cure. Because his explanation of the source of the crisis in the classroom was so flawed (as the first two chapters of this book, among many other sources, show) he provided only a shaky basis from which to improve the conditions described in his blistering and accurate attack.[1]

Crisis in the Classroom (1970), the result of the Carnegie Corporation's Study of the Education of Educators, directed by Silberman, was an authoritative, severe indictment of American education. First, Silberman correctly argued, schools fail, and indeed have always failed, to equalize opportunity. Their rhetoric of social mobility notwithstanding, schools have done remarkably little to counteract racial, social, and other inequities within American society, and their failure, he noted, had touched off "burning anger," especially among "Negro Americans...Puerto Ricans, Mexican Americans, and Indian Americans."[2] Silberman also indicated the schools for their repressive and spirit-breaking quality, preoccupation with order and control, and antagonistic, authoritarian atmosphere. Deprived even of the freedom to go to the bathroom at will, students usually became unnecessarily dependent on authorities for direction and unable to assume the few responsibilities offered them. They learned that docility and conformity were the best strategies for survival.

Noting correctly that throughout the twentieth century school reformers, including those in the 1960s, accomplished remarkably little, Silberman analyzed acutely the failures and weaknesses of several widely proclaimed but ultimately disappointing curricular reforms: team teaching, the nongraded classroom, and computer-assisted instruction. Of all the institutions of American education, one early twentieth-century innovation, the junior high school, was the worst: "the junior high school, by almost unanimous agreement, is the wasteland, one is tempted to say cesspool—of American education."[3]

Schools failed in every respect. They neither taught skills nor produced knowledge in the conventional sense; they reinforced the handicaps of poverty and race; and they tried to root out whatever traces of independence and individuality they could find in the personalities of their students. The weaknesses of teacher education, Silberman bluntly but fairly claimed, compounded all these problems. Intellectually vapid, inheriting a tradition that neglected questions of purpose, nearly useless in a practical sense, teacher education was a disgrace.[4]

How were we to account for this awful situation? Here Silberman had much less to offer the troubled and confused observer, consumer, or casualty of American education. His straightforward view of the cause of educational failure asserted, "what is mostly wrong with the public schools is due not to venality or indifference or stupidity, but to mindlessness." Mindlessness is "the failure or refusal to think seriously about educational purpose, the reluctance to question established practice." According to Silberman, mindlessness pervades all American society, accounting not only for its bad schools but for other major social difficulties as well. We simply have been too preoccupied, too lazy, or too self-interested to think seriously and reflectively about the purposes of our activities and institutions.[5]

A 125-year fit of mindlessness is a startlingly simple explanation for the persistent failure of a major social institution. As an explanation, however, mindlessness serves two purposes. First, it removes the hint of personal threat at least implicit in most social criticism. No one in particular is at fault for what happened. We can all—educator, parent, citizen—rest comfortable in the knowledge that our motives and intentions deserve no blame. Second, and more serious, the attribution of educational failure to mindlessness removes blame not only from individuals but also from the larger social and economic context in which schools operate. (In this way, mindlessness is the functional equivalent of the theory of unintended consequences popular among liberal social analysts searching for explanations that locate institutional or political failure outside the intrinsic properties of social and economic structures or individual intentions.) Without question, in Silberman's view schools could be reformed without a major overhaul of the structures that surrounded and sustained them. Neither America's long-term obsession with law and order on the cheap, labor markets, occupational structures, the harsh impacts of industrial capitalism nor biases of race, gender, and class had contributed greatly to educational disaster.

Although it would be comforting to believe Silberman right, no one reasonably versed in the history of education should accept mindlessness as the root of America's educational problems. To the contrary, educators always considered the relation of the details of curriculum, pedagogy, and structure to larger social and educational objectives. Nor does the historical record support his complaint that the balance in American education had slipped too far toward the cognitive. It would be more accurate to argue that most public schools have been so deeply concerned with the affective, so committed to the primacy of attitude over intellect, that they never paid sufficiently serious attention to cognitive skills or to knowledge. (The major exceptions are the famous selective city high schools of the nineteenth and earlier twentieth centuries.)[6]

Silberman's diagnosis of mindlessness as the cause of the crisis in the classroom underlay his prescriptions for educational change. "If mindlessness is the central problem, the solution must lie in infusing the various educating institutions with purpose, more important, with thought about purpose, and about the ways in which techniques, content and organization fulfill or alter purpose."[7] This prescription misses the point that the problem with American schools has been not their lack of purpose but their continued commitment to purposes rooted in social inequality and its attendant culture. His argument, therefore, did not offer a new direction for American education. His stress on the importance of the affective reflected a very old tradition. The problem with the tradition, put most bluntly, is that poor people did not (and do not) need another lesson in how to behave, even if that behavior was to be liberated rather than repressed. They needed (and still need) the knowledge and skills to move out of poverty.

The Results of Public Education

How might a historian approach the questions Silberman asked: what accounts for the current failure of the schools, and what should be the goals of reform? One way to begin to look for answers is to think about the results of public education. Without tests, questionnaires, or direct and systematic classroom observations, historians can approach the results of education only indirectly. But they can compare roughly the explicit purposes of schooling and social trends over time. As Chapter 1 showed, nineteenth-century school promoters argued that public education would alleviate five problems: crime and poverty, cultural heterogeneity, poor work habits, "idle youth," and the anxieties of middle-class parents about their children's future. Despite school promoters' rhetoric, public education had very little effect on crime, delinquency, and poverty, which did not disappear or even significantly diminish. Indeed, little connection ever existed between the extent of public education and the amount of distress and disorder in social life. Schools have dealt more successfully with some of the other problems that spurred their creation. Schooling did alleviate a good deal of middle-class parental anxiety by providing a public institutional setting for adolescence and a mechanism for the transmission of status. They also reduced the problem of idle youth, because, whatever else they do, compulsory schooling takes young people off the street.[8]

Schools also undoubtedly helped diffuse new work habits during the transition to industrialism. Exactly how they accomplished this purpose, however, remains a complicated question, for even contemporary scholars cannot say with certainty what children learn in school. One of the most persuasive answers consistent with the history of schooling is in Robert Dreeben's important book *On What Is Learned in Schools*, which argues that schools teach children how to behave. Within them, they learn the norms that differentiate public from private life, that govern the way people are treated in institutions and at work as opposed to within their families. The source of these important messages, Dreeben stresses, is not the curriculum or what teachers say. Rather, the structure and organization of public schooling transmit its most important messages.[9] Nineteenth-century educators also recognized the impact of organizational structure on individual personalities and fiercely debated the social implications of pedagogical practice and motivational technique. Although contemporary discussions have replaced nineteenth-century moral categories with universalism, independence, and achievement, the messages transmitted by the organization of schooling have remained similar throughout the past hundred years. (My favorite example is this: schools are where children learn that helping your friend is cheating.)[10]

Ultimately, as educators recognized, the social implication of schooling was a political issue shaped by ideas about the behavior and role of citizens and their relation to the state. Nonetheless, educators remained mostly silent about one political consequence of the organization of schooling: its contribution to the legitimation of inequality. As Stanislaw Ossowski argued in a brilliant book, *Class Structure in the Social Consciousness*, the reigning image of social structure in America (and in the Soviet Union, too) is "nonegalitarian classlessness." Reasons for the hegemony of an ideology that accepts inequality but rejects class lie buried deep within the history of political culture and political economy, and relative weights cannot be assigned authoritatively to socialization within the family, the organization of work, patterns of property distribution and social mobility, transmission of messages through religion, literature, advertising, and other media, and formal education. Nor can a sequence, an interrelation of factors woven into an explanation, be offered with any confidence. Still, public schools have played an important, if indeterminate, role among the panoply of mechanisms that have secured the loyalty of citizens to a competitive system in which, by and large, they have been losers.[11]

Schooling has legitimated inequality, to take one example, by teaching children to blame themselves for failure. Starting in the second quarter of the nineteenth century, schoolmen waged a campaign to base promotion on achievement. Over the complaints of parents and students, they emphasized that promotion from one grade or educational level to another should be earned. The system owed them nothing: children who did not pass examinations remained responsible for their own failure. In this way, schools have taught children their first lesson in political economy: the unequal distribution of rewards mirrors the unequal distribution of ability. Those who achieve deserve their success; those who fail are, very simply, less worthy.

Both popular thought and political rhetoric have measured the moral worth of American society by equality of opportunity, not equality of condition. The test has been the degree to which the individual has remained free to rise as far as his talents could take him. (I deliberately use the male pronoun here. Until very recently, occupational mobility largely has been a game restricted to men.) The value of social policy, in this view, lies in the extent to which it removes barriers to individual achievement, not primarily in the degree to which it reduces inequality. Opportunity, not equality, ranked high among the goals of early school promoters in the nineteenth century; it ranked equally high among the goals of the War on Poverty in the 1960s. Indeed, contemporary resistance to affirmative action, which is the first sustained attempt in American history to give priority to the reduction of inequality of condition even at the expense of individual merit, only underlines the strength of popular commitment to an individualist definition of equality.

This long-standing individualist emphasis on equality of opportunity misdirected the debate about equity in education that surfaced two decades ago and, despite the current stress on excellence, still lingers around issues of busing, bilingualism, gender, and policy toward the handicapped. Despite the inability of schools by themselves to reduce poverty, overcome racism, and eliminate gender bias from American life, efforts to combat the inequities that remain embedded in their structure and performance retain an important purpose. That purpose, however, is not the promotion of individual social mobility; for the equation of mobility with the good society only reinforces a sense of worthlessness in many people. To some extent mobility is a zero-sum game; most people must always lose. If they believe their loss reflects their own inherent worth, they remain systematically robbed of their self-esteem.

Aside from its consequences for individuals, a preoccupation with individual equality of opportunity engenders frustration. When each new cycle of reformers learns that schools cannot alter the structure of inequality, it leaves the scene of the action, cynical or defeated, and without the reformers' harassment the system's biases flourish more easily. Those biases—discrimination based on class, race, and gender; inequality of resources, access, and achievement—remain critical because they represent a contradiction between political values and social institutions. American society remains committed to a definition of citizenship that denies the legitimacy of discrimination based on race, class, or gender. The reason for promoting integration and attempting to equalize the achievement of races or genders and to eliminate discrimination in schools is that institutions should reflect, not contradict, the concept of citizenship that gives American society what moral worth it retains. The failure to pursue egalitarian policies consistently and firmly is a tacit admission that the values that underlie democratic citizenship have become hollow shells, resonating a rhetoric without substance.

The Social Policy Dialectic

Social policy is dialectical, as the early history of public schooling illustrates nicely. Early nineteenth-century social and economic development created novel problems, which public school promoters viewed through a lens that reflected the limitations of their culture and the anxieties of their class. As a result, new school systems (like other social institutions) did not represent a wholly appropriate response to the problems that troubled their creators. Indeed, they won acceptance through promises that could be fulfilled only partially, and from their inception they suffered serious contradictions between explicit purposes and actual results.

As the cost of schooling increased, the contradiction between promise and reality erupted into serious attacks. Beginning in the aftermath of the depression of 1873, across the continent a series of critics (discussed in Chapter 3) ruthlessly began to dissect the bureaucratic urban school systems that had mushroomed in the preceding two decades. Their themes would be familiar to anyone today: schools had become too rigid; they did not lessen crime; they were unresponsive to the community; they taught reading and writing less effectively than had little country schools earlier in the century; they cost too much; they required too many administrators; educators had become martinets, unwilling to tolerate criticism and defensive of their systems.

Although the contradiction between purpose and realization emerged quite quickly in public education, a similar dialectic always inheres in the policy process, because the implementation of a policy alters the context in which it originated. The creation of school systems, for example, altered the objective educational situation in the same way that the creation of mental hospitals altered the relation between mental illness and society. In time, altered circumstances make the original policy obsolete; a new contradiction surfaces and a demand for innovation or reform starts anew. Of course the dialectic varies in its pace and in the conflict it generates. The appropriateness of the original policy to the circumstances surrounding its formulation is one important influence; another is the degree of commitment to existing policy by various interest groups. However, the general moral is clear: no policy can be expected to last forever; policymakers should learn to build impermanently.[12]

The point seems almost commonsense; nonetheless, it requires emphasis. For failure to appreciate the dialectical nature of institutional development has been a major recurrent weakness of social policy. Certainly, to take an important example, it has added bitterness to the often unproductive arguments between proponents of centralization and decentralization in the administration of public education. Neither side has appreciated that no particular balance will remain appropriate forever, and each has invested its administrative proposals with transcendent virtue. In the process, both sides have missed the point: administrative arrangements should be judged by the extent to which they foster or retard particular goals and values at a given historical moment. Those goals—such as equality of access to public facilities and the reduction of differential achievement between children of varied social origins—require a policy sensitive to the contradictions that emerge between principles and administrative arrangements, not one frozen for all time and defended as sacred.

By definition, the existence of institutions has created new groups. In education, truants as a category are impossible without compulsory schooling. Inmates cannot exist apart from jails, mental hospitals, or poorhouses. Institutions also created new classes: managers and managed. School superintendents and superintendents of insane asylums were among the first chief executives of the nineteenth century's new institutional state. This managerial class developed a vested interest in the expansion of institutions, the avoidance of criticism and change, and the justification of institutional policy. Early superintendents of insane asylums, for instance, fended off critics of institutionalization in the 1870s and defended the treatment of mental illness in large residential institutions. Similarly, as Chapter 3 has shown, in the same years school superintendents banded together to fight the first critics of public educational systems and to justify the large, expensive, public bureaucracies over which they presided.[13]

The managerial class has supplied institutions with a built-in capacity to mobilize resistance to serious reform. The result is a complicated, subtle, perhaps even superhuman task: the development of policies which will self-destruct and the formation of a core of committed managers who gracefully will dismantle their own creations.

A dialectical conception of policy has four major problems. One is implementation, exacerbated by the tenacious hold of institutional beneficiaries on the status quo. A second is the contradiction that frequently exists between principles themselves. For instance, many educational reformers in the 1960s and 1970s hoped both to increase parental influence on schooling and to reduce racial segregation. The implementation of one principle required radical decentralization; the implementation of the other often led to larger and more heterogeneous schools.

The third problem is the susceptibility of a dialectical conception of policy to a strictly pragmatic or technocratic point of view. The measure for policy should not be simply political acceptability or what works most easily at a given moment. Rather, policy should be evaluated according to the extent to which it expands the influence of a principle within social life. The point of a dialectical view is that institutionalized policy will develop contradictions to the principles it is supposed to promote. At that point policy shifts become urgent.[14]

Institutionalized policies shape the categories in which we think. Thus the fourth problem with the dialectical approach is the difficulty of transcending in our imagination the set of arrangements that actually exists at any given moment. Consider the question of adolescence. Defined as a stage of prolonged, institutionalized dependence, adolescence emerged only in the late nineteenth century. G. Stanley Hall's treatise *Adolescence* (1904) did not mark the belated recognition of a permanent phase in the life course. Rather, it reflected the shift in demographic experience that began as young people started to live longer than ever before in the homes of their parents and to spend large portions of their lives in specially designed institutions called schools. Yet prolonged institutionalized dependence now seems natural, and policy addresses the question of how to make the experience more pleasant and worthwhile. Not nearly enough, however, does anyone ask if prolonged institutionalized dependence itself is necessary or appropriate. We are unable to transcend the categories with which nearly a century of social policy has described the life course of young people. The same point, as I will argue later in this chapter, can be made about the very definition of "public," as in "public education."[15]

Failure to transcend obsolete policies and the definitions on which they rest fueled the crisis of legitimacy that struck most major social institutions in the 1960s and early 1970s. The American Federation of Teachers, for example, documented widespread violence—rapes and assaults by students on one another and on teachers—within the Houston public schools. Although it also attacked self-serving school officials who refused to report incidents to the police and intimidated teachers who did, the AFT's report placed the blame for violence on the inadequate financial support provided the schools by the community. Underpaid teachers faced overcrowded classrooms in which they were unable to keep order. The result was violence.[16]

Contrary to the report, violence, class size, and teacher salaries have no necessary connection. In the nineteenth and early twentieth centuries miserably paid teachers fought for the right to teach classes of sixty or seventy students in urban schools. In the monitorial schools serving poor children in the late eighteenth and early nineteenth centuries, one master sometimes presided over hundreds of pupils. Most accounts report these schools as being remarkably orderly. Violence and disruption did not pose serious problems in city schools, and pupils generally accepted the authority of teachers. Therefore, the source of contemporary violence within the schools must be sought in the recent reluctance to accept teachers and administrators as bearers of legitimate authority.

(Discipline problems apparently were worst in rural schools, as Edward Eggleston's *The Hoosier Schoolmaster* shows in such graphic and humorous detail; in cities a chronic shortage of school places probably contributed to the perceived value of schooling and the maintenance of order.)[17]

In the 1960s and 1970s, serious attendance problems, assaults on students and teachers, and the need for police to patrol school corridors signaled not only a failure of customary modes of ensuring order but also a broader rejection of the authority of social and political institutions. Students who rioted had not learned docility, reliability, and restraint. They had not learned to accept the unequal distribution of power and rewards with grace and a fitting self-effacement. In the same way, poor parents who attempted to make schools legally responsible for the achievement of their children rejected a fundamental premise of the system: individual responsibility for failure. By their demand that the schools actually teach, they made a powerful political protest that struck directly not only at schools but also at the ideology that legitimizes inequality in America. The rise in malpractice suits, the attack on the welfare system, and the disillusionment following Watergate were three other examples that showed how the contradiction between the promise of institutionalized power and its results finally had begun to penetrate popular consciousness. By the 1980s, however, responses had bifurcated into cynicism and apathy about social issues among many citizens and sustained, often grassroots political activity among others. Whether the immediate future belongs more to the private cultivation of consumption or to Common Cause remains uncertain.[18]

One conclusion, however, does stand out clearly. The forces most powerfully shaping schools do not flow from educational planning or deliberate policy. Nor have they ever. Rather, the source of contemporary pressure for change lies, as it always has, in the contradictions between the schools and the social order. I am not optimistic enough to predict an unprecedented resolution of contradictions in the interests of the poor and powerless. Rather, most responses will attempt to defuse their explosive potential with a series of mimetic or diversionary reforms.[19]

Consider open classrooms and related soft, permissive innovations. Whatever their pedagogical merits, they could diffuse conflict by containing emotions within a setting where controls have been hidden more subtly and power relations not altered at all. "The appearance of permissiveness," observes Christopher Lasch, "conceals a stringent system of controls, all the more effective because it avoids direct confrontations between authorities and the people on whom they impose their wills." What Lasch calls the "therapeutic view of authority" permits the preservation of "hierarchical forms of organization in the guise of 'participation.' " The danger is that permissive innovations, like the advertising in the Sunday newspaper, could promote the illusion of freedom in the interests of corporate capital and the state.[20]

In the 1960s and 1970s, advocates of permissive innovations often unknowingly echoed one important strand in the history of educational reform; like Silberman, they stressed the affective results of schooling and worried more about emotions than about intellect. A radical revolution in American education would reverse the emphasis. Of course no clean line separates the moral and intellectual aspects of curriculum or pedagogy. But it does matter whether the primary emphasis of schooling is the development of cognitive skills or the inculcation of political and social attitudes.

Nonetheless, the fashionable contemporary call for a return to basics in education rarely rejects the fundamentally moral mission of the schools. The clue is that improvement in the teaching of reading, writing, and mathematics often is sought in authoritarian pedagogy. The advocates of basic education frequently also champion rigidity, conformity, and corporal punishment. They seek not the intellectual emancipation of students but a solid return for their dollars invested in schools and an end to the freaky, subversive behavior they associate with progressive educational reform. The problem is that the old methods did not work very well. No evidence exists, for instance, that schools ever promoted higher reading levels among the entire population. In fact the opposite probably was the case. There is therefore a danger in the turn toward basics in education. The mild but unmistakable increase in the concern with human dignity, honesty, and compassion within the schools during the last two decades could be lost without any corresponding gain in students' ability to read, write, or think critically and analytically about their lives. The problem is how to tilt the emphasis of schooling away from character and toward cognitive ability without returning to the repressiveness whose effective exposure remains the best legacy of the romantic reform that flourished not all that long ago.

Coping with Failure

Throughout the history of American educational reform, one theme has remained constant: the grandiose and unrealistic expectation that schools can solve America's social, economic, cultural, political, and moral problems.[21] Most teachers and administrators have probably always realized schooling's inherent limitations, but only occasionally have they tried to moderate the millenial faith that many Americans have placed in formal education since early in the nineteenth century. Exactly why Americans have placed such a trust in formal schooling remains far from clear and a central question for educational historians. Whatever its sources, however, one consequence is clear: the disillusionment that periodically arises when a new generation discovers that schools cannot fulfill the mission with which they have been entrusted.

In response, school promoters have developed a repertoire of strategies for coping with failure. One of the first was the discovery of learning problems. In his brilliant book *The Intelligence of a People*, Daniel Calhoun showed that eighteenth-century teachers assumed that when children did not learn, the fault lay with the method or quality of instruction, not with the intelligence of the child. Calhoun argues that learning problems—defined as individual inability to master what is taught—were discovered in the nineteenth century partly as a response to the problems encountered by defensive educators.[22]

Hereditarian thought supplied another strategy. Most educational reform movements have exuded optimism about human capacity. In the 1830s and 1840s, confidence in the ability of institutions to reduce ignorance, poverty, crime, mental illness, and juvenile delinquency fueled the creation of school systems, mental hospitals, penitentiaries, and reformatories. In each case, it was thought, the institutions' environment, coupled with mild educational and rehabilitative techniques, would transform personalities and eradicate deficiencies originating in a faulty home life, parental ineptitude, or the pressures of modern civilization. All the new institutions failed to reach their goals. Inadequately financed, overcrowded, poorly conceived, inherently punitive, few of them had a chance. Within a couple of decades at most all turned from reform to custody, and, as their sponsors sought the reasons for their failure, in the 1860s hereditarian thought made its first prominent American appearance. Mental hospitals could not cure their inmates because mental illness was inherited, an incurable disease. The same could be said of poorhouses and poverty, of reformatories and delinquents, of jails and prisoners, even of schools and children.[23]

Commentators outside the system offered different explanations. In the 1870s school critics, as Chapter 3 shows, ruthlessly dissected the bureaucratic urban school systems that had mushroomed in the preceding two decades. Some of their criticisms lingered and gathered strength, coalescing into the complex late nineteenth- and early twentieth-century movement for educational change known as progressivism. Despite the variety in their views, many progressive era reformers shared their antebellum predecessors' optimism about the capacity of schools to solve social problems. Once again, the inability of schools to reach those goals contributed to the pessimism about human ability and the stress on heredity reflected in the eugenics movement, new concepts of intelligence, and immigration restriction, all frequently advocated and fostered by the same people. Indeed, Stephen Jay Gould has shown how early twentieth-century psychologists and educators distorted Binet's concept of an intelligence quotient into a unitary, genetic quantity with which to classify and stratify the new ethnic, working-class children flooding the schools.[24]

The most recent burst of optimism based on faith in the influence of environment over heredity exploded in the 1960s and propelled the War on Poverty and other reform movements. Writing in 1968, I predicted that if the current initiative should fall far short of its goals, then hereditarian theories of intelligence would reemerge. Within a year Arthur Jensen's now famous argument for inherited intellectual differences based on race had appeared in the *Harvard Educational Review*.[25]

For more than a century, many reformers explained failure as the result of excessively decentralized and unprofessional administration, and they usually equated improvement with centralization. Because schools suffered from a lack of professionalism and central direction, reform consisted of tightened administrative procedures and professionally directed, systemwide innovation. This model scored some impressive achievements, because reformers reached many of their structural goals. The first generation of school promoters successfully created urban school systems, age-graded, hierarchical, centrally administered, tax-supported, and compulsory, taught by specially trained teachers. In the Progressive era advocates of kindergartens, industrial education, and a revised high school curriculum attained most of their goals, thereby creating the differentiated educational structure that has remained largely in place ever since. After World War II, to take one major example, educational promoters successfully persuaded the federal government to spend large amounts of money on public education. Within a century virtually all children between the ages of six and sixteen began to spend a decade of their lives mostly in schools, whose collective costs were enormous. These were major accomplishments.[26]

But a sense of failure lingered. Many people had hoped that new educational structures, an expanded clientele, and increased resources would improve learning and solve fundamental social problems. The history of the last two decades has crushed those expectations. For it seems that schools can neither alleviate inequality and injustice nor impart instruction effectively.

Effective Schools

This sense of failure is the context in which a new reform strategy—the effective school movement—emerged. It began with the observation that even in the worst systems some schools succeed, and it attempted to identify the qualities that make those schools work. Committed to the key role of local instructional leadership, it eschewed systemwide reform strategies in favor of empowering coalitions of principals, teachers, and parents to improve individual schools. The effective school strategy separates the goals of educational reform. Implicitly, it accepts one moral of educational history: schools by themselves cannot be effective weapons with which to fight the inequality and racism endemic to American social structure. By thus attempting to distinguish between what schools can and cannot be expected to accomplish, the effective school strategy offers a creative response to the failure of the last two decades. Still, its task is extraordinarily complex because of the multilayered composition of the failure to which it is a response.[27]

First is the failure of schools to meet their social goals. Second is the bankruptcy of the top-down, centralized model of reform. Third is the inadequacy of material resources to provide a solution. After the large social science surveys (such as the one by James Coleman) in the late 1960s and early 1970s, it is difficult to believe that, important as adequate finances are, by itself a massive infusion of cash will solve the schools' problems. Fourth is the weakness of research. One major tradition in social research—large-scale aggregate analysis—has reached its limits. In education, this brand of research has revealed very little about why some schools work better than others. In an analogous way, its attempts to analyze social mobility have shown remarkably little about the interconnection among local labor markets, social structure, and individual work histories. The reason in both instances is the lack of attention to context inherent in most large aggregate analyses.

Specific local contexts mediate great social forces. Class, race, gender, and ethnicity assume configurations shaped by a host of factors such as local labor markets, residential patterns, socialization processes within families, and political structures. No analysis can estimate accurately the impact of any pedagogy, curriculum, or mode of school organization unless it accounts for the particular context through which it is mediated. Of course, an unreflective ethnography that describes behaviors without attention to the way in which general and powerful influences affect actors and institutions cannot provide a useful or coherent guide to action, either. Nor is it helpful to view schools as autonomous units capable of self-regeneration despite the forces that impinge on them. Rather, the challenge is to formulate theory that understands schooling as a process shaped by history, great social forces, and particular contexts.

Class and conflict are two great forces to which American social science and reform have responded weakly, and this failure to deal forthrightly and adequately with them is the fifth component of the failure that underlies the effective school movement. Viewed from one angle, American social science since early in the twentieth century seems an elaborate dance away from the idea that social conflict is normal, not unusual or pathological, and that class is something other than inequality or stratification. (As the next chapter will show, writers have recently mounted an attack on the key role that critical historians of education have attributed to social class.) In one important strand within American social thought, conflict reflects contending parties' lack of information. In this view, rational analysis, education, and planning can resolve conflict and reconcile apparently opposing interests by exposing strife as irrational, an egotistical and unenlightened refusal to realize that advancement of the common good best serves individual interests.

These assumptions have not withstood recent history very well. During the last two decades, conflict has been the norm rather than the exception, for antagonisms have exposed the fault lines deeply etched within American society. As resources have become scarce, as choice strikes close to home when racial justice means busing in Boston not marching in Alabama, or public housing in South Philadelphia not rehabilitating the ghetto, reform, at last, stands exposed as the zero-sum game it is, if it moves beyond cosmetics. No theory that considers conflict exceptional, pathological, or ephemeral or denies the structural roots of conflicts or class differences on major issues can explain the strife that ripped apart American social institutions, including schools and universities, in the decade after 1963.

The effective school strategy represents a response to all five components of educational failure. It moderates educational goals, rejects the centralized model of reform, looks for solutions in human rather than material resources, exchanges the macro for the micro level as a focus of action and research, and attempts to sidestep the educational issues that pit groups against one another. Still, as a strategy, it has serious limits.

First, it places responsibility for failure squarely on teachers and administrators. Although schools have avoided responsibility for too long, reformers must ask whether the job of teaching or administering effectively in urban schools has become impossible for the ordinary person. The reason some succeed so well may be their extraordinary reserves of energy or charisma. Indeed, in his assessment of progressivism in education, Lawrence Cremin pointed out that progressive theory often could not be implemented, simply because it placed impossible demands on teachers.[28] Therefore, the effective school strategy must avoid the elaboration of impossible demands whose imperfect implementation would be viewed as the fault of individual teachers.

More serious, the effective school strategy marks a break with the notion that schools are prisoners of social structure. The optimistic, upbeat side of the new strategy mutes the role of political, social, economic, and demographic factors in shaping what happens within individual schools. But it would be a mistake to draw the line too sharply, for the problems within individual schools cannot be severed from their origins in forces over which teachers and administrators have no control. Conflicts over racism offer one example; another is the problem of school violence, discussed earlier.

Despite its limits, reform that begins by empowering parents and teachers to change their own schools and stresses the possibility of effective education for everyone represents a radical break with the past. It modestly redistributes power and challenges the notion—reinforced by promotion practices, the distribution of rewards, and the pattern of everyday life in schools—that those who achieve deserve their success and that those who fail are, very simply, less worthy. Because the belief that success reflects merit is serviceable, just as the low educational achievement of poor children has been serviceable in its way, too, the implementation of an effective schools policy faces enormous obstacles. If it can overcome political resistance, avoid the isolation of schooling from its social context, restrain the temptation to blame individuals, and overcome the limits of past research and theory—and these are great though not insurmountable challenges—then a commitment to effective schools represents a creative response to failure, indeed a genuine and welcome initiative within American education.

The Social Implications of Excellence

The effective school movement no longer represents the cutting edge of reform. Within only a few years it lost its place to a hard new emphasis on "excellence." In retrospect, the effective schools movement was one of the last and most interesting products of the concern with poverty and civil rights that surfaced in the 1960s; "excellence" is a product of the revived Cold War and its new domestic agenda.

With the 1983 report of the National Commission on Educational Excellence, *A Nation at Risk: The Imperative of Educational Reform*, excellence skyrocketed to first place among the goals of public education.[29] In slightly more than thirty pages of military metaphors, the report blamed American education for the decline in the nation's economic and military preeminence. The report represents one strand in educational criticism—our children aren't learning as well as they used to—that has reappeared periodically since the 1870s (see Chapter 3). The report levels its charges with little supporting evidence; and it fails to consider how the great forces affecting American life in the last few decades have buffeted educational institutions. In its pages, American schools are products of energy, will, and competence. Smart, committed teachers motivated by merit pay can turn them around and save the country, especially if they increase the amount of homework.

Many criticisms can be leveled at the report, which, in the end, substitutes a mixed metaphor, "a rising tide of mediocrity," for an analysis of what's wrong with public education.[30] Here I want to focus on just one: its total neglect of context. The National Commission fails to diagnose accurately the causes of the malady— low achievement—that it purports to find everywhere. It ignores the altered demography of schooling (the great increase in the proportion of young people in secondary and higher education), which contributes to changes in test scores, and the altered social ecology of cities, which has changed the class and racial composition of urban schools. It neglects the interaction of class, gender, and race with schooling. It bypasses the conflicts that have undermined the legitimacy of educational authorities and increased the difficulty of teaching and learning. It does not even acknowledge its precursor, the deployment of education as a weapon in the Cold War in the panic that followed Sputnik's launch in 1957, or ask why, with goals so parallel to its own, the earlier reform movement failed. Instead, we are told once more that the schools can save us.[31] The targets this time are not crime, poverty, and ignorance. Rather, as in the post-Sputnik reforms, they are the Russians, national honor, and first place in power among nations.

By tapping widespread, diffuse anxieties about education, the commission won support from a broad coalition: parents, rich, poor, and middling, disgusted with the failure of schools to teach their children; industrialists worried about productivity, labor discipline, and wages; Cold Warriors anxious about America's alleged decline in international stature; and university representatives concerned with declining enrollments. To all of them, the National Commission's simple slogans offer some reassurance. Whose interests the report serves best, is, however, another question.

One code word, "excellence," leads straight to the report's major social implications. By definition, excellence implies stratification. To excel is to achieve at a level beyond the ordinary. Within schools, excellence implies the recreation of hierarchies that give primacy to academic achievement and link achievement more closely to rewards in the world of work. It calls, in short, for a rigid meritocracy. For many reasons, meritocracies usually serve best those who enter them with a favored position, and it is not hard to predict who will appear most excellent and garner most rewards. A policy stressing excellence, therefore, is another way of redistributing resources upward. As has usually happened in the past, a new educational policy proposed in the interests of everyone would serve best those already privileged.

Of course, all is not well with the schools. They do fail their students, and they fail most badly those with the least ability to look for help elsewhere and with the fewest resources to help compensate for an inadequate education. But there are alternatives to excellence that describe educational goals more usefully and equitably. One of these is competence. Instead of concentrating on excellence, a limiting idea, reform might focus on the development in all children of competence in crucial cognitive abilities. Competence reflects the faith at the core of any democratic educational ideal: the educability of everyone. Certainly, competence, like excellence, could become little more than a slogan. I advance it not so much because of its great merit but in contrast to excellence as a focus for thinking about the goals of educational reform.

Debating goals, however, may not be the most effective way to start improving education. The more important, prior question is

who should decide what the schools should do? The control of
education is an issue about which the National Commission was,
for understandable reasons, silent. Its implicit mission, after all,
was the reinforcement, not the redistribution, of power. But the
question of control is crucial, for it determines whose interests
schools will serve best. With the notable exception of advocates
of community control, most debates about control have stayed
within narrow boundaries. Should school boards be elected or
appointed? Should they be based on ward or at-large representation? Should city councils retain the power to appropriate school
funds? Should the mayor appoint the superintendent? Should principals and teachers be allowed to choose the textbooks and plan
the curriculum for their schools?[32] Important as these issues are,
they have deflected attention from more far-reaching questions
about control. An alternative way to reexamine questions about
control is to think about the meaning of "public" in public education. Here, once more, historians can make an important
contribution.

Toward Redefining Public Education

Historians can make three useful observations about the current
crisis in education, especially in urban schools. Each of them points
to the way in which most debate and commentary remains trapped
within categories that are historical and contingent rather than
permanent, immutable, or inevitable.

First is the distinction between public and private. Most discussions draw a sharp line between the two and assume that public
includes both finance and management, the funding of schools
through taxes, and their management through centralized bureaucracies. In fact the combination of the two emerged only in the
nineteenth century (as Chapter 2 showed). In the seventeenth and
eighteenth centuries, "public" implied education carried on in a
school rather than in a home. By the late eighteenth and early
nineteenth centuries it had come to mean schooling open to a broad
cross-section of the community, even though administered by self-
perpetuating boards of trustees (as in the example of paternalistic
voluntarism). Indeed, states provided for secondary education by

giving money to academies (which today we would call private schools), religious groups, and voluntary bodies that tried to supply nondenominational schools for the poor.

Only later, for a combination of social and political reasons, did public education begin to mean schools supported by taxes and controlled and managed by public authorities. A growing educational establishment (see Chapter 3) that saw in the development of large school systems excellent opportunities for careers, mobility, and power vigorously promoted the equation of management and finance in the definition of "public." At the same time, the line between public and private has been much less clear in other sectors of American social life. In welfare, for instance, the mixture always has been complex and the boundaries vague. The same can be said of higher education because nominally private colleges and universities have long received public funding of one sort or another. Indeed, since World War II even the most famous and independent universities have become dependent upon federal money.

The point is that we can divorce the public funding from the public control and management of schools without destroying public education. To have schools funded by taxes but owned by boards of parents, for example, would not destroy public education. Rather, it would change it. Consider an analogy. Suppose individuals remain at liberty to choose their physicians, and physicians continue to operate autonomously, only all medical expenses are paid through public funds. This, it would rightly be thought, would be a form of public medicine. Why would not schools that operate under similar principles be equally public?

The second important point about the history of education is that a variety of types of schools existed before the creation of public educational systems. For instance, contrary to myths fostered by early public school promoters, the many academies scattered throughout towns and cities were not undemocratic elite institutions that restricted access to secondary education to the wealthy. Rather, as Chapter 2 observed, they were schools often closely attuned to the rhythms of popular life. They allowed students to enter and leave in a flexible way; they were hospitable to older students; they accommodated the seasonal labor demands of agricultural communities; and they were very inexpensive.[33] One historian has estimated, to take another example, that the same proportion of children went to school in New York City in the late eighteenth century, before the introduction of a public school system, as did in the mid-nineteenth century after one had been established.[34] Even in rural Massachusetts, according to another careful analysis, school attendance was remarkably high in the early nineteenth century.[35] These examples show that public control and management of schools are not necessary to assure that schooling will be widespread and easily accessible or that attendance will be high.

Third, the history of urban education is littered with successful attempts to alter the composition of school boards. These have had very little effect upon what goes on in individual classrooms. Small boards are expanded; large boards are reduced; elected boards become appointed; appointed boards become elected; ward representation is changed to at-large representation. Usually these attempts are led by first-citizens convinced that sound, honest management can fix the schools, or at least lower taxes.[36] The problem with this position is its innocence about how schools work, the factors that condition teaching and learning, and the problems involved in initiating change.

Both historical and contemporary social research show that attempts to change or radically improve the quality of schooling by systemwide directives almost always fail. Reform from the top down simply does not work very well. What does work sometimes, as the effective school movement reveals, is reform undertaken at the level of the individual school. Change, many educators have begun to realize, proceeds best on a school-by-school basis, initiated by strong and effective principals, supported by teachers, parents, and students.

By ignoring history, we have replicated the same unsuccessful reform strategies over and over again. We also have reified a definition of public education forged to fit antebellum America and ignored the contingent, protean meaning of "public" in America's past. We have refused to recognize that the dream of common schooling is dead, first wounded by differentiation between and within schools early in the twentieth century, then killed by the social ecology of cities and suburbs after World War II.[37] In the process we have ceded authority to bureaucracies, remote from children and parents, buffeted by politics and self-interest. We have allowed the recreation of pauper school systems within large cities; now, we realize, the schools do not serve even our affluent youngsters very well. None of the reform energy lavished on schools throughout their history, none of the federal dollars poured into them in recent years, none of the professors of education who have trained their staffs and studied their operation, have been able to prevent this disaster. Is it not time to stop wandering within the same debates? History will not dictate new answers, but it can liberate us from old questions. Surely this is not a trivial contribution.

5

The Politics of
Educational History

In the 1960s American historians began to overturn celebratory versions of history with accounts that tried to explain the origins of the Vietnam War; the persistence of racism and segregation; the distribution of power among gender and classes; intractable poverty and the decay of cities; and the failure of social institutions and policies designed to deal with mental illness, crime, delinquency, and education. Conservative rejoinders emerged first in the history of foreign policy and political history, where tough, sometimes vicious wars have divided the profession. Later they spread to education, and there, too, the battle remains joined.

However, even critics of the new history of education admit that a simple narrative of the triumph of benevolence and democracy can no longer be offered seriously by any scholar even marginally aware of recent writing in the field. The problem for critics, therefore, has been twofold: the destruction of the critical historians' credibility and the construction of an alternative and equally plausible interpretation of the educational past. They have not succeeded with either task. I do not want to ascribe more unity to recent critics than to the historians they oppose. They differ greatly; no unified antirevisionist movement exists. There is, however, a wide audience eager for reassurance that the critical historians are wrong. At their worst, the new critics have descended to falsification, distortion, and ad hominem attacks as they have tried to build an apologist case for American education. At their best, they have tried to assemble counterevidence through intensive research. Even then, too often, otherwise careful scholars cannot resist the creation of straw men as they engage in a new sport I call revisionist-bashing.

One major intellectual goal has animated the work of the new critics since the 1970s: as much as possible, they want to loosen the connections between education and social class in America's past and present. They are not alone. The interpretation and role of class is one of the core issues shaping the politics of American history. In the 1980s some of the critics adopted a new goal not entirely compatible with their old one: the construction of an educational past that legitimates the new conservative educational agenda, by which I mean the replacement of equity and compassion with toughness and excellence. Both the assault on class and the assault on equality have shared the pretense of objectivity. Critics have not discussed their own politics. They present themselves as fair, dispassionate scholars interested only in the facts and in finding out and reporting what really happened. In truth, usually they are as partisan as the critical historians they attack, and even their most sophisticated quantitative work cannot sustain the illusion that numbers are neutral.

Numbers Are Not Neutral

Advanced statistical techniques cannot transcend or resolve the issues that underlie the politics of historical scholarship. Consider Carl Kaestle's and Maris Vinovskis' study of education in antebellum Massachusetts. Kaestle and Vinovskis deploy a statistical barrage to demonstrate the complex character of social behavior and the inadequacy of single factor explanations. "We do not," they write, "present a theory of educational development in this volume."[1] Rather, their book probes several discrete questions that center on one historical problem: "How did the changing extent, structure, and control of schooling relate to the social, economic, and cultural features of different nineteenth-century communities, and how did these relationships change over time?"[2] Their answers attempt to detach education from class and to loosen the links critical historians have found between the development of public

schooling and the economic and social transformation of antebellum America.

Kaestle and Vinovskis explore trends in school attendance; the
rise and decline of early childhood education; the determinants of
school-leaving among teenagers; the nature of urban-rural differences in schooling in two very different, neighboring communities;
trends in educational finance; and the social and ecological character of support for and opposition to the Massachusetts State
Board of Education in 1840. With the exception of the two case
studies, all these explorations are primarily quantitative, supported
with appropriate nonquantitative source material, and frequently
use multivariate procedures.

The expansion of enrollment, they argue, preceded state intervention in schooling or the takeoff to industrialization. The greatest upsurge in schooling, they find, happened between 1750 and
1830. After about 1830 the proportion of children attending
school leveled off and even dropped a bit by later in the century.
The initial increase came not within the cities but in rural areas.
After 1840, however, the amount of education received by the
average child, as measured by length of school year and regularity
of attendance, increased. This increase took place more often in
urban than in rural areas. By arguing that rural attendance rose
first, Kaestle and Vinovskis are able to loosen the connection between educational expansion, state policy, and the urban and industrial development of the twenty years before the Civil War.
Their conclusion, however, is partly an artifact of their method.
For the subsequent stagnation of rural enrollment reflects another
development they document in the book: a very large decline in
the number of children under the age of five or six attending school
after 1840. The enrollment of other age groups did not decline, a
point they acknowledge only in passing. Indeed, they do not dis-
aggregate figures by age. By including under-five-year-olds in their
analysis, Kaestle and Vinovskis are able to exaggerate the magnitude of the rise in school attendance before the creation of the
state board of education and to underemphasize the rise thereafter.

Similarly, their analysis of school-leaving is based on young
people aged thirteen to nineteen. In their multiple classification
analysis, the dependent variable is school attendance; the independent variables include a number of factors, among them age,

which proved the most powerful influence on attendance, thereby allowing Kaestle and Vinovskis to deemphasize the force of social factors. By definition, however, age had to be the most influential variable (more important than occupation, wealth, or other indexes of class, for instance), because school attendance differed markedly at each age, dropping off notably after fourteen. About half the children ceased to go to school by the age of fifteen, and very few attended after the age of seventeen. It would have been better to have analyzed only fifteen-to-seventeen-year-olds, about 20–50 percent of whom attended school. In brief, they entered age in their analyses in a way that maximized its influence and minimized that of other, more theoretically promising variables.

In their analysis of the relation between socioeconomic groups and school-leaving, Kaestle and Vinovskis lump together white-collar and skilled workers into one category. They defend their scheme with reference to work on occupational classification in history (including my own, which does not in any way support their procedure). Every piece of evidence available from this period shows marked distinctions between white-collar and skilled workers, including different rates of fertility, school attendance, and property ownership. Nor do they differentiate between masters and journeymen (employers and their employees in the same trades), whose resources and behavior also differed significantly. In short, they lump together occupations in a way certain to obscure important variations that contradict their argument.

Kaestle and Vinovskis do not distinguish capitalism from either industrialization or urbanization (which, as I argued in Chapter 1, is critical) or understand it as a concept embracing a pattern of social relations, not simply a way of organizing production. Consequently, their presentation is innocent of any attempt to describe, let alone analyze, the social structure in which educational development took place. Lacking any conception of class, their assertions of the absence of connection between education, manufacturing, or capitalism founder. Despite the sophistication of their quantitative methods, they do not effectively damage the core of the existing major arguments (which certainly do have flaws) or offer a coherent and convincing alternative.

It is difficulte to pin down Kaestle's and Vinovskis' theoretical position for two reasons. First, they hedge so much on every major question that it is impossible to ascertain what they actually do believe. Second, they self-consciously disclaim any attempt to write theory or to offer a coherent interpretation. Yet theoretical assumptions are embedded in all writing, whether or not they are made explicit. Here, the guiding assumption reflects the idea of interdependence, a strand dominant in American social science since early in the twentieth century. Early twentieth-century social scientists, as Thomas Haskell observed, adopted the concept of interdependence to explain social phenomena. Whereas an earlier generation had sought direct and superficial causes—such as an unmediated link between immoral behavior and poverty—the first academic social scientists in the 1890s viewed the world as an immensely complex series of interconnecting variables mutually reacting on one another. In this situation direct causal attribution and simple explanation were impossible. The task of social science became, instead, to trace the intricate connections between all social phenomena. Kaestle and Vinovskis stand firmly within this tradition. They write that "education itself is so complex that it cannot be treated as a single variable and then pegged to a single historical development out of which all other concerns flowed."[3]

Although social institutions always relate in complex ways to their contexts, interdependence is an interpretative strategy that signals a retreat from any attempt to find a principle or core within a social system. Its world lacks a center, a driving force. Social development comes simply from the reciprocal effects of the many factors operating within a complex network. It becomes impossible to say what gives coherence or shape to any social system. Hence the levers of change remain obscure and no basis exists for moral judgment.

In the early twentieth century, the adoption of interdependence signaled not only a change in causal attribution but also the retreat of the social sciences from their early concern with social reform. Closely tied to the ideology of objectivity, interdependence formed part of the package that social scientists offered in exchange for limited academic freedom, professional standing, and respect within the worlds of university, policy, and business. As such it has been associated with the disengagement of social science from concern with critical analysis or moral judgment. When Kaestle and Vinovskis state, "we do not argue that the development of public schooling in Massachusetts was fundamentally unjust, or that it was fundamentally just," they are attempting to move educational history in the same direction.[4]

Building on his earlier work in Essex County, Massachusetts, Vinovskis has continued to challenge the importance of social class in antebellum educational history by reexamining my conclusions about an important incident in the town of Beverly, Massachusetts, in 1860.[5] The event in question is the vote to abolish the Beverly high school at a town meeting on March 14, 1860. The event is noteworthy because the town clerk recorded the name of every voter and how he voted. No one has been able to locate a similar nominal-level record of voting on another nineteenth-century educational issue. The vote took place in a highly charged atmosphere: the great shoemakers' strike in Essex County, where Beverly is located. Most of the shoemakers and other working-class voters cast their votes against the high school; professionals and businessmen more often supported it. The question is, why? More precisely, to what extent was the vote related to social class? My interpretation gave class a prominent place. Vinovskis says I exaggerated.

Vinovskis emphasizes the role of the town's geography (which, though he does not mention it, I noted as well) and ongoing local controversies over the politics of education, which were played out in the high school vote. He combines a detailed narrative history of the town's educational politics (based on impressive and thorough research in local primary sources) with several statistical studies, the most important of which for his purposes was a multivariate analysis of the vote on the high school issue.

Ultimately Vinovskis contradicts none of my findings, which were based on descriptive rather than multivariate statistics. Rather, he reorders their importance. He argues that the part of the town in which voters lived was exceptionally important. Wealth also was critical. Occupation worked in the way I predicted, but in his multiple classification analysis (MCA) it had a much lower influence (as measured by its beta weight). Age and family size were reasonably close to what could be expected from my results. Despite his attempt to distance himself from my argument (and his claims that he succeeded), Vinovskis writes, "Overall the MCA results confirm Katz's findings."[6]

Vinovskis' occupation variable in the MCA might not fully reflect occupation's influence. One other variable, town officeholding, is weighted by the importance of office, which in turn is estimated by the occupation of officeholders. So occupation is introduced twice. (Vinovskis reports that this makes little practical difference in the outcome of the analysis.) In the same way, wealth cannot be completely separated from occupation, and Vinovskis reports some statistical interaction between the two. For instance, no shoemakers had $5,000 or more in property.[7] Also, the occupational scale contains a residual category, "other," with ninety members, or about 25 percent of the total, making it the second largest category. Vinovskis created this large residual category to reduce the number of degrees of freedom in the analysis by eliminating small groups. The category includes laborers (all of whom opposed the high school), nonshoemaker artisans, and others. It, too, might reduce the summary weighting of occupation.

Despite his multiple classification analysis, no one can deny that over 70 percent of voting farmers, mariners, and shoemakers and all the voting laborers (not broken out into a separate category by Vinovskis) cast their votes against the high school. Vinovskis attempts to mute the influence of working-class opposition to the high school by arguing that not all mariners, shoemakers, artisans, and farmers opposed it. However, most analysts consider a 70 or 80 percent vote by a group reasonable evidence of the attitude of its members.

The more serious issue is conceptual. The argument in favor of multivariate analysis is that it enables one to sort out the relative influence of various factors on a dependent variable. Especially as applied to persons, multivariate analysis, when not used sensitively, can create arbitrary and meaningless distinctions because identity has multiple, overlapping, and inseparable components. Vinovskis found poor, working-class men, many of them from the town's outlying districts, opposing the high school. Do his statistics automatically and irrefutably tell us that one factor alone dominated their vote? How would these voters have identified themselves? Would they, for instance, have separated their income from their occupation from their residence and told an interviewer, "I really voted against the high school, not because I'm a mariner, but, first, because I live in an outlying district and, second, because

I'm poor"? (The same difficulty bedevils attempts to sort out occupation and ethnicity in discussions of the American working class, whose ethnic affiliations have been part of its class definition.) By implication, Vinovskis defines class as a wooden, static variable whose influence in American history hinges on a beta weight. In the process he ignores the direction of contemporary work on antebellum America, which considers class a social relation and searches for ways to discover and portray its shifting forms and meanings.[8]

Vinovskis describes a Beverly filled with tension, conflict, and bitterness. He shows in far more detail than I did how conflicts and animosities shaped educational politics. He argues that the majority of Beverly's citizens did not want a high school and voted for it only because they were forced to by state law. He comments on the "anger felt by many voters toward the imposition of an expensive and seemingly unnecessary institution by a determined minority using the threat of a court indictment against the town," and of "the tremendous amount of bitterness that must have been generated by the imposition of this institution on the citizenry."[9] But what were the social sources of this bitterness?

The problem, as in the book he coauthored with Kaestle, is that despite his attention to the history of town politics, Vinovskis' account floats in a curious contextual vacuum. For it devotes little attention to the social and economic history of the town, and without a social and economic context, he is unable to explain his major findings in a coherent way, let alone reduce the influence of social class in antebellum American history. He cannot account for the interest in education he documents or tell readers why some reformers wanted a high school. Indeed, he does not systematically lay out (as does *Irony*) the pro–high school case. Nor is he able to account for reformers' passionate hostility to the district system (also a theme of *Irony* that he does not acknowledge) or to interpret one of his most perceptive observations: namely, that the argument in Beverly was about priorities. How much money should be spent on common schools and how much on a high school? Although the issue polarized the town, he does not explore its social roots or sources. If he had, questions of class would have been hard to avoid.

Vinovskis objects to the tenor of recent debates on educational historiography. He dislikes the strident political attacks on those historians inaccurately lumped together as "revisionists," and he thinks angry responses are inappropriate. Instead, he calls for a "scholarly and objective" reexamination of important issues to which, presumably, he hopes his book contributes.[10] But politics cannot be divorced from scholarship, and numbers are no more neutral than words. Vinovskis is as partisan as the rest of us. I mean this as no criticism. Rather, I only wish he would make his assumptions and commitments more explicit and drop the fiction of neutrality. For history, after all, is about questions that matter.

The Attack on Critical History

Vinovskis' complaint about strident and unscholarly attacks on the critical historians of education refers primarily to Diane Ravitch's book *The Revisionists Revised*.[11] He is right about the ideological content of her assault but, I think, mistaken when he asserts that "raising questions about why someone was asked to do a particular review of the field [which is how her book originated] ... is not likely to advance scholarship any further than the original accusations."[12] The reasons why a book was written remain central to its interpretation. In Ravitch's case, they raise disturbing questions about power relations within the politics of scholarship and important issues of academic freedom and integrity.

Ravitch argued that through shoddy scholarship or political motivation revisionist historians had deployed incomplete evidence, bad logic, and poor theory to present a simpleminded, conspiracy-ridden, and thoroughly negative portrait of America's educational past. Written in the service of un-American political ideals, their work had not only distorted the past but also exacerbated the problems of low morale and declining standards in American education. Ravitch wanted to substitute a story of progress, a sustained attempt to realize democratic-liberal aspirations in a pluralist society. Despite unfortunate lapses, including slavery and McCarthyism, the fundamental openness of society and the steady improvement in the lot of minorities remained indisputable hallmarks of America's past, evidence of the fundamental soundness of American institutions. Progress could be continued through a steady application of the democratic-liberal tradition of reform—in particular of representative rather than participatory democracy.

Ravitch's book added nothing to the historiography of education. Nonetheless, it requires extended discussion because it represents the current backlash against dissenting scholarship and social reform. *The Revisionists Revised* has received a great deal of attention and favorable comment. Many reviewers have accepted its description of revisionist scholarship without further scrutiny. It seems clear that the book's message is one that many wanted to hear. At the time Ravitch wrote, the mood of the country had shifted in a more conservative direction, with budget-cutting as the most popular electoral slogan, and a general backlash against radical ideas evident in many quarters. Still, the economy stagnated, inflation increased, and the condition of the cities deteriorated. In these circumstances, myths about the credibility of social institutions and the reality of social progress served to protect professionals and to bridge the distance between mood and actuality.

The history of Ravitch's book shows that it was not simply a straightforward attempt "to contribute to the lively debate that American education needs at all times."[13] In 1975 the National Academy of Education with a grant from the Ford Foundation invited Ravitch to review the literature on the history of American education. This review was expanded into *The Revisionists Revised*. Copies of the review were sent to the publishers of the historians attacked, deans of education, and some professors of education, not all historians. I received copies from my publishers, none directly from the Academy. So did most of those attacked.[14]

This incident raises troubling questions. Why was Ravitch, rather than one of the more obviously established scholars in the field, selected to write the review in the first place? Was the Academy's intent to review the field, or did it want a critique of the revisionists? How was the mailing list for distribution chosen? Why did it include publishers, deans, and influential professors but not the authors attacked? If the connection between Ravitch and the National Academy has left the "revisionists" uneasy, they should be pardoned: whatever the motivation behind the incident, a deliberate and well-financed attempt to discredit them could not have been initiated more effectively.[15]

Ravitch attempted to construct a group she called "radical revisionists" and, despite a token acknowledgment of distinctions among them, to portray them as intellectually and politically unified. In fact, sharp differences of method, interpretation, and politics separate the historians she attacked, although each has offered a critical version of the past. Ravitch scarcely mentions that her "radical revisionists" have often sharply criticized each other.

Ravitch falsely homogenized the historians she criticized into a set of straw men not only by ignoring the differences and controversies among them but also by distorting their viewpoints, omitting important aspects of their arguments, and inventing positions they had not taken.[16] Her tactics were precisely those she attributed to the "radical revisionists": omission, distortion, the creation of straw men, ideological bias, and unjust and unwarranted impeachment of motive. Although she deprecated the "revisionists'" alleged attack on the motives of earlier educational reformers, Ravitch herself assaulted the motives and integrity of the historians she criticized.[17] Referring to Bowles and Gintis, she stated, "one might wish that the authors showed some slight appreciation for the democratic-liberal values that preserve their freedom to publish a call to revolution against democratic liberalism."[18] Yet a central premise of Bowles and Gintis is that a contradiction exists between the democratic character of the political process and the hierarchical organization of economic life. Contrary to what Ravitch implied, they defined socialism "as an extension of democracy from the narrowly political to the economic realm."[19] Her remark impugned two scholars' commitment to academic freedom, democracy, and intellectual dialogue, demonstrable in both their published work and their lives.

By attempting to substitute a different version of the American past, Ravitch became one of the most articulate exponents of what I call the apologist case for American education, past and present (although, as I shall show, her subsequent work has abandoned even an implicit defense of education's present). Like Vinovskis, the overriding goal of her argument was the detachment of educational history from questions of social class.[20] She also drew a sharp distinction between representative and participatory democracy, presenting only the former as in the American liberal tradition. Advocating participatory democracy put "the educational radical at odds with the mainstream of liberalism."[21] Ravitch's animosity toward decentralization and the dispersal of power not only underlay her critique of the revisionists but also was the hidden agenda of *The Great School Wars*, a thinly veiled attack on decentralization efforts in the New York City schools from the early nineteenth century to the present, and is one of the central themes of her history of American education since 1945. Hers was an odd position for an admirer of John Dewey and Jane Addams, both of whom attempted to demonstrate the centrality of process to democracy. After all, Jane Addams' observation that "unless all men and all classes contribute to a good, we cannot even be sure that it is worth having" most simply and eloquently states the assumption on which efforts to make democracy more participatory have rested.[22] More serious, Ravitch located the position she contested outside the American tradition and hence implied that it was both alien and dangerous.[23]

Ravitch's apologist case reflected a tenuous grasp of social theory as well as a skewed definition of the American democratic tradition. For example, she neither defined class explicitly nor showed that she was aware that more than one conception exists. Nonetheless, she asserted that class analysis is largely inappropriate to American history, and she supported her position with the claim that most Americans regard themselves as middle class. Her definition of the revisionists' position on class caricatured and travestied their analyses. In radical history, serious class analysis rejects purely subjective definitions or arbitrary divisions of people according to solely quantitative criteria such as wealth or prestige scores. Rather, it attempts to view class as a relation, instead of as bumps in a system of stratification or as the artifact of an opinion poll. Class embraces social relations broader than simple economic self-interest, as all the historians Ravitch attacked realized quite well. Nonetheless, she distorted their arguments and failed to marshal any effective counterevidence.[24] Nor did she define bureaucracy, although she discussed it extensively. Her point appeared to be that, although bureaucracy may be unpleasant, it is inevitable and not an organizational embodiment of bourgeois social values. In support of her point, Ravitch noted that bureaucracy "is a characteristic organizational form in social and communist nations" and criticized Bowles and Gintis for failing to make the same observation. Yet they had faced the issue directly and effectively in a way that affirmed their commitment to democratic values. Contrary to what Ravitch maintained, moreover, nearly everybody (including the revisionists) has recognized that bureaucratic forms emerged from a response to complex social problems (see Chapter 3); the point is that those responses, all contested by rational people, embodied particular values and priorities.[25]

Ravitch's analysis of social mobility was no more useful or accurate than her interpretation of class or bureaucracy, and one should not accept her argument that "widespread" upward mobility would destroy the radical case.[26] Revisionists would probably all agree that schooling has served the well-to-do better than the poor and, by and large, has helped reproduce rather than alter class structure. They would not deny that substantial individual mobility has always occurred. But there are two additional, vital points. First, social mobility has been largely structural. An expanding economy produced more white-collar, technical, professional, and managerial positions than could be filled by the children of people already holding similar occupations. Second, rates of occupational attainment have differed sharply by class. Working-class children always have done less well economically.[27]

Ravitch contended that education has fostered high rates of mobility. To support her point she used Blau and Duncan's findings about occupational mobility to suggest that education matters more than social origins. However, their data show that although education plays a critical role in occupational attainment, social origins strongly influence the amount and nature of the education young people receive. Working-class children are much less likely to receive the type of education that leads to the most desirable jobs. Thus Ravitch ignored the class distribution of education, the structural basis of mobility (the number of openings), and the question of proportions (not the number but the share of children from various social backgrounds who reach different occupational levels).[28]

Ravitch's most forceful argument for the apologist position were her assertions that the gap between white and black income had been narrowing, that the general situation of blacks had been improving, and that education had played a key role in the process.[29] These claims concluded a chapter that omitted any mention of unemployment, inflation, racial tension, trends in residential segregation, or the debased value of higher degrees on a tight job market. To understand her image of black progress one need look no further than Ravitch's source, a Census Bureau report, and her distortion of it. The report showed an increase between 1970 and 1974 in the ratio of black to white family income only among husband-wife families headed by a person under the age of thirty-five. Among all families with husband and wife present, the ratio declined. Moreover, the proportion of families with both husband and wife present declined among blacks and remained stable among whites. Partly as a result of the increase in female-headed households, the proportion of married black women in the labor force increased. Thus between 1970 and 1974 the income of black families decreased relative to that of whites, from .61 to .58.[30]

Ravitch did not cite the evidence in the same publication that between 1967 and 1973 black family income had decreased relative to white family income. Nor did she note that black unemployment is usually about twice as high as white; that black infant mortality in 1973 was only slightly lower than the white rate in 1950; or that black males in every age category from one year through twenty-five could expect to live longer in 1959–1961 than they could in 1973.[31]

The situation had not changed materially between 1974 and 1976, according to a report by the U.S. Commission on Civil Rights.[32] Between 1960 and 1976, black college attendance increased. The proportion of black males aged twenty-five to twenty-nine who completed college rose from 4 percent to 11 percent, while the white male college attendance rate increased from 20 percent to 34 percent. The ratio of black to white thus rose from .20 to .32. However, most black males who had attended college were unable to find work to match their qualifications. The proportion in jobs that typically required less education than they had received was 58.5 percent in 1960 and 55.0 percent in 1976. Similarly, the proportion of black male high school graduates with jobs typically requiring no high school diploma shifted only from 70.2 percent in 1960 to 67.2 percent in 1976.[33] Despite the civil rights movement and the War on Poverty, despite more years of education, black men were unable significantly to increase their chances for jobs for which they were qualified, and unemployment among them had worsened.

Ravitch's complacent view of America's past, present, and future, a story marred by unfortunate "lapses from the standard," left her unable to explain the origins of the problems that she did admit existed. Her list of America's educational problems included "a decline in educational standards, as evidenced by policies of automatic promotion in elementary and secondary schools, and at the post-secondary level, by the acceptance of grade inflation, diploma mills, and term-paper factories." Ravitch's only explanation of these problems was as startlingly simplistic as Charles Silberman's (see Chapter 4): "These changes did not come about solely because of the way history has been written in recent years, but the repeated assertions by historians and social scientists that schooling was of little or no intrinsic value has had its impact on policy makers." Although she did not state what that impact had been, perhaps she had in mind her earlier assertion, "to sap the political will that is necessary to effect change."[34]

Ravitch's assumption that the average policymaker had been influenced by revisionist historians is a claim I find impossible to believe, and for which no evidence of any sort is offered. No more accurate is her fabricated claim that revisionists believe schooling has no intrinsic value.[35] Even more serious, Ravitch tried to turn the revisionists into scapegoats for serious social and educational problems. By placing responsibility for the problems of American education on a group of historians and neglecting unemployment, inflation, and racism, Ravitch displaced the blame from where it should rest. The problem, she implied, lay not in the distribution of power and resources, but rather with those carping critics who had sown disaffection and eroded the will to action.

The apathy and hostility, even violence, encountered daily in schools, public anger and disillusionment with public education, educators' sense of impotence and rage—none of these can be explained by the apologist case. By offering a more realistic explanation of the situation, the "revisionists" actually have helped at least some students and teachers survive their daily lives with their sanity and self-esteem intact. All that Ravitch and other apologists have done is to attempt to kill the messenger who brings bad news and to spin illusions of social progress.

It is important to understand why the apologist case surfaced in the late 1970s and why it was welcomed in many quarters. During that decade, one key message of social science research was that educational innovation and reform had failed. The War on Poverty and its related educational spinoffs seemed to have missed their goals. As so often in American history, education had been deployed as the primary weapon to fight poverty, crime, and social disorder, and, as before, schools were unable to alleviate these great problems whose structural origins lie in the distribution of power and resources. Reform (as I argued in Chapter 4) usually has rested on environmental assumptions that are inherently optimistic: altered environments can change character and behavior. As reforms have failed, hereditarian theories have surfaced: problems of crime, poverty, and ignorance are not environmental but genetic. This familiar pattern in American history recurred during the 1960s and 1970s as the environmental theories underlying the War on Poverty's optimism gave way to the hereditarian arguments of Jensen and Herrenstein. Those who want to resist genetic arguments have two alternatives. One is to recognize the structural origins of social problems and the inherently ineffectual nature of the reforms that have been attempted. The other is to argue the case for social progress, regardless of what the evidence shows. The latter was Ravitch's course; it is what makes the apologist case so appealing.

Ravitch subtitled her last chapter "Limitations of the Ideological Approach," but she did not define ideology. Presumably, it is bad, an attempt to put scholarship to the service of political goals whatever the evidence might show. Her assertion that the books she attacked, and not her own, were ideological was disingenuous at best. It was also dangerous, and this is why such a slight, polemical book needs a lengthy discussion. Ravitch's book will be used again, as it already has, as ammunition by those who want to assert the apologist case for American social institutions and to dampen the prospects for structural reform. Her sponsorship by the National Academy of Education gave her work greater legitimacy than the ordinary polemic. Once it is believed that critical history will meet

with official disfavor, young scholars facing a tight job market will
be reluctant to deviate far from center. Indeed, evidence exists that
this has already begun to happen, as part of the turn to the right
that has created a climate receptive to Ravitch's message. That is
why Ravitch's credibility is an important issue.[36]

The Legitimation of the Conservative Educational Agenda

Four years after *The Revisionists Revised*, Ravitch published a
history of education in America since 1945 in which she shifted
from apologist to critic.[37] Once again, she clothed her attack in
an illusory mantle of objectivity and continued her assault on both
participatory democracy and the alleged decline in educational
standards. But her objective had shifted from an attack on revisionist historians to a historical account that legitimates the current
conservative educational agenda with its stress on excellence and
a refurbished meritocracy.

The Troubled Crusade discusses:

Urban riots without reference to police brutality or the Kerner
Commission

White movement to the suburbs without reference to government mortgage policies, urban renewal, or the interstate highway program

The recent history of American education with hardly a mention
of standardized testing

Factors influencing the postwar development of American education with no consideration of the role of corporations, labor
markets, or the changing nature of work

The development of teacher unionism without mention of the
substantive conditions to which it was a response

The increase in black educational attainment without mention
of trends in comparative black and white family income over
time

The comparative experience of blacks and early twentieth-century immigrant groups in American cities with no reference to
the work of any of the scholars who have attempted systematic
comparative analyses[38]

The controversy over the Moynihan report without reference to the serious historical criticism of its premises by Herbert Gutman and many others

The effects of desegregation without reference to the work of Robert Coles

The removal of Harold Rugg's books from libraries with no indication that they were burned in bonfires

Black English without reference to the work of William Labove

Recent educational theory with only one brief reference to Piaget

The relation of education to class and race without any reference to the work of Bowles and Gintis and with only a fleeting bibliographic reference to Christopher Jencks

Twentieth-century liberalism and educational theory and the formation of post-1945 national educational policy without reference to the major historical work on either subject[39]

To show why each of these omissions is serious and how they skew Ravitch's history would be tedious. Should it in fact be necessary to say that recent historical work completely undercuts the last of the immigrants thesis by showing that the experience of early twentieth-century immigrants and blacks differed in fundamental and incommensurate ways? Or that the desire for home-ownership, combined with government mortgage policies, bank redlining, and the interstate highway system, not just fear of blacks, stimulated the suburbanization of the middle class? Or that the Kerner Commission showed that an incident of police brutality preceded virtually every major urban riot? Or that the median income of black families relative to white in 1960 and 1982 was an identical .55?[40] Or that deindustrialization, automation, and unemployment have profound implications for urban education? Or that corporate goals have had some influence on educational policy? Rather than rehearse the answers to these questions, which are largely self-evident to anyone moderately well informed about current historical scholarship or social trends, it is more useful to reflect on the content, method, and tone of Ravitch's book.

First, the content lacks context. Despite the book's attempts to situate education within the great political struggles of its day, it lacks any systematic analysis of the relation of education to social

structure, the labor market, work, social mobility, corporate capital, or foreign policy, all subjects about which an abundant, respectable, recent literature exists, even if Ravitch would disagree
with many of its conclusions. As a result, her book lacks any
consideration of the political economy of American education.
This absence of economic and social context (as with Vinovskis'
work) is intrinsic to the new conservative educational historiography, because a systematic exposition of education's political
economy would undermine the attempt to detach schooling from
class, conflict, and other dynamic forces of social change.

Even more, Ravitch's book is curiously ahistorical. It makes an
odd and undocumented assertion that the schools really did adopt
the progressive agenda in the years after World War II.[41] Not where
I went to school, and not, I think, nearly as often as Ravitch implies.
More important, implicit in the book is the idea that the goals of
American schools once were primarily cognitive rather than social,
affective, or, in nineteenth-century terms, moral. This is a myth,
as I have argued throughout this book, but a serviceable one.
History as the story of lapsed virtue is common to conservative
causes (as in the laments that pass for family history in political
discourse) because it sets a standard that justifies change as a return
to the normal rather than as a radical departure from precedent.

Next, method. In recent decades, historians of education have
been among the pioneers within the historical community in using
new methods and applying social theory. Ravitch's book draws
on none of the recent trends in educational or, for that matter,
any other branch of historical writing. It is traditional narrative.
Her book "contains no policy recommendations, no visions of the
future (corporate or otherwise), no pedagogical prescriptions. It is
a history."[42] Despite this statement, whenever possible she deals
with people with whom she disagrees by ignoring them. Some of
them, such as the progressives who are part of the story, cannot
be omitted. But she can pretend that the social scientists and historians whose work contradicts or qualifies her interpretation simply don't exist.

The book strives for the illusion of balance. Ravitch claims:
"One's first obligation as a historian is to represent the past accurately, not to present a party line ... When I record a debate
that occurred 30 years ago ... I set forward as honestly as I know

how what the views of the antagonists were."[43] Certainly, each of Ravitch's accounts of an issue consists of a list of arguments made by each side. The question is, which arguments has she selected? What has she emphasized?

Sometimes, funny things sneak in and tilt the reader's view. Sometimes it's only a word, phrase, or list. Consider, for example, the following: "Well before the war in Vietnam actually ended, the era of disruptive campus protests faded, and student activists became involved in feminism, ecology, mysticism, and religious cults."[44] Are we supposed to think that feminism has the same intellectual substance and seriousness as a religious cult? Or that the Vietnam protest was just another adolescent fad? Or ponder this sentence: "Confidential personnel records, rigorously protected from the eyes of the FBI and state investigators during the McCarthy years, were opened to investigators from EEOC and the Department of Labor who were looking for evidence of sex discrimination."[45] Why is the comparison between McCarthyism and the investigation of alleged sexual discrimination necessary? What is it trying to say?

The story of the civil rights movement from *Brown* to affirmative action is described repeatedly as the transition from "color-blindness" to "color-consciousness."[46] Even if the labels are accurate, which is arguable, is it not tinting the story to cast it in those terms? Similarly, Ravitch's discussions of progressivism, the McCarthy period, the feminist movement, student radicalism, and so on chronicle excesses, idiocies, and mistakes in great detail. But they say less about the meaning of those movements, why they captured the hearts and minds of so many intelligent and decent people, or their real contributions and lessons. As I have already made clear, I have no quarrel with a historical account that reflects political, social, or moral views. Indeed, historical neutrality is impossible, even, I would argue, morally offensive. My objection, rather, is to the pretense of objectivity or impartiality, which has become the leading characteristic of the new conservative educational historiography.

As for tone, Ravitch's book lacks empathy. This is a very subjective criticism, for which there is no empirical demonstration. I only can say that it strikes me as though Ravitch read the writing of student protesters, feminists, black militants, and other social

critics well enough to summarize their arguments but without any
sense of what they felt, with no empathy with their rage, alienation,
or despair. One simply cannot grasp the existential meaning or
the significance of any of these protests by listing arguments pro
and con and presuming to reach a detached, rational evaluation.
They are the great issues of our time. They are responded to,
appropriately, with passion.

Ravitch is very critical of any attempt to deflect schools' primary
emphasis from a structured approach to the mastery of skills and
subject matter defined in a conventional, disciplinary way. She is
no friend of affirmative action, efforts to promote community
control, or (except for the early civil rights movement) attempts
to stimulate educational or social change through protest or direct
action. Indeed, these are the sources of her "troubled crusade."
Ravitch's title expresses one of her primary theses. America's "crusade against ignorance," for which Thomas Jefferson called in
1786, has been in trouble since the end of World War II. I take
her use of trouble to have three meanings: declining educational
achievement, the politicization of virtually every educational issue,
and the loss of a clear and appropriate educational purpose. Above
all, the great theme of these years has been the translation of the
"crusade against ignorance" into "a crusade for equal educational
opportunity," which became the "overriding goal of postwar educational reformers. Sometimes those who led the battles seemed
to forget why it was important to keep students in school longer
. . . that the fight for higher enrollment was part of a crusade against
ignorance, and that institutions would be judged by what their
students had learned as well as by how many were enrolled."[47]

Ravitch does not want to be pinned down too closely on any
of these points or on any specific point of view. She does not want
to be associated with any of the recent reports on education, which,
she points out, appeared after her book was written (although she
did participate in the Twentieth Century Fund's report). Nor does
she want to be labeled "neoconservative" or anything else. She
can't have it both ways. Whatever her intentions or her preferences,
she unavoidably will find herself in the camp calling for a return
to "excellence" in education, represented by *A Nation at Risk*.
(Ravitch's protests against association with this movement ring
especially hollow considering the title of a recent book that she

coedited, *Against Mediocrity*.)[48] The implications of her story lead
logically to that association. This is the important point made by
Deborah Meier in her criticism of *Troubled Crusade*. Meier argued
that Ravitch's interpretation supported the movement created by
several convergent developments: the recent spate of reports on
education, the increased use of standardized testing, the emphasis
on tough promotional policies, homework, and rigor, and the
current manpower goals of corporate America. "Ravitch's book,"
writes Meier, "is not written in a vacuum. A lot of action is going
on out there in the real world... Under the mantle of disinterested
historian, Ravitch presents a version of the recent past that lends
support to a whole set of existing proposals that will drag us not
so slowly off in what, I strongly believe, is the wrong direction."[49]

In the end, what fascinates me about Ravitch's book are its
central contradiction and its essential nihilism, both of which show
the bankruptcy of the new conservative educational history. Despite its potshots at critical historians and progressive reformers,
its vigorous assertions of its own objectivity, and its claim to have
set the record straight, conservative educational history cannot
offer a coherent version of the past or a position on the present
that follows logically and consistently from its conclusions.

In her introduction, Ravitch made the point (which virtually
every reviewer has cited) that throughout American history,
schools "sometimes... have been expected to take on responsibilities for which they were entirely unsuited. When they have
failed, it was usually because their leaders and their public alike
had forgotten their real limitations as well as their real strengths."[50]
Throughout *The Troubled Crusade*, she attempted to document
the problems created by trying to use schools as agencies of social
reform, but she never asked why Americans have placed so many
burdens on their schools. Why have they turned to schools instead
of to more direct methods of social, economic, or political change?
The answer is, in part, that educational reform has substituted for
social and economic reform. In the nineteenth century, Americans
learned to deflect their problems onto their schools rather than
confront the painful task of actually trying to solve them, especially
when those problems involved the redistribution of power and
resources. Ravitch showed no interest in redistributive public policy, but she did reveal a decent concern with poverty, racism, and

injustice. Therefore, she had a problem. Unwilling even to discuss the political economy of the schools, let alone consider the roots of the problems with which, as she said, schools have been left to grapple, Ravitch retreated to a sentimental emphasis on the possibilities of education as social reform, hardly consistent with the preceding 329 pages of her book: "To believe in education is to believe in the future, to believe in what may be accomplished through the disciplined use of intelligence, allied with cooperation and good will. If it seems naively American to put so much stock in schools, colleges, universities, and the endless prospect of self-improvement and social improvement, it is an admirable, and perhaps even a noble, flaw."[51]

But what does *The Troubled Crusade* really imply about the prospects for reform? If Ravitch is right, nearly everyone who has tried has failed. The progressives may have been well intentioned but their efforts were disastrous. Certainly, we cannot rely on the educational establishment, represented by schools of education, that supported them. The reforms of the 1960s accomplished very little. The federal government is more a hindrance than a help. Community control is a menace. Teachers' unions are concerned primarily with the welfare of their members. Where, then, is the impetus for reform? What is the source of change? There is no answer in Ravitch's book. Indeed, despite its last few sentences, its implications are profoundly pessimistic.

In her earlier attack on revisionist historians, Ravitch blamed them for inciting pessimism. They had supposedly taught a generation of education students that they could not educate their pupils or change their schools. Consequently, they bore a heavy responsibility for the decay of teacher morale and educational quality. The attribution of such influence to a handful of diverse historians missed the point of their work and incorrectly understood its meaning for those relatively few people in the schools who took it seriously. In *The Troubled Crusade*, Ravitch adopted the viewpoint of her former enemies and wrote a book more glum, less hopeful, than any of them.

Where do the attacks and counterattacks of the last several years leave the writing of educational history? Two points drift up from the rhetorical dust. First, the new conservative educational history has accomplished very little. Aside from poking holes in a few weak points, its major goal, the detachment of education from class, has failed. Its practitioners (even Paul Peterson, the most recent and sophisticated) have offered no coherent alternative to nearly a generation of critical history.[52] And its hallmark, the pretense of disinterested objectivity, is transparent. Revisionist-bashing has become a semipopular sport, but it is a dead end.

The second point, then, is the need to recast the debate. The question is not whether some illusory group, called revisionists, is right or wrong. It is, rather, how to build on their insights. Certainly, individual work should be scrutinized, though not for the purpose of tearing it to shreds and proudly waving its fragments at the end of a pole, conservative, radical, or liberal. Rather, the task is to create a stronger framework, one that incorporates new directions in historical writing (such as the emphasis on republicanism in early America), theoretical advances, and good research. Here, the model is Ira Katznelson's and Margaret Weir's brilliant recent book *Schooling for All*, which elevates debate on education's past to a new plane by showing how the practice and ideal of democracy combined with class formation and the persistence of social inequality to shape the history of schooling.[53] Katznelson and Weir neither reject class, pretend objectivity, nor disguise their politics. They show that the cutting edge of educational history will remain critical. For it is the only kind that makes sense of the disaster that surrounds us.

6

The Moral Crisis
of the University

Prologue

On Tuesday, February 22, 1983, an undergraduate at the University of Pennsylvania reported that she had been raped by a group of fraternity students early the previous Friday morning after a party at their house. After more than a month of hesitation, the university's administration charged the individual men with a violation of the university's code of conduct (a brief statement requiring students to behave in a mature and responsible fashion) and prepared for hearings before the University Court, composed solely of students. However, before any hearing took place, the university reached settlements with the men. Although the terms are secret, it is known that the settlements required the men to undergo a process of reeducation through reading, essay writing, discussion, and community service. Because settlements reached under the university's judicial charter preclude expulsion or suspension as sentences, these sanctions were not available.

The settlements were reached in May, just before graduation, a time when it is virtually impossible to mobilize opinion around any issue. Therefore, the grumbling among many faculty, staff, and students about the secrecy and apparent leniency of the sanctions dissipated. However, when the *Philadelphia Inquirer*'s Sunday magazine carried an extensive and, as it turned out, reasonably accurate account of the event the issue exploded again. As a result of concern on the campus, early in the fall the Executive Committee of the Faculty Senate voted to establish a committee of senior faculty to investigate the administration's handling of the case against the individual men and its treatment of the woman.

The Senate Executive asked me to chair the committee, and the task consumed all its members' lives for the fall semester. Our report did not speculate on the motives for administrative actions. Instead, we concerned ourselves only with what had been done and with evaluating those choices and outcomes. Although there are a variety of plausible, if sometimes contradictory, theories about the issues, one of them seems to me clearly wrong—that this event was an isolated, if tragic, phenomenon, divorced from the mainstream of campus life and of no general significance. To the contrary, I believe the incident raises fundamental issues about the character of universities in the late twentieth century. My reflections as a historian on those issues have prompted this chapter, which argues that this incident is one example of a powerful and disturbing trend that has robbed universities of the capacity to answer questions critical to their own future. I refer to the assimilation of universities to the marketplace and the state.

Origins of the Multiversity

In his 1963 Godkin Lectures at Harvard, Clark Kerr, then president of the University of California, announced the birth of the multiversity. "The basic reality for the university," he said, "is the widespread recognition that new knowledge is the most important factor in economic and social growth." Because they now were "required to produce knowledge as never before," universities had assumed an unprecedented role, "with little but platitudes to mask the nakedness of the change."[1] In the 1960s, as Paul Axelrod has shown for Ontario, public recognition that knowledge had become a new and vital form of capital also shaped the development of Canadian higher education. In both countries one result was the accelerated assimilation of universities to the marketplace and the state.[2]

To Kerr, the structure of the multiversity reflected "competing visions of true purpose, each relating to a different layer of history, a different web of forces... The university is so many things to so many different people that it must, of necessity, be partially at war with itself." Kerr celebrated this lack of a common center as an expression of a healthy, vital pluralism that enhanced both creativity and freedom. Any university, he wrote, could "aim to be no higher than to be as British as possible for the sake of the undergraduates, as German as possible for the sake of the graduates and research personnel, as American as possible for the sake of the public at large—and as confused as possible for the sake of the preservation of the whole uneasy balance." Universities, he said, might be defined "as a series of individual faculty entrepreneurs held together by a common grievance over parking."[3]

Kerr stressed the massive post–World War II increase in the federal financing of universities; the multiversity could also be called the "federal grant university." As early as 1960, he pointed out, federal support accounted for 75 percent of all university research expenses and 15 percent of total university budgets. The emergence of the federal grant university, he observed, had been eased because it took place without planning. With no "overall view" of what had "been happening to them," universities had made "piecemeal adjustments." As a consequence, "the federal government and the leading universities entered into a common-law marriage unblessed by predetermined policies and self-surveys—but nonetheless they formed a very productive union." The paradox, as Kerr pointed out, was that "the federal colossus had the power to influence the most ruggedly individual universities." "The better the university," he commented wryly, "the greater its chances of succumbing to the federal embrace." Even as it snuggled up to the federal government, the university managed at the same time to keep at least one arm around the corporate world. "The university and segments of industry," wrote Kerr, "are becoming more alike." The professor was assuming "the character of an entrepreneur. Industry, with its scientists and technicians, learns an uncomfortable bit about academic freedom and the handling of intellectual personnel. The two worlds are merging physically and psychologically."[4]

One lesson was clear. The dynamic forces shaping universities (like the forces shaping schools) have come from outside their walls. "The location of power has generally moved from inside to outside the original community of masters and students. The nature of the multiversity makes it inevitable that this historical transfer will not be reversed." Those faculty who longed for a quiet, self-contained world were guilty of a "guild" mentality; they were romantics, unaware of, or unwilling to accept, the transformation of the higher learning. To be sure, faculty still exercised authority "over admissions, approval of courses, examinations, and granting of degrees," and they had achieved "considerable influence over faculty appointments and academic freedom." But "organized faculty control or influence over the general direction of the growth of the American multiversity" remained limited, and it would not grow larger. Therefore, whether or not faculty approved of the multiversity was beside the point; its emergence was inevitable. To oppose it would be to stand in the way of history. The legitimacy of the multiversity rests, in the final analysis, not on its worth but on its necessity.[5]

Kerr intended his remarks as an analysis and celebration of the multiversity. Although he did not try to mask its internal tensions, he viewed its evolution as a great triumph. Its loosely coupled structure, internal diversity, human and financial resources, and protection of academic freedom released an unprecedented burst of intellectual energy and creativity that spread beyond the boundaries of the university to invigorate, instruct, and improve the world around it. "The campus and society," according to Kerr, "are undergoing a somewhat reluctant and cautious merger, already well advanced." Implicit and unanswered in Kerr's account are critical questions: Where are the boundaries of the university? Are there any principles that distinguish the conduct and development of universities from other social institutions? Are they anything more than sites of advanced teaching and research? What principles and criteria guide their activities?[6]

In Kerr's account, the principles and criteria underlying the recent development of universities reveal a process that a less sanguine observer can term the assimilation of the university to the marketplace and the state. Although this process has been in effect for a long time, it has always met resistance from those who believed that neither the needs of the state nor the criteria of the marketplace should be allowed unmediated power to shape the organization and conduct of the higher learning. Universities have been "contested terrain" where the forces of resistance have won important, if partial, victories. There is nothing inevitable about the shape of the higher learning. It is (like the structure of public education, discussed earlier) the result, if not of planning, of human agency. It is the product of compromise, conflict, and, above all, choice.

The conflict between what, for shorthand, I will call the forces of marketplace and community in higher education echoes an old struggle. For centuries, faculty argued that universities should be self-governing communities of scholars and tried to resist the pull of church or state, which sought the inculcation of orthodoxy and the training of loyal servants. However, the ascendancy of liberal economics in the nineteenth century reshaped the ancient tensions within higher education. For liberal economics substituted the demands of an impersonal marketplace for the intrusive authority of church or crown. Under the mantle of service to the whole community and relevance to contemporary life, some university reformers attempted to apply the principles of supply and demand to the evaluation of academic institutions. A clear example was Francis Wayland's attempt to reform Brown in the 1850s. Wayland argued that colleges were suffering a decline in popularity because they remained aloof from popular desires and changing tastes, and he proposed their transformation into educational supermarkets governed by laws of supply and demand where students would come and go at will, choosing as many or as few courses as they wished.[7] Essentially, he proposed remodeling colleges along the lines of academies, as described in Chapter 2. Both, after all, were structured on the same organizational model: corporate voluntarism.

Even in the heady, early nineteenth-century days of liberal economics, some faculty resisted the application of a market model to higher education, and, for a variety of reasons, Wayland failed to implement his vision of a free-market university.[8] Although nineteenth-century liberal economics added the laws of supply and demand as enduring arbiters of academic life, the great attempt to press higher education into the service of the market and the secular state began with the creation of modern universities in the late nineteenth and early twentieth centuries. The process took only twenty or thirty years in the United States and somewhat longer in Canada. The major new features in universities were: graduate and professional schools; lectures and seminars; the elective system; a strong, nonclerical president; an emphasis on public service; internal bureaucracy; specialized academic departments; a commitment to research; and expanded size. By the early twentieth century, commentators pointed to the presence of a new and distinctive institution. American universities, wrote Edward Slosson, a professor of chemistry, in 1910, "are very much alike; more alike, doubtless, than they claim to be... The American university tends to be a specific type, very different from that of England, Germany or France."[9]

In a recent, important book Colin Burke has contended that historians have overstated the extent of the "university revolution." He finds, first, that enrollment increased much less than has usually been imagined. Second, most students chose traditional curricula and underenrolled in the newer, more innovative ones. The factors accounting for changing enrollment levels, he argues, were the increasing incorporation of college education into the training of lawyers, ministers, and educators and the entrance of a much larger number of women. At the same time, the age range of entering students narrowed and assumed a much more—by our standards—modern pattern. Still, a number of outside forces (the cost of college, apprenticeship, patterns of entry to many occupations) retarded the pace of enrollment growth.[10]

Despite the continuities Burke and others have found between antebellum and late nineteenth-century higher education, no one denies that great changes occurred. But they were centered in a relatively few institutions that transformed academic life only gradually. As Laurence Veysey pointed out, in the late nineteenth and early twentieth centuries a variety of ideals—utility, service, culture, and research—competed for dominance in American universities. Clark Kerr observed correctly that decades later, none of these four ideals ever triumphed completely, and as a result the organization of the new or transformed universities reflected no central purpose. Rather, universities had become federations whose components were coupled by bureaucracy, which was grafted onto their earlier corporate voluntarist structure. According to Veysey, "Bureaucratic administration was the structural device which made possible the new epoch of institutional empire-building without recourse to specific values. Thus while unity of purpose disintegrated, a uniformity of standardized practices was coming into being."[11]

Market principles invaded universities in various ways. "Losing a clear sense of purpose," observed Veysey, "spokesmen for the American university around the turn of the century ran the danger of casually, even unconsciously, accepting the dominant codes of action of their more numerous and influential peers, the leaders of business and industry." The invasion of universities by the market "excited more heated comment at the time" than any other "academic trend." Lamenting the new business ethic in higher education, in 1902 John Dewey wrote that universities "are ranked by their obvious material prosperity, until the atmosphere of money-getting and money-spending hides from view the interests for the sake of which money alone has such a place."[12] The classic attack on the relations between business and universities came from Thorstein Veblen in *The Higher Learning in America* (1910), a tough, satirical, and penetrating critique that introduced the phrase "captains of erudition" to describe the new, entrepreneurial university leaders who had replaced the clergymen presidents of American colleges before the Civil War.[13]

As Veysey pointed out, contacts between universities and the marketplace took place at many levels. Presidents and professors attempted to recruit students by writing articles about the economic utility of collegiate education. At the same time, support for the creation, maintenance, and expansion of universities came from philanthropists, who frequently and often successfully tried to influence the internal life of the institutions they supported. "Of more consequence than donors for the actual conduct of affairs at most universities," in Veysey's view, "were boards of trustees," composed largely of businessmen or other nonacademic professionals, who often stressed the importance of athletics, businesslike management, and a conservative faculty. Presidents, in turn, often viewed their faculty as employees. "Like shrewd businessmen, university presidents and trustees sought to pay their faculties as little as the 'market price' demanded; both Eliot [Harvard] and Gilman [Johns Hopkins] were more parsimonious in this respect than the financial condition of their institutions required. Similarly, most presidents favored (and practiced) a policy of paying professors unequal salaries, so that 'market price' might obtain on an individual basis."[14] In other words, the labor of faculty had been transformed into a commodity whose price was determined by its value in a novel arena: the academic marketplace.

The transformation of the leading universities signaled a new era in the history of capital. In a dramatic and novel way, knowledge—advanced technical and managerial knowledge—had become a resource essential to the progress of the vast new corporations and bureaucracies that dominated economic and social life. Science and technology, production and administration, coordination and marketing: all required experts and expert knowledge. Until the late nineteenth century, most experts and expert knowledge had been produced outside universities. By capturing the process through which they were produced and transferring the actual production of much new knowledge from outside their walls to within them, universities staged one of the great coups in the history of capitalism. However, they met only minimal resistance because the imperial interests of universities and the self-protective instincts of professionals reinforced each other nicely. Together, they made credentials dispensed by universities the hallmark of professional expertise. Universities thereby became the gatekeepers of the advanced technical-managerial society.[15]

Before the late nineteenth century, professional education had taken place in a wider variety of settings. Engineers, for instance, frequently were trained in shops; lawyers often had begun their careers as apprentices in law offices; most nurses and social workers received no professional training whatsoever. Although the increasing formalization of training within universities followed a different pace for each occupation, in all of them great changes took place between about 1870 and World War I, especially during the 1890s. Enrollment in law schools more than tripled, and in medical and nursing schools it more than doubled. About twenty-five law schools existed in 1860 and over one hundred in 1900, of which thirty had been founded in the 1890s. But the profession that accounted for the greatest number of students was education. According to Burke, normal schools enrolled 4 percent of all students in higher education in 1860, 16 percent in 1870, and 30 percent in 1900. One quarter of the graduates of regular colleges became teachers or professors. The increased dependence of colleges and universities on teacher training heightened their efforts to attract women and fueled the rapid rise in female college attendance in the same years. In the 1890s, over half the undergraduates at the University of Michigan were women and over 45 percent of its alumni were teachers.[16]

The expansion of professional education irreversibly blurred the boundaries of universities. Professional schools are dependent on the fields they serve. Because their graduates must be prepared to assume specific occupational roles and to perform competently, professional training is driven by criteria derived from practice and by the nature of the division of labor within specific occupations. For example, the history of curricula in schools of education in the early twentieth century mirrored the history of the educational bureaucracy. As specific jobs proliferated within expanding school systems, schools of education offered courses and degree sequences that paralleled them exactly.[17] University-based professional schools find it difficult to challenge conventional practice without leaving their students at a disadvantage in the job market, and, because they are dependent upon the good opinion of the field, they often are reluctant to make sharp criticisms of professionals or their work. This field-dependence undercuts their capacity to lead, rather than follow, the development of their fields and mutes their potential as professional critics.

By the late nineteenth century, many universities had already established separate departments of education, and by 1920 separate schools of education had started to appear on campuses across the country. Within these new departments and schools, universities hatched educational research as a new academic field and developed graduate programs for administrators, researchers, and other educational specialists. Through training, textbooks, and consulting, professors of education forged close links with public school systems and thus strengthened the connections between universities and the state.

Of course, in these years universities began to serve the state through many other channels, too. Faculty (most notably at the University of Wisconsin) became increasingly active as expert advisers on governmental policy. Because state and federal governments played such a minimal role in social policy before World

War I, university faculty directed their efforts toward urban problems and city government. The relation between Chicago and its universities provides a vivid case in point. Clearly, one hallmark of the progressive era was the attempt to link universities and public service through the application of specialized, expert knowledge to the solution of public problems. Once again, though, circumspection became the price of public trust. Professionals in the service of the state learned to confine themselves to areas in which they possessed recognized technical expertise and to keep their recommendations within the boundaries of acceptable alternatives for public policy. This lesson was one consequence of the great academic freedom cases of the late nineteenth and early twentieth centuries.[18]

Universities, the Marketplace, and the State

The academic freedom cases that rocked Stanford, Wisconsin, Cornell, Pennsylvania, Chicago, and other schools reflected the heightened influence of the marketplace and the state on universities and the transmutation of universities into great bureaucracies led by "captains of erudition." Like corporate executives, university presidents in the late nineteenth and early twentieth centuries tried to increase their control over their workers. Within industry, management increased its control of the workplace by reorganizing production in ways that eroded the customary autonomy of skilled workers in several trades. Though blocked by constraints that did not exist in industry, university presidents tried to exert their direct authority over faculty in a variety of ways. One (noted earlier) was to keep faculty salaries secret. Another was to demand that professors not offend trustees or influential sectors of the public. Because of their great dependence upon private donors or legislative goodwill, the early "captains of erudition" combined their entrepreneurial zeal with political caution.

During this period, capital controlled labor primarily by breaking strikes with impunity and blackballing labor leaders; and it controlled universities primarily by engineering the dismissal of dissident faculty and trying to block their appointment elsewhere. Thus, when some professors (including Henry Carter Adams at Cornell, Richard Ely at Wisconsin, Edward W. Bemis at Chicago,

John R. Commons at Indiana, and Edward A. Ross at Stanford) refused to curtail their advocacy of free silver, the right of labor to organize, and other causes unpopular in conservative circles, or to restrain their criticism of industries or municipal franchises in which trustees had a direct interest, they were attacked and, in many cases, fired. These sad, sordid, even craven violations of academic freedom have been chronicled often, and I will not rehearse their details.[19] The important point here is what these cases illustrate and their consequences. First, they point to the erosion of the boundaries between the university and the marketplace. As university presidents tried to behave like industrialists who could exact obedience from employees and fire them at will, one of the criteria for dismissal became endangering the financial health of the university by damaging its reputation in influential circles. In these early cases, faculty members fired for openly stating their opinions on public issues received almost no support from colleagues. Nor had they any legal protection. In truth, they were more vulnerable for publicly stating unpopular opinions than for incompetence.

Faculty mobilized slowly and timidly in response to capital's assault. The conventional landmark in the history of academic freedom is the founding of the American Association of University Professors in 1915. In its early years the AAUP moved cautiously not only because of public hostility but also because of conservatism among faculty. Nonetheless, at its inception the association adopted a statement supporting academic freedom and tenure. Also in 1915, college presidents organized the American Association of College Presidents. In its early years, the AACP rejected the AAUP position on academic freedom and tenure and vigorously asserted the right of presidents and trustees to exercise their independent authority in decisions to hire or dismiss faculty. Although the AACP nearly reversed this stance in 1922, not until 1940 did the two associations agree on a set of principles governing academic freedom and tenure that colleges and universities were willing, albeit gradually and grudgingly, to incorporate into their statutes.[20]

The early AAUP position did not reflect an unlimited commitment to academic freedom. As Mary Furner has shown, during the years of the great academic freedom cases, university faculty had goals beyond protection from arbitrary administrative action. They were also working actively for recognition as professionals with valuable, expert skills. As they maneuvered to create new disciplines and sell their services to government and industry, faculty developed a defense of academic freedom based on technical expertise and objectivity, and they defended only colleagues threatened with dismissal for exercising their professional judgment. Objectivity itself became an ideology deployed in the service of professionalization. Indeed, as Furner has observed, "As professionalization proceeded, most academic scientists stopped asking ethical questions. Instead they turned their attention to carefully controlled, empirical investigations of problems that were normally defined by the state of knowledge in their fields rather than by the state of society. Professional social scientists generally accepted the basic structure of corporate capitalism. Abandoning their pretensions to a role as arbiters of public policy, they established a more limited goal: recognition as experts with extraordinary technical competence in a highly specialized but restricted sphere."[21]

Academic mobilization resulted in a compromise. Administrators could not control faculty in the same way that corporate presidents could control manufacturing. Veysey pointed to the "sense of informal limitations" that constrained the "exercise of power" at all major institutions. These limits, he observed, became especially obvious when the "Taylorite 'efficiency' craze began to seek academic targets just after 1910." Even if faculty were unwilling to support unrestrained academic freedom, they "guarded certain symbols of self-respect" and believed that universities "differed significantly from manufacturing concerns." However, academics were ambivalent about the invasion of the university by the market and the state. Even as they resisted attempts to circumscribe their academic freedom, they sought closer ties with government and industry as consultants and expert advisers, and they solicited outside funds that made possible the expansion of their research activities and graduate training programs.[22]

The influence of the state on universities became especially evident during World War I. Few professors protested when their colleagues were fired for opposition to the war, and many others behaved supinely. Professional historians, as Carol Gruber has shown, were especially culpable in their role as propagandists; they violated the elemental criteria of their profession by producing patently false and distorted material attacking America's enemies.[23] (Relations between universities, the marketplace, and the state differed in Canada and the United States in at least one important respect: the relative influence of the private and public sectors. In Canada, the private sector has exerted far less influence. For reasons analyzed by Paul Axelrod, private and corporate contributions to Canadian universities have been much lower, and, even more telling, a far higher proportion of Canadian university graduates have been employed in the public and a far lower in the private sector than in the United States.)[24]

By the end of World War I, many administrators as well as faculty had become alarmed by the fragmentation of universities. Rapid expansion, academic and professional specialization, the proliferation of the elective system, and the disintegrating boundaries between universities, the marketplace, and the state, had robbed curricula of their coherence. University education appeared to have lost any sense of purpose, and educational programs reflected primarily the demands of disciplines and professions for specialized or technical training. One response—in both undergraduate and professional education—was the general education movement, which attempted to define a core of knowledge essential to an educated person. The movement's first major achievement was Columbia College's Contemporary Civilization Course, initiated in 1919. It affected graduate and professional training as well; in the field of education one of its major achievements was the introduction of the "foundations of education" as a required subject at Teachers College, Columbia, in the 1920s. The general education movement gathered steam in the 1940s, coasted in the 1950s, and began to come under attack in the 1960s. Only in the last few years has it reappeared as administrators and faculty have once again voiced alarm over the fragmentation, specialization, and lack of coherence in university programs. This oscillation between a search for coherence and either a purely elective system or a pattern of fragmented, specialized programs represents the way in which the tension between marketplace and community has been expressed in the history of curriculum.[25]

By the start of World War II, within universities a compromise had been reached between the forces of the marketplace and community. Its hallmarks were a core curriculum and an official commitment to academic freedom and tenure. This is the context from which Clark Kerr's multiversity emerged in the next two decades. Despite the accuracy of his analysis, Kerr's description of the multiversity underestimated the forces that would disrupt campuses not long after his lectures were published. Of course it would have been difficult to foresee the turmoil to be caused by the Vietnam War or the extent to which the civil rights movement would spread to campuses. But Kerr did not realize the explosive force of the internal contradictions he so actively championed. More concerned with the faculty, he missed the next great challenge to the major tendencies in the history of the higher learning, which came, unexpectedly, from the students.

Student revolts on campuses in the 1960s were complex events with several sources, including the Vietnam War, the civil rights movement, disenchantment with technology and material progress, and even socialization patterns within upper-middle-class families. Most important for my purposes here, student radicals attacked the multiversity for neglecting its distinctively educational purposes and for its assimilation to the marketplace and the state. This general criticism underlay many specific complaints: professors who neglected teaching, the presence of secret defense research on campus, restrictions on public advocacy of unpopular causes, and the lack of student participation in university governance. However strident, intellectually fuzzy, or disruptive they were, student radicals were the vanguard of the resistance to the multiversity. As faculty donned their entrepreneurial and bureaucratic roles, it was left to students to take up the task of resistance. One student demand was "relevance," which in practice has proved an ambiguous goal. "Relevance" has had two major meanings. One is the demand for a closer link between university education and jobs. In this sense, students helped accelerate the erosion of the boundaries between universities and the marketplace. The other meaning, however, is more consistent with the radical student critique; it reflects a demand that universities incorporate the great moral and social issues of the day into their curricula.

For many reasons, students could not seriously change the direction of university development or retard the pace of assimilation. The major institutional legacy of their activities was the development of formal participatory structures that included university administrators, faculty, students, and, sometimes, support staff. However, these structures have been unable to transform the spirit of academic decision making or to inject a sense of community into campuses.

Let me draw on one example from my own experience. In the early 1960s the Province of Ontario created the Ontario Institute for Studies in Education (OISE) to do research, development, and graduate training in education. The province had been far behind American states in these respects, and, through a rapid infusion of money, it hoped to improve its position rapidly and effectively. OISE affiliated with the University of Toronto for instructional purposes, and all graduate degrees were awarded by the university. The faculty of OISE grew rapidly from about 20 in its first year, 1965–66, to over 40 in its second, and about 140 a few years later. With nearly unlimited funding for a few years, the province had managed to create a major graduate school of education. OISE's budget included not only money for faculty but also internal research and development funds and generous assistance for students. With these resources, the support staff grew as rapidly as the faculty, and the student body—composed mainly of part-time students—mushroomed. OISE experienced all the predictable pains of rapid growth. But what I want to concentrate on here is the issue of governance.

OISE was staffed mainly by young faculty deeply affected by the criticism of universities prevalent in the 1960s. They chafed against what appeared to be the authoritarian and bureaucratic patterns of administration, and they fought for a new form of academic government that would draw on every constituency. The result of their efforts was an experiment: the creation of an Institute Assembly designed to be the precursor of a unicameral form of academic government. The assembly consisted of representatives from every constituency, including the board of governors; although its powers were only advisory to the administration and board, it was clearly a major force. In an effort to permit everyone who wanted to participate in academic government the opportunity for a meaningful role, the assembly included four major standing committees, each with subcommittees. Each committee and subcommittee was to be composed of assembly members plus elected representatives of every OISE constituency. The whole structure was to be presided over by a faculty member chosen by the assembly as its speaker; the speaker was also to serve as an unofficial ombudsman. I was the first speaker and served for one memorable year.

In a formal sense, we made the assembly work. It took a position on every major decision facing OISE; no major decisions contrary to its wishes were taken by either the board of governors or the administration. As ombudsman, I mediated some major conflicts and listened to many grievances. Because elections were held to fill every committee vacancy, ballots had to be sent to several hundred part-time students for every subcommittee opening. Not surprisingly, the proportion who voted was very small, and the cost of operating the structure—in terms of both money and time—was very great. The issues with which the committees and assembly dealt were almost entirely budgetary and structural. Almost no issues of educational or substantive research policy were discussed. Most decisions about what to teach remained confined to the academic divisions of OISE, and research policy expressed the wishes of individual faculty or was made in the process of awarding internal research funds within the research committee. By the end of the first year, enthusiasm for participation in the assembly had begun to wane, and it continued to slide. The faculty is now unionized and the dream of a unicameral governing body is dead.

The assembly's history offers several lessons. One involves the connection between democracy and bureaucracy. In a large organization, democratic procedures require bureaucratic forms. Without a widespread sense of commitment and purpose among the participants, form triumphs over substance, practice is governed by routine, and a small number of interested people effectively exert control. Even a new and relatively small academic institution, such as OISE, could not arouse the sustained commitment essential to participatory government in spirit as well as in form. One reason is that, like the multiversity it was in miniature, OISE lacked a core. Faculty had closer ties with their disciplinary colleagues around the continent than with each other. Their first loyalty was to their professional work, defined as research and specialized teaching. Many faculty sought to influence public education directly, which meant muting criticism and building links with the educational bureaucracy. Internal views of what OISE should do were diverse. Few people wanted to take the time to hammer out a coherent statement of purpose or to risk the conflict that a discussion of educational policy entailed. A relatively decentralized system of academic divisions loosely coupled by a bureaucracy remained, in the end, the best assurance of independence. At the same time, students had their own lives to worry about. Most were trying to balance their obligations to jobs, families, and graduate study; few wanted to help run the institution. For a variety of reasons, the support staff probably remained the most interested, but to the administration and the board of governors, the assembly was a nuisance and sometimes a menace.

I suspect that academic governance traveled a similar trajectory in many places. The legacy of the experience is a collection of structures in which previously excluded groups have a place. In most instances, a relatively small proportion of each constituency probably participates in central, universitywide governance, and the reality is far different from the hopes of the reformers who fought for new governing bodies ten or fifteen years earlier. Nonetheless, central, participatory assemblies remain important. Even if they have little impact on routine operations or on major questions of educational policy (which remain decentralized), they serve as channels through which resistance can be mobilized quickly and effectively in crises or in reaction to events or decisions that outrage the campus. They are, if nothing else, a conscience always brooding over the shoulder of the central administration. This is an honorable and necessary role, though quite different from real communal governance. (Perhaps widespread participation and community can be sustained only within relatively small units where all members are immediately affected by most major decisions. This, of course, is why departmental politics remain so much more lively than central administrative ones. Where central bodies remain most active, they consist of single constituencies, such as faculty senates or undergraduate assemblies. The reason, again, is the greater commonality of interest among members.)

With its only effective challenge deflected, denatured, or accommodated, the assimilation of the university to the marketplace and the state accelerated. The unionization of faculty on many campuses, which reflects a wage-labor model, is one example. Others are the increased dependence on federal funds and the recent increase in formal ties between universities and the corporate world. Some universities have even based their internal budgetary procedures on a market model. Responsibility-based budgeting, as the model is called, ties the allocation of resources to the enrollment of individual schools and departments and thereby fosters competitive, entrepreneurial activity on individual campuses. Some of these developments, of course, reflect the precarious situation of universities caught by inflation, decreased government funding, and a smaller cohort from which to draw students. But they also reflect the lure of government contracts and private-sector money. Committed to research, tempted by opportunity, tied more closely to their profession than to their institution, faculty have willingly and eagerly facilitated the erosion of the boundaries of the university and the obliteration of its distinctive features.

The Moral Crisis of the University

Until now, I have deliberately avoided an explicit definition of the key process described here: the assimilation of the university to the marketplace and the state. Its meaning, which I hope has emerged from my account, has four components: first, the increasing similarity in the principles that underlie the organization and operation of universities and corporations, especially the application of the law of supply and demand to internal decisions. Two consequences of the adoption of market principles are the determination of educational and scholarly worth by market value and the transformation of faculty scholarship into a commodity. Second is the increased determination of internal priorities and lines of development by the requirements of corporations and the state. The dictation of research directions by the availability of funds and the structuring of educational programs by the division of labor within professions are two results of this aspect of the process. Third, the activities of faculty members increasingly resemble those of entrepreneurs or bureaucrats. Faculty reap their greatest rewards outside the university. Their primary loyalties are to their professional peers around the world and to their clients and sponsors. Fourth, the direction of university development is justified by appeals to the "needs" of the economy, society, technology, or some other great force. A reified imperative drives the history of the higher learning and narrowly constricts the availability of alternatives at any point in time. The character of universities becomes inevitable, and their legitimacy rests on their service to the great forces over which they have no control.

What is wrong with this process? After all, Clark Kerr saw in it the triumph of a democratic pluralism and the unprecedented release of energy and creativity in the public service. However, as Robert Paul Wolff pointed out in *The Ideal of the University*, Kerr "commits exactly the same error which lies at the heart of classical laissez-faire theory," that is, the identification of "effective market demand with true human need." The result is "a covert ideological rationalization for whatever human or social desires happen to be backed by enough money or power to translate them into effective demands." In Kerr's analysis, "national needs" assume the role of the market in classical economic theory. They are above politics, beyond intervention, an inexorable force shaping the higher learning. Thus, the responsiveness of the multiversity to "national needs" is "nothing more than its tendency to adjust itself to effective demand in the form of government grants, scholarship programs, corporate or alumni underwriting, and so forth." Although Kerr's analysis invested these demands with moral worth, in truth the university is only accepting the priorities of the government or of some other body for space research, weapons systems, or other goals. Universities, it follows, cannot be genuine critics of the "national purpose" of which they are an instrument, and their independent role in social and political analysis is badly, if not fatally, damaged. The question Wolff posed is: "at the present time is . . . there a greater social need for full-scale integration of the resources and activities of the universities into existing domestic and foreign programs, or for a sustained critique of those programs from an independent position of authority and influence?"[26]

The answer must reflect a position on a difficult question: what is it exactly that makes a university distinct from other social institutions? Wolff offered a compelling definition based on a conception of the ideal university as a "community of learning." The ideal university, he argued, should be "a community of persons united by collective understandings, by common and communal goals, by bonds of reciprocal obligation, and by a flow of sentiment which makes the preservation of the community an object of desire, not merely a matter of prudence or a command of duty."[27] Community implies a form of social obligation governed by principles different from those operative in the marketplace and state. Laws of supply and demand lose priority; wage-labor is not the template for all human relations; the translation of individuals into commodities is resisted. The difficult task of defining common goals or acceptable activity is neither avoided nor deflected onto bureaucracy.

Nonetheless, modern universities do remain distinct from both the corporate and governmental worlds, and, for all its force, the process of assimilation remains incomplete. The great barriers to the total victory of the marketplace and the state are academic freedom and tenure. Although tenure decisions often reflect marketplace criteria, tenure is critical for four reasons. First, it restricts the major principle of economic relations in the marketplace: free wage labor. Tenure rejects the prerogative of management to dismiss employees at will; it affirms alternative principles to supply and demand; it rests on an expansive, rather than a restrictive, definition of the reciprocal obligations between workers and employers. Second, it lessens the translation of faculty into commodities whose value is determined solely by their current market price. It prevents the dismissal of academics solely because their work has gone out of fashion. In this way, it protects academics from each other as well as from the marketplace. Without tenure, competent academics whose work no longer appeared at the cutting edge of their fields would no doubt find themselves increasingly without work. Tenure thus restrains the application of pure market value as the sole criterion of continued academic employment. Third, tenure protects academic freedom. Before the introduction of tenure, university administrations succumbed to pressure to fire faculty members with unpopular ideas. There is no doubt that the same process would happen again. Tenure, therefore, is essential if universities are to play any meaningful role as social critics. Finally, tenure permits internal self-criticism. No other institutions permit the attacks on their policies and administration that characterize universities. True, even in universities criticism is muted for various reasons, but without tenure there would be almost none.

Despite the existence of tenure—which recent history shows is itself a reversible gain—the forces of community are fragile, and they are losing. Their weakness leaves universities unable to define their purpose; they are increasingly vulnerable because they are unable to mount a credible defense against those intrusions of the marketplace and state that most faculty and administrators even now sense as dangerous or excessive. Universities are less able than ever to define the ways in which they are distinct from other social institutions, how the principles on which they operate differ from those in business and government, and why they should enjoy special privileges. Therefore, the next great crisis of the university may not be demographic, fiscal, or organizational. Instead, it may be moral.

The moral flabbiness of the university weakens every aspect of its life. Consider the example of the alleged rape with which I began this chapter.[28] Most people who comment on the issues surrounding this incident offer one of three explanations. First, until the 1960s, colleges and universities officially exercised a close watch over the sexual behavior of their students. After the attack on these restrictions by students in the 1970s, rules were abandoned with stunning speed. Dormitories became coeducational; restrictions on the presence of men and women in each other's rooms disappeared; universities dropped almost all specific rules of conduct; and faculty generally left students alone to do what they chose. Now, so it is argued, we are reaping the consequences of neglect.

A second explanation is that students now suffer from extraordinary stress. Anxious about admission into a top professional school, worried about a tight job market, facing a future in which annihilation seems more possible than fulfillment, their behavior combines an explosive, periodic release of tension with a nihilism deeply disturbing in the young. Of course, and this is the third argument, some would say that there is little especially new in student behavior. The heavy-drinking students of the 1980s seem more rowdy and noisy than the stoned students of a decade or two ago. Men have always abused and raped women. What has changed is the willingness of women to suffer in silence and the emergence of supportive networks that encourage and help those who are victims to press their case.

Although each of these points has merit, by themselves they are only partial. What needs explaining is not only student behavior but also university response. Whatever motivates students, it is a university's capacity for appropriate, effective, and collective response that is at issue, and this has been eroded by the processes underlying the modern history of the higher learning. Let me illustrate with six questions that emerge from the incident.* The first concerns the distinction in the treatment of men and women. No assertion angers administrators who handled the case more than the claim that they treated the men involved more fairly than the woman. There can be no doubt of the administration's sincerity on this point. Yet the process and results best served the interests of the men. The men remained on campus and suffered no interruption in their studies and no disruption of their future plans. The sanctions they received were, at worst, an inconvenience. The woman withdrew from the university and suffered greatly. Why did the victim fare so much worse than her alleged assailants? The answer lies in the myriad ways in which the structure of institutions and the nature of legal processes still discriminate by gender. In truth, whatever our intent, there are differences in the way we treat our sons and daughters.

Second, what sort of conduct is acceptable on campus? At the University of Pennsylvania, the brief general statement about mature and responsible behavior signals an unwillingness or inability to confront the difficult and divisive ethical issues that an answer requires. One reason the question is so difficult is that the university, like its counterparts, lacks a common center or any effective sense of community. There are no accepted core principles around which a statement about the limits of acceptable behavior can be framed. Some faculty are reluctant to agree even that the university

---

*In fairness, it should be pointed out that after the incident described earlier the university administration introduced a strong policy on sexual harassment, initiated a review and reform of internal judicial procedures, and stimulated increased faculty-student contact in various ways, such as making attractive apartments in student residences available to faculty. The administration also tried, though with only partial success, to remove the offending fraternity chapter from the campus.

can legitimately proscribe activities that are not clearly illegal. If there are not boundaries between the university and the state, then the state may as well set and enforce all standards of conduct.

Third, what is the responsibility of the faculty for the nature and quality of undergraduate life? The university rewards faculty on market principles, that is, for the quantity and perceived value of their professional productivity. There are no rewards for attention to undergraduate life. To the entrepreneurial and bureaucratic faculty member, undergraduates tend to be a distraction; there is no incentive to think about their lives outside the classroom; and, even if there is a fleeting interest or concern, there is no time. Every sort of professional pressure in modern universities pulls energetic, active, ambitious faculty away from a concern with student life. Relations between faculty and students have become increasingly analogous to wage labor: contractual, specific, and delimited.

Fourth, is justice within universities different from justice in a court of law? Do the same rules of evidence, due process, and right to counsel apply in university settings as outside them? Again, without a clear sense of how universities differ from other social institutions, no answer to this question is possible. Yet it is central to the way in which universities respond to misconduct among students, staff, or faculty.

Fifth, what should be the balance between decentralization and central leadership within universities? The administration's inability to take clear and decisive control of the case described here reflects structural dilemmas endemic to modern universities as well as to the responses of particular individuals. Universities remain remarkably decentralized institutions, for the multiversity is a loosely coupled federation. Critical decisions about educational policy and personnel are made in departments and schools, and every incursion by a central administration is resisted fiercely. Faculty whose own entrepreneurial and bureaucratic activities reduce the boundaries between the university, the marketplace, and the state are quick to invoke the ancient traditions of the university whenever they disagree with an initiative taken by a president, provost, or dean. Yet they also want an administration that can react effectively to crises, raise money, and mediate equitably among the various interests on the campus. With few, if any, common values or shared purposes to which to appeal, only extraordinary leaders can summon the loyalty and commitment necessary to galvanize faculty sentiment around decisive, controversial, or risky actions. The result is a kind of administrative schizophrenia, which, as in this incident, can cripple administrative effectiveness.

Sixth, how do we balance the protection of the institution's reputation with the preservation of its integrity? Or, what are the limits of expediency? Every institution tries to protect itself. Self-preservation is as fundamental an institutional as a human instinct. Therefore, institutions (and universities are no exception) prefer to keep embarrassing incidents or facts about themselves private. Allegations of gang rape on campus do not help raise money or attract students. They do not enhance the image and reputation of the university. The expedient course, therefore, is to deal quietly and privately with the problem. In itself, privacy and institutional protection are not ignoble criteria. The difficulty is their consequence. For the price of privacy often is moral compromise.

Moral compromise is an especially troublesome course for universities. For all their problems, universities and their faculties remain immensely privileged. They retain a freedom of activity and expression not permitted in any other major social institution. There are two justifications for this privilege. One is that it is an essential condition of teaching and learning. The other is that universities have become the major source of moral and social criticism in modern life. They are the major site of whatever social conscience we have left; without them the civil rights movement, the protest against the Vietnam War, modern feminism, and the antinuclear movement would have been immeasurably weaker. If the legitimacy of universities rested only on their service to the marketplace and state, internal freedom would not be an issue. But their legitimacy rests, in fact, on something else: their integrity. Like all privileges, the freedom enjoyed by universities carries correlative responsibilities. In their case it is intellectual honesty and moral courage. Modern universities are the greatest centers of intellectual power in history. Without integrity, they can become little more than supermarkets with raw power for sale. This is the tendency in the modern history of the higher learning. It is what I call the moral crisis of the university.

Notes

1. The Origins of Public Education

1. Two notable exceptions were Frank Tracy Carlton, *Economic Influences upon Educational Progress in the United States, 1820–1850* (1908; reprint, New York: Teachers College Press, 1965), and Merle Curti, *The Social Ideas of American Educators: with a Chapter on the Last Twenty-Five Years* (1935; reprint, Totowa, N.J.: Littlefield, Adams, 1959). For a discussion and criticism of the older method, see Lawrence A. Cremin, *The Wonderful World of Elwood Patterson Cubberly: An Essay on the Historiography of American Education* (New York: Teachers College Press, 1965). The works especially important in the rejuvenation of the history of education are: Paul H. Buck, Clarence Faust, Richard Hofstadter, Arthur Schlesinger, Jr., and Richard Storr, *The Role of Education in American History* (New York: Fund for the Advancement of Education, 1957); Bernard Bailyn, *Education in the Forming of American Society: Needs and Opportunities for Study* (Chapel Hill: University of North Carolina Press, 1960); Lawrence A. Cremin, *The Transformation of the School: Progressivism in American Education, 1876–1957* (New York: Random House, 1961).

2. Hayden V. White, "The Burden of History," *History and Theory*, 5 (1966), 132.

3. Carl F. Kaestle, *Pillars of the Republic: Common Schools and American Society, 1780–1960* (New York: Hill and Wang, 1983); David Tyack, *The One Best System* (Cambridge, Mass.: Harvard University Press, 1974); Carl F. Kaestle, *The Evolution of an Urban School System: New York City, 1750–1850* (Cambridge, Mass.: Harvard University Press, 1974); Stanley K. Schultz, *The Culture Factory: Boston Public Schools, 1789–1860* (New York: Oxford University Press, 1973); Selwyn Troen, *The Public and the Schools: Shaping the St. Louis System, 1838–1920* (Columbia: University of Missouri Press, 1975).

4. Richard L. McCormick, *From Realignment to Reform: Political Change*

in New York State, 1893–1910 (Ithaca: Cornell University Press, 1979), pp. 11–24; Ira Katznelson, *City Trenches: Urban Politics and the Patterning of Class in the United States* (New York: Pantheon, 1981), esp. chap. 3; Ira Katznelson and Margaret Weir, *Schooling for All: Class, Race, and the Decline of the Democratic Ideal* (New York: Basic Books, 1985), pp. 28–57.

5. Michael B. Katz, "Secondary Education to 1870," in *The Encyclopedia of Education* (New York: Free Press, 1971), 8: 159–165.

6. Oscar Handlin and Mary Flug Handlin, *Commonwealth: A Study of the Role of Government in the American Economy: Massachusetts 1774–1861* (New York and London: Harvard University Press, 1947); David Roberts, *Victorian Origins of the British Welfare State* (New Haven, 1960); Karl Polanyi, *The Great Transformation: The Political and Economic Origins of Our Time* (1944; reprint, Boston: Beacon Press, 1957).

7. Carroll Smith-Rosenberg, *Religion and the Rise of the American City* (Ithaca: Cornell University Press, 1971); Raymond Mohl, *Poverty in New York, 1783–1825* (New York: Oxford University Press, 1974); Paul Boyer, *Urban Masses and Moral Order in America, 1820–1920* (Cambridge, Mass.: Harvard University Press, 1978); Michael B. Katz, *The Transformation of the Poorhouse: A Social History of Welfare in America* (New York: Basic Books, 1986), chaps. 1–4; Susan E. Houston, "The Impetus to Reform" (Ph.D. diss., University of Toronto, 1974).

8. See the suggestive comments on institutional alternatives in Sean Wilentz, *Chants Democratic: New York City and the Rise of the American Working Class, 1788–1850* (New York: Oxford University Press, 1984), p. 288.

9. David J. Rothman, *The Discovery of the Asylum: Social Order and Disorder in the New Republic* (Boston: Little, Brown, 1971); Gerald N. Grob, *The State and the Mentally Ill: A History of Worcester State Hospital in Massachusetts, 1830–1920* (Chapel Hill: University of North Carolina Press, 1966) and *Mental Institutions in America: Social Policy to 1875* (New York: Free Press, 1973); W. David Lewis, *From Newgate to Dannemora: The Rise of the Penitentiary in New York, 1796–1848* (Ithaca: Cornell University Press, 1965); Robert M. Mennel, *Thorns and Thistles: Juvenile Delinquents in the United States, 1825–1940* (Hanover, N.H.: University Press of New England, 1973).

10. Charles Loring Brace, *The Dangerous Classes of New York and Twenty Years' Work among Them* (New York, 1872); Michael B. Katz, *The Irony of Early School Reform: Educational Innovation in Mid-Nineteenth Century Massachusetts* (Cambridge, Mass.: Harvard University Press, 1968), part 3.

11. Houston, "Impetus"; Alison Prentice, "Education and the Metaphor of the Family: The Upper Canadian Example," *History of Education Quarterly*, 12 (1972), 281–303; Barbara Brenzel, *Daughters of the State: A Social Portrait of the First Reform School for Girls in North America, 1846–1905* (Cambridge, Mass.: MIT Press, 1983).

12. Peter Laslett, ed., *Household and Family in Past Time* (Cambridge: Cambridge University Press, 1972), pp. 1–148; Michael B. Katz, *The People of Hamilton, Canada West: Family and Class in a Mid-Nineteenth Century City*

(Cambridge, Mass.: Harvard University Press, 1975), chap. 5; Michael B. Katz, Michael J. Doucet, and Mark J. Stern, *The Social Organization of Early Industrial Capitalism* (Cambridge, Mass.: Harvard University Press, 1981), chap. 5.

13. Katz, *People of Hamilton*, chap. 5; Katz, Doucet, and Stern, *Social Organization*, chap. 6; John R. Gillis, *Youth and History: Tradition and Change in European Age Relations, 1770–Present* (New York: Academic Press, 1974), pp. 1–3; Joseph K. Kett, *Rites of Passage: Adolescence in America 1790 to the Present* (New York: Basic Books, 1977).

14. Yasuckichy Yasuba, *Birth Rates of the White Population in the United States, 1800–1860* (Baltimore: Johns Hopkins University Press, 1962); Colin Forster and G. S. L. Tucker, *Economic Opportunity and White Fertility Ratios* (New Haven: Yale University Press, 1972); Mark J. Stern, *Society and Family Strategy, Erie County, New York, 1850–1920* (Albany: SUNY Press, forthcoming); Viviana A. Zelizer, *Pricing the Priceless Child: The Changing Social Value of Children* (New York: Basic Books, 1985).

15. Barbara Welter, "The Cult of True Womanhood: 1820–1860," *American Quarterly*, 18 (Summer 1966), 151–174; Kathryn Kish Sklar, *Catharine Beecher: A Study in American Domesticity* (New Haven: Yale University Press, 1973); Nancy Cott, *The Bonds of Womanhood: "Women's Sphere" in New England, 1780–1935* (New Haven: Yale University Press, 1977).

16. Katz, *Irony*, pp. 56–58; Alison Prentice, "The Feminization of Teaching in British North America and Canada, 1854–1875," *Histoire Sociale–Social History*, 8 (1975), 5–20; Daniel Calhoun, *The Intelligence of a People* (Princeton: Princeton University Press, 1973), esp. pp. 188, 195, 204; Richard M. Bernard and Maris A. Vinovskis, "The Female School Teacher in Ante-Bellum Massachusetts," *Journal of Social History*, 10 (1977), 332–345.

17. Carl F. Kaestle and Maris A. Vinovskis, *Education and Social Change in Nineteenth-Century Massachusetts* (Cambridge: Cambridge University Press, 1980), esp. pp. 154–156.

18. For a vivid example of how a young woman welcomed the chance to teach, see Anna Fuller, "The Schoolmarm," in *Pratt Portraits* (New York: G. P. Putnam's Sons, 1892), excerpted in Nancy Hoffman, *Woman's "True" Profession: Voices from the History of Teaching* (New York: Feminist Press and McGraw-Hill, 1981), pp. 74–79.

19. See, for example, Herbert Gutman, "Work, Culture, and Society in Industrializing America," *American Historical Review*, 78 (1973), 540.

20. Martha Branscombe, *The Courts and the Poor Laws in New York State, 1784–1929* (Chicago: University of Chicago Press, 1943); David M. Schneider, *The History of Public Welfare in New York State, 1609–1866* (Chicago: University of Chicago Press, 1938); Katz, *Transformation of the Poorhouse*, chap. 1.

21. Maurice Dobb, *Studies in the Development of Capitalism*, rev. ed. (New York: International Publishers, 1963), p. 7; Karl Marx, *Capital*, trans. Frederick Engels (1887; reprint, Moscow: Progress Publishers, 1954), pp. 318–347; Wilentz, *Chants Democratic*, pp. 107–144; David M. Gordon, Richard Edwards,

and Michael Reich, *Segmented Work, Divided Workers* (New York: Cambridge University Press, 1982), pp. 48–99.

22. Kaestle, *Evolution of an Urban School System*, p. 102; Douglas Lamar Jones, "The Strolling Poor: Transiency in Eighteenth Century Massachusetts," *Journal of Social History* (1975): 28–55; Handlin and Handlin, *Commonwealth*; Wilentz, *Chants Democratic*; Daniel Rodgers, *The Work Ethic in Industrial America, 1850–1920* (Chicago: University of Chicago Press, 1978), p. 30; Gordon, Edwards, and Reich, *Segmented Work, Divided Workers*, pp. 48–99.

23. Ian E. Davey, "Educational Reform and the Work Class: School Attendance in Hamilton, Ontario, 1851–1891" (Ph.D. diss., Univ. of Toronto, 1975); Stephan Thernstrom and Peter Knights, "Men in Motion: Some Data and Speculations about Urban Populations in Nineteenth-Century America," in Tamara K. Hareven, ed., *Anonymous Americans: Explorations in Nineteenth-Century Social History* (Englewood Cliffs, N.J.: Prentice-Hall, 1971), pp. 17–47; Katz, *People of Hamilton*, chap. 3; Katz, Doucet, and Stern, *Social Organization*, chap. 3.

24. Christopher Lasch, "Origins of the Asylum," in Christopher Lasch, ed., *The World of Nations: Reflections on American History, Politics, and Culture* (New York: Basic Books, 1973); Harry Braverman, *Labor and Monopoly Capital: The Degradation of Work in the Twentieth Century* (New York: Monthly Review Press, 1974), pp. 279–280.

25. Tyack, "Kingdom of God and the Common School"; Timothy Smith, "Protestant Schooling and American Nationality," *Journal of American History*, 53 (1967), 679-695; Kaestle, *Pillars of the Republic*.

26. Katznelson and Weir, *Schooling for All*, pp. 9–10. See also Rush Welter, *Popular Education and Democratic Thought in America* (New York: Columbia University Press, 1962).

27. Houston, "Impetus"; Harold Schwartz, *Samuel Gridley Howe: Social Reformer, 1801–1876* (Cambridge, Mass.: Harvard University Press, 1956); Katz, *Irony*; Mohl, *Poverty in New York*; Boyer, *Urban Masses in America: 1820–1920* (Cambridge, Mass.: Harvard University Press, 1978).

28. Kaestle, *Evolution*; Harvey J. Graff, *The Literacy Myth: Literacy and Social Structure in the Nineteenth-Century City* (New York: Academic Press, 1979); Oliver MacDonagh, "The Irish Famine Emigration to the United States," *Perspectives in American History*, 10 (1976), 357–448; Frank F. Furstenberg, Jr., Theodore Hershberg, and John Modell, "The Origins of the Female-Headed Black Family: The Impact of the Urban Experience," in Theodore Hershberg, ed., *Philadelphia* (New York: Oxford University Press, 1981).

29. Katz, *Irony*; Oscar Handlin, "The Horror" in *Race and Nationality in American Life* (Boston: Little, Brown, 1950), esp. p. 125.

30. E. P. Thompson, "Time, Work Discipline, and Industrial Capitalism," *Past and Present*, 38 (1967), 56–97; Gutman, "Work, Culture, and Society."

31. Leo Marx, *The Machine in the Garden: Technology and the Pastoral Ideal in America* (New York: Oxford University Press, 1964), p. 248; Katz, *Irony*, pp. 45–46.

32. Katz, *People of Hamilton*, chap. 5; Katz, Doucet, and Stern, *Social Organization*, chap. 6.

33. On the decline of apprenticeship in New York City, see Wilentz, *Chants Democratic*, p. 33.

34. Katz, Doucet, and Stern, *Social Organization*, chap. 6.

35. Stephan Thernstrom, *Poverty and Progress: Social Mobility in a Nineteenth-Century City* (Cambridge, Mass.: Harvard University Press, 1964), and *The Other Bostonians: Poverty and Progress in the American Metropolis, 1880–1970* (Cambridge, Mass.: Harvard University Press, 1973); Katz, Doucet, and Stern, *Social Organization*, chaps. 1–5. There is a large recent historical literature on social and geographic mobility.

36. The best discussions of the uneven erosion of the crafts are in Wilentz, *Chants Democratic*, esp. chap. 3, and Clyde Griffen and Sally Griffen, *Natives and Newcomers: The Ordering of Opportunity in Mid-Nineteenth-Century Poughkeepsie* (Cambridge, Mass.: Harvard University Press, 1978), chaps. 2 and 7. On shoemakers, see Alan Dawley, *Class and Community: The Industrial Revolution in Lynn* (Cambridge, Mass.: Harvard University Press, 1976), chap. 3. Comparative figures on the occupations of fathers and sons are from my research in Katz, Doucet, and Stern, *Social Organization*, chap. 5.

37. On boarding schools, see James McLachlan, *American Boarding Schools: A History Study* (New York: Scribner, 1970). The best history of adolescence is Kett, *Rites of Passage*. See also Prentice, "Education and the Metaphor of the Family," and Katz, *Irony*, pp. 50–52.

38. The phrase is from Richard C. Edwards, *Contested Terrain: The Transformation of the Workplace in the Twentieth Century* (New York: Basic Books, 1979).

2. Alternative Models for American Education

1. My thinking on this issue was stimulated by Lynn L. Marshall, "The Strange Stillbirth of the Whig Party," *American Historical Review*, 72 (1967), 445–468.

2. For a contemporary debate that echoes similar issues, see Richard Berube and Marilyn Gittel, *Confrontation at Ocean-Hill Brownsville* (New York: Praeger, 1969).

3. William Olan Bourne, *History of the Public School Society of the City of New York* (New York: Wm. Woodland, 1870), p. 7. On the NYPSS see also Carl F. Kaestle, *The Evolution of an Urban School System: New York City, 1750–1854* (Cambridge, Mass.: Harvard University Press, 1974).

4. Bourne, *History*, pp. 6–7, 85–94.

5. Ibid., pp. 85–94.

6. Ibid., pp. 373–402.

7. Ibid.

8. Ibid., pp. 6–7, 36–39.

9. Ibid., pp. 18–20. On the monitorial system see Carl F. Kaestle, ed., *Joseph Lancaster and the Monitorial School Movement: A Documentary History* (New York: Teachers College Press, 1973).

10. Bourne, *History*, pp. 18, 20.

11. Ibid., pp. 359–373.

12. Ibid.

13. Ibid.

14. Ibid., pp. 202–224. On the religious controversy, see also Vincent P. Lannie, *Public Money and Parochial Education: Bishop Hughes, Governor Seward, and the New York School Controversy* (Cleveland: Case Western Reserve University Press, 1968).

15. *American Annals of Education and Instruction*, 6 (1836), 440.

16. *Proceedings and Debates of the Convention of the Commonwealth of Pennsylvania, 1837–1839* (Harrisburg, 1837–39), p. 290.

17. Ibid., p. 310. See also Joseph J. McCadden, *Education in Pennsylvania, 1801–1835 and Its Debt to Robert Vaux* (Philadelphia: University of Pennsylvania Press, 1937), and Joseph M. Wightman, *Annals of the Boston Primary School Committee from Its First Establishment in 1818, to Its Dissolution in 1855* (Boston: Rand and Avery, 1860).

18. Bourne, *History*, pp. 359–373.

19. Allen Dodge, "The Expediency of Abolishing the Board of Education and the Normal School," Massachusetts House Document 49, 1840. On the politics of the attempted abolition of the Board, see Carl F. Kaestle and Maris A. Vinovskis, *Education and Social Change in Nineteenth-Century Massachusetts* (Cambridge: Cambridge University Press, 1980), pp. 213–232.

20. Dodge, "Expediency."

21. Orestes Brownson, "Article 1—Second Annual Report of the Board of Education...," *Boston Quarterly Review* (1839), 393–434.

22. Ibid.

23. Dodge, "Expediency."

24. *Proceedings of Convention of Pennsylvania*, pp. 354–355, 392.

25. Ibid., pp. 245, 385.

26. Edward Eggleston, *The Hoosier Schoolmaster* (1871; reprint, New York: Hill and Wang, 1957), pp. 1–2.

27. Throughout this volume, *schoolmen* refers to the career educators (grammar school masters, high school teachers and principals, school superintendents, journal editors), almost exclusively male, of the nineteenth century. It is a term they would have used to describe themselves.

28. Brownson, "Article 1."

29. Most states seem to have supported academies with public funds for some time. See James Mulhern, *A History of Secondary Education in Pennsylvania* (Lancaster, Pa.: Science Press, 1933); James Pyle Wickersham, *A History of Education in Pennsylvania* (Lancaster, Pa.: Inquirer Publishing, 1886); Conrad E. Patzer, *Public Education in Wisconsin* (Madison: Wisconsin Department of

Education, 1924); William Warren Ferrier, *Ninety Years of Education in California, 1846–1936* (Berkeley: Sather Gate Book Shop, 1937); Emit Duncan Grizzell, *Origins and Development of the High School in New England before 1865* (New York: Macmillan, 1923); Harriett Webster Marr, *The Old New England Academies Founded before 1826* (New York: Comet, 1959); George F. Miller, *The Academy System of the State of New York* (Albany: J.B. Lyon, 1922); Alexander James Inglis, *The Rise of the High School in Massachusetts* (New York: Teachers College Press, 1911).

30. "Norwich Free Academy, with an Account of Recent School Movements in Norwich, Connecticut," *Journal of Education*, 2 (1856), 665–694.

31. "Norwich Free Academy"; "High Schools and Endowed Academies," *Massachusetts Teacher*, 10 (1857), 321–336; "High Schools in Massachusetts," ibid., pp. 182–185.

32. "High Schools in Massachusetts."

33. Ibid.

34. Edward Hitchcock, "The American Academies System Defended," in Theodore R. Sizer, ed., *The Age of the Academies* (New York: Teachers College Press, 1964), pp. 92–106.

35. The best discussion of academies' flexibility is in Joseph K. Kett, *Rites of Passage: Adolescence in America, 1790 to the Present* (New York: Basic Books, 1977).

36. For the shift in policies regarding corporations, see Oscar Handlin and Mary Flugg Handlin, *Commonwealth: A Study of the Role of Government in the American Economy, Massachusetts, 1774–1861* (New York: New York University Press, 1947).

37. George S. Boutwell, *Thoughts on Educational Topics and Institutions* (Boston: Phillips, Sampson, 1859), pp. 188–189.

38. Letter from Horace Mann to Frederick A. Packard, July 22, 1838, in Raymond Culver, *Horace Mann and Religion in the Massachusetts Public Schools* (New Haven: Yale University Press, 1929), p. 73.

39. Bourne, *History*, p. 235.

40. Henry Barnard, "Sixth Annual Report of the Superintendent of Common Schools of Connecticut to the General Assembly for 1851," *Journal of Education*, 5 (1865), 309–310.

41. Boutwell, *Thoughts on Educational Topics*, pp. 182–183.

42. Barnard, "Sixth Annual Report," pp. 309–310.

43. Ibid., pp. 293–295.

44. Ibid.

45. Ibid., p. 318.

46. Michael B. Katz, *The Irony of Early School Reform: Educational Innovation in Mid-Nineteenth Century Massachusetts* (Cambridge, Mass.: Harvard University Press, 1968), Part I; David F. Labaree, "The People's College: A Sociological Analysis of the Central High School of Philadelphia, 1838–1939" (Ph.D. diss., University of Pennsylvania, 1983).

47. Barnard, "Sixth Annual Report," p. 318.

48. *Reports of the Annual Visiting Committees of the Public Schools of the City of Boston* (1845).

49. "The Necessity of Restraint," *Massachusetts Teacher*, 4 (1851), 37.

50. David Tyack, "The Kingdom of God and the Common School," *Harvard Educational Review*, 36 (1966), 447–469; Timothy L. Smith, "Protestant Schooling and American Nationality, 1800–1850," *Journal of American History*, 53 (1967), 679–695.

51. "The Necessity of Restraint," pp. 33–34.

52. *Report of the School Committee of the City of Boston, 1857–1858* (1858), p. 50.

53. For a general discussion of the values implicit in nineteenth-century textbooks, see Ruth Miller Elson, *Guardians of Tradition: American Schoolbooks of the Nineteenth Century* (Lincoln: University of Nebraska Press, 1964).

54. *Proceedings of Convention of Pennsylvania*, pp. 223–224, 202.

55. *Reports of Annual Visiting Committees* (1845), pp. 10–11.

56. A. P. Peabody, "The Relation of Public Schools to the Civil Government," *Unitarian Review*, 6 (1876), 24–39.

57. Editorial, *Massachusetts Teacher*, 1 (1848), 134.

58. Horace Mann to Henry Barnard, June 23 and July 9, 1838, Fales Library, New York University.

59. Mann to Barnard, March 2, 1840, Fales Library, New York University.

60. *Report of the School Committee of the City of Lawrence, 1857–1858* (1858), p. 48.

61. Board of Public Charities of the State of Pennsylvania, "Compulsory Education," in *Report of the Board for 1871* (privately printed and distributed, 1872), p. 18.

62. Massachusetts Senate Document 10 (1847), p. 17.

63. Board of Public Charities, "Compulsory Education," pp. 20–21.

64. *Proceedings of Convention of Pennsylvania*, pp. 383–384, 366.

65. Katz, *Irony*, pp. 155–188, 319–357.

66. For a documentary history of the Primary School Committee, see Wightman, *Annals*.

67. Thomas H. Barrows, "Supplementary Report of the Superintendent of Common Schools," *Pennsylvania Senate Journal*, 2 (1836), 354–356.

68. For perceptive remarks on these issues see Jonathan Messerli, "Localism and State Control in Horace Mann's Reform of the Common Schools," *American Quarterly*, 17 (1965), 104–118.

69. Thomas E. Finegan, *Free Schools: A Documentary History of the Free School Movement in New York State* (Albany: University of the State of New York, 1921).

70. Brownson, "Article 1," pp. 408–409, 415.

71. Ibid., p. 412.

72. For a provocative formulation relevant to this point, see Seymour Martin

Lipset, *Revolution and Counterrevolution: Change and Persistence in Social Structures* (New York: Basic Books, 1968).

3. How Urban School Systems Became Bureaucracies

1. For other discussions of the bureaucratization of urban education, see David B. Tyack, *The One Best System: A History of American Urban Education* (Cambridge, Mass.: Harvard University Press, 1974), and Selwyn Troen, *The Public and the Schools: Shaping the St. Louis System, 1838–1920* (Columbia: University of Missouri Press, 1975).

2. Exeter (pseud.), "Boston Gossip," *New England Journal of Education*, 14 (November 1881), 331. On Parker and Quincy see M. B. Katz, "The 'New Departure' in Quincy, 1873–1881: The Nature of Nineteenth Century Educational Reform," *New England Quarterly* (March 1967), 3–30.

3. I have analyzed the Mann-Masters episode in *The Irony of Early School Reform: Educational Innovation in Mid-Nineteenth Century Massachusetts* (Cambridge, Mass.: Harvard University Press, 1968).

4. This essay is in no sense an attempt at a complete history of education in Boston in these years. For instance, I touch only marginally on the problems of Catholics, a major source of conflict during these years; I hardly mention either technical education or drawing and music, subjects that aroused much heat and spurred curricular and institutional innovations. Likewise, the whole issue of the defensibility and role of public high schools, not discussed here, was critical in these years, though more problematic in places other than Massachusetts.

5. Carl J. Friedrich, *Constitutional Government and Democracy*, rev. ed. (Boston: Ginn and Co., 1950), pp. 44–57.

6. For a chronological account of the history of education in Boston, see "A Chronology of the Boston Public Schools," *Annual Report of the Superintendent* (Boston, 1930), pp. 91–126. This account also contains the references in the school documents for each item in the chronology.

7. B. A. Hinsdale, *Our Common-School Education; with a Digression on the College Course* (Cleveland, 1877), p. 9; Roger Lane, *Policing the City: Boston, 1822–1855* (Cambridge, Mass.: Harvard University Press, 1967).

8. For an example of the argument that the old arrangements were grossly inefficient see John Dudley Philbrick, "The New Departure," *New England Journal of Education* (January 1877), 9. The growing complexity of administering the city is well described throughout Lane, *Policing the City*. Lane attributes the development of the police force largely to this source.

9. *Annual Report of the School Committee of the City of Boston, 1865* (Boston, 1865), pp. 44–49; *Annual Report of the School Committee of the City of Boston, 1866* (Boston, 1867), pp. 42–43; "Report of Special Committee" and "Superintendent's Reports," ibid., pp. 45–59 and 150–55.

10. William H. Payne, *Chapters on School Supervision* (Cincinnati and New

York: Wilson, Hinckle, 1875), pp. 15–17. See also Aaron Gove in *Journals and Proceedings and Addresses of the National Education Association of the United States, Session of the Year 1884* (Boston, 1884), p. 27 (hereafter cited as *NEA 1884*), and "City Superintendents," *New England Journal of Education* (April 1878), 264.

11. Payne, *Chapters*, pp. 15–17; also John Dudley Philbrick, "The New Departure," *New England Journal of Education* (February 1880), 116.

12. See, for example, "City Superintendents," *NEA 1884*.

13. Payne, *Chapters*, pp. 6, 13, 17, 30, 53.

14. John Dudley Philbrick, "How Shall We Get Good Teachers?" *Journal of Education* (June 1881), 367–368; J. L. Pickard, "City Management of Public School Systems," *Education* (September 1883), p. 98; *New England Journal of Education* (November 1880), 344.

15. For an interesting insight into the relation of superintendents to politics, see the discussion reported in "New England Association of School Superintendents," *Journal of Education* (June 1881), 377.

16. John Dudley Philbrick, "Remarks to Principals," *Thirty-second Semi-Annual Report of the Superintendent of Public Schools of the City of Boston, September, 1877* (Boston, 1877), pp. 64–74.

17. Thomas Bicknell, "The National Council of Education," *NEA 1882*, pp. 86–87. On the problem of individualism in relation to the growth of the professions see Daniel H. Calhoun, *Professional Lives in America: Structure and Aspiration, 1750–1850* (Cambridge, Mass.: Harvard University Press, 1965), especially pp. 178–97.

18. For an account of one such episode see Katz, *Irony*, Part II.

19. *Expenditures for the Public Schools: Report of the Committee on Accounts* (Boston, 1885), p. 33; *Boston Evening Transcript*, January 22, 1875; *Annual Report of the School Committee of the City of Boston, 1875* (Boston, 1876), pp. 9–11.

20. Hinsdale, *Common-School Education*, p. 18.

21. Richard Grant White, "The Public-School Failure," *North American Review*, 131 (1880), 538.

22. Gail Hamilton, *Our Common-School System* (Boston: Estes and Lauriat, 1880), pp. 204–205.

23. *Boston Evening Transcript*, January 22, 1875.

24. *Boston Pilot*, May 22, June 5, and December 11, 1875.

25. *Boston Evening Transcript*, May 27, 1875.

26. Tyack, *The One Best System*, pp. 126–176.

27. *Boston Evening Transcript*, January 31, 1876.

28. "Report of the Superintendent of the Public Schools for the Year Ending July 31, 1876," *Annual Report of the School Committee, 1875*, p. 153; *New England Journal of Education* (January 1876), 30; *Boston Evening Transcript*, February 9 and 16, 1876; *Boston Daily Globe*, March 1, 1876.

29. "Report of the Committee Appointed to Represent the School Committee before the Legislature," *Annual Report of the School Committee, 1875*,

p. 176; *Report of the Special Committee on Changes of Regulations of Superintendent and Supervisors* (Boston, 1877).

30. *Boston Daily Globe*, March 1, 1876.

31. *Boston Evening Transcript*, March 2, 1876.

32. *Boston Daily Globe*, March 1 and 15, 1876; *Boston Evening Transcript*, March 22, 1876.

33. John Tetlow, "Lecture Eulogizing Ellis Peterson," Tetlow Papers, 1904(?), Houghton Library, Harvard University; *Boston Evening Transcript*, February 23, 1876.

34. *Thirtieth Semi-Annual Report of the Superintendent of Public Schools, Boston, September 1876*, published separately; "Report of the Superintendent of the Public Schools for the Year Ending July 31, 1876," *Annual Report of the School Committee, 1876*; Philbrick, "The New Departure."

35. Ibid.

36. *Report of the Superintendent, 1876*, pp. 81, 147. Philbrick's description of western school systems is one of the most useful sources describing urban educational administration at this time.

37. "The Case from the Supervisors' Point of View," *New England Journal of Education* (January 1877), 9.

38. *Report of the Special Committee on Changes of Regulations; Report of the Special Committee on the Plan of Work of the Superintendent, Supervisors and Board of Supervisors* (Boston, 1877); Philbrick, "Remarks to Principals," p. 73.

39. *Boston Evening Transcript*, January 23, 1878; *Boston Daily Globe*, January 23, 1878; *New England Journal of Education* (January 1878), 73.

40. *New England Journal of Education* (January 1878), 56, 73.

41. *Boston Evening Transcript*, January 21, 1878.

42. *New England Journal of Education* (March 1878), 168.

43. *New England Journal of Education* (January 1878), 56; *Thirty-fourth Semi-Annual Report of the Superintendent of the Public Schools* (Boston, 1878), pp. 25–26, 28–30; *Thirty-fifth Semi-Annual Report of the Superintendent of Public Schools* (Boston, 1879), p. 28; *Thirty-sixth Semi-Annual Report of the Superintendent of Public Schools of the City of Boston* (Boston, 1879), p. 17. Samuel Eliot was the superintendent at this time.

44. *New England Journal of Education* (February 1878), 102; (May 1878), 328–329; (December 1878), 388.

45. Hinsdale, *Common-School Education*, pp. 19–23.

46. Hamilton, *Our Common-School System*, p. 91.

47. Charles Francis Adams, Jr., "The Development of the Superintendency," Paper read before the National Educational Association at Chautauqua, New York, July 14, 1880; reprinted in *The New Departure in the Common Schools of Quincy and Other Papers on Educational Topics* (Boston, 1881), pp. 60–63.

48. B. A. Hinsdale, *Our Common-Schools: A Fuller Statement of the Views Set Forth in the Pamphlet Entitled, "Our Common-School Education," with Especial Reference to the Reply of Supt. A. J. Rickoff* (Cleveland, 1878), pp. 27–

29. For this insight into the effects of bureaucracy I am indebted to Robert Merton, "Bureaucratic Structure and Personality," in Robert K. Merton et al., *Reader in Bureaucracy* (New York: Free Press, 1952), pp. 361–371.

49. Hamilton, *Our Common-School System*, pp. 96–97.

50. Hinsdale, *Common-School Education*, p. 24.

51. Ibid., p. 26; Hamilton, *Our Common-School System*, pp. 249–250; White, "Public-School Failure," pp. 549–550.

52. Adams, "Development of the Superintendency," pp. 66–73.

53. *First Report of the Committee on Revision of the School System* (Boston, 1879); *Annual Report of the School Committee of the City of Boston, 1879* (Boston, 1879), p. 6.

54. *Annual Report of the School Committee, 1879*, pp. 7–29.

55. *Fourth Report of the Committee on Revision of the School System* (Boston, 1879), pp. 5–7.

56. Ibid., pp. 7–9.

57. Ibid., pp. 9–10.

58. Ibid., p. 10.

59. Ibid., p. 11.

60. *Report of the Joint Committee and Revision Committee on the Permanent Supervision of the Primary Schools* (Boston, 1879); *Thirty-sixth Semi-Annual Report*, pp. 14–19.

61. *Boston Evening Transcript*, February 5, 1880.

62. For a theoretical statement of the way in which bureaucracy fosters rigidity of behavior and a sense of unity among its members, who tend to defend each other against criticism from outside the organization, see the discussion of Merton's ideas in James G. March and Herbert A. Simon, *Organizations* (New York: John Wiley & Sons, 1958), pp. 38–39.

63. *New England Journal of Education* (April 1879), 264; (May 1879), 281; (October 1879), 181.

64. Joshua Bates, *Our Common Schools* (Boston, 1879); reprinted from the *Sunday Herald*, November 30, 1879.

65. *Boston Evening Transcript*, February 25, December 13 and 29, 1880; John Dudley Philbrick, "The New Departure in Boston," *New England Journal of Education* (February, March, April, and May 1880).

66. Andrew J. Rickoff, *Past and Present of Our Common-School Education: Reply to President B. A. Hinsdale with a Brief Sketch of the History of Elementary Education in America* (Cleveland, 1877).

67. Richard Grant White, "Public-School Failure," pp. 537–546.

68. Ibid., pp. 548–550.

69. "The New Obscurantists," *New England Journal of Education* (December 1880), 396–397. Those who used the census of 1860 to refute White were Carroll D. Wright, *The Results of the Massachusetts Public School System* (Boston: Rand, Avery, 1879), which originally appeared as part of the *42nd Annual Report of the Board of Education, 1879*; B. G. Lovejoy, "Mr. Richard Grant White vs. The Public Schools of the United States: A South-Side View,"

Education, 1 (March 1881), 340–342; George J. Luckey, "Is Our Public-School System a Success? A North-Side View of Richard Grant White," *Education*, 1 (March 1881), 348–355; John Dudley Philbrick, "The Success of the Free-School System," *North American Review*, 32 (1881), 249–262; George Hicks, "The Public School System," *Education*, 1 (July 1881), 583; J. P. Wickersham, "Education and Crime," *NEA 1881* (Boston, 1881), pp. 46–55.

70. Quoted in Lawrence A. Cremin, ed., *The Republic and the School: Horace Mann and the Education of Free Men* (New York: Teachers College Press, 1957), p. 80.

71. *A Statement of the Theory of Education in the United States of America, as Approved by Many Leading Educators* (Washington, D.C.: Government Printing Office, 1874).

72. On the sociological concept of goal displacement see, for example, Amitai Etzioni, *Modern Organizations* (Englewood Cliffs, N.J.: Prentice-Hall, 1964), pp. 10–12.

73. Bicknell, "The National Council of Education," pp. 78–87.

74. *Boston Evening Transcript*, February 5 and 25, 1880; December 9, 1881.

75. Exeter, "Boston Gossip," p. 311; *Boston Evening Transcript,* October 6 and (quoting *Advertiser*) November 9, 1880.

76. *New England Journal of Education* (November 1880), 344.

77. *New England Journal of Education* (December 1880), 415.

78. On Parker in Quincy see Katz, "The 'New Departure' in Quincy."

79. Exeter, "Boston Gossip"; *Boston Evening Transcript*, March 28, 1880.

80. *Boston Evening Transcript*, March 28, 1880.

81. *Boston Daily Globe*, April 10, 1881.

82. *Boston Evening Transcript* (quoting *Herald*), April 11, 1881; *Boston Daily Globe*, April 10, 1881.

83. *Boston Daily Globe*, April 10, 1881.

84. *Boston Evening Transcript*, April 12, 13, and 27, 1881.

85. *Journal of Education*, 14 (November 1881), 311; (April 1881), 222; Exeter, "Boston Gossip," p. 223.

86. *Boston Evening Transcript*, November 29, 1882; Folkstone (pseud.), "Boston Letter," *Journal of Education* (November 1882), 313; ibid., p. 344.

87. *Journal of Education* (January 1881), 44; (December 1881), 420–421; (January 1889), 25; *Boston Evening Transcript*, December 1, 9, and 12, 1881.

88. *Boston Evening Transcript*, February 2 and 15, 1882; Exeter, "Boston Gossip," *Journal of Education* (January 1882), 9, 25; *Report of the Special Committee upon Primary Schools and other Supervision* (Boston, 1882).

89. *Boston Evening Transcript*, February 28 and March 1, 1882; Exeter, "Boston Gossip," *Journal of Education* (February 1882), 107; (March 1882), 154–155.

90. *Second Annual Report of the Superintendent of Public Schools of the City of Boston, March, 1882* (Boston, 1882), especially pp. 13–14.

91. Ibid.

92. *Boston Evening Transcript,* March 15, 1882; *Journal of Education* (March 1882), 186; (April 1882), 222, 238.

93. *Annual Report of the School Committee of the City of Boston, 1883* (Boston, 1884), pp. 19–23.

94. *Journal of Education* (November 1884), 296; *Report of the Special Committee on Method and Work of Superintendent and Supervisors* (Boston, 1884).

95. *Journal of Education* (November 1884), 296.

96. Etzioni, *Modern Organizations,* pp. 98–99.

4. History and Reform

1. Charles Silberman, *Crisis in the Classroom: The Remaking of American Education* (New York: Random House, 1970).

2. Ibid., p. 69.

3. Ibid., p. 324.

4. Ibid., pp. 380–381.

5. Ibid., pp. 10–11.

6. David F. Labaree, "The People's College: A Sociological Analysis of the Central High School of Philadelphia, 1838–1939" (Ph.D. diss., University of Pennsylvania, 1983); Joel Perlmann, *Send These to School: Ethnicity, Schooling, and Social Destinations in Providence, R.I., 1880–1935* (forthcoming).

7. Silberman, *Crisis,* p. 11.

8. On the contemporary relation between education, social mobility, and income, see Christopher Jencks et al., *Inequality: A Reassessment of the Effect of Family and Schooling in America* (New York: Basic Books, 1972); Raymond Boudon, *Education, Opportunity, and Social Inequality* (New York: John Wiley & Sons, 1973), pp. 77, 200–201; Robert M. Hauser, "Review Essay: On Boudon's Model of Social Mobility," *American Journal of Sociology,* 81 (1975–76), 1175–1187. Joel Perlmann's work in progress will be the first large-scale study of the relation between education and social mobility in nineteenth-century America. For a case study of the problem of youth and the educational response in one city see Michael B. Katz, Michael J. Doucet, and Mark J. Stern, *The Social Organization of Early Industrial Capitalism* (Cambridge, Mass.: Harvard University Press, 1981), chap. 5; on school attendance and industrialization see Michael B. Katz and Ian E. Davey, "School Attendance and Early Industrialization: A Multivariate Analysis," *History of Education Quarterly,* 18 (1978), 271–293. The best account of child-raising ideas in the nineteenth century is in Daniel Calhoun, *The Intelligence of a People* (Princeton: Princeton University Press, 1973).

9. Robert Dreeben, *On What Is Learned in Schools* (Reading, Mass.: Addison-Wesley, 1968). On the content of nineteenth-century instruction, see the thorough analysis of school textbooks in Ruth Miller Elson, *Guardians of Tradition: American Schoolbooks of the Nineteenth Century* (Lincoln: University of Nebraska Press, 1964). See also the interesting discussion of the content of text-

books used in the Freedmen's Bureau schools in Robert C. Morris, *Reading, 'Riting, and Reconstruction: The Education of Freedmen in the South, 1861–1870* (Chicago: University of Chicago Press, 1981).

10. Michael B. Katz, *The Irony of Early School Reform: Educational Innovation in Mid-Nineteenth Century Massachusetts* (Cambridge, Mass.: Harvard University Press, 1968), Part II.

11. Stanislaw Ossowski, *Class Structure in the Social Consciousness* (London: Routledge and Kegan Paul, 1963); Michael Lewis, *The Culture of Inequality* (Amherst: University of Massachusetts Press, 1978); Michael Buroway, "Toward a Marxist Theory of the Labor Process: Braverman and Beyond," *Politics and Society*, 8 (1978), 262–265.

12. For a more formal discussion of the application of a dialectical approach to institutional analysis, see J. Kenneth Benson, "Organizations: A Dialectical View," *Administrative Science Quarterly*, 22 (March 1971), 1–21.

13. Gerald N. Grob, *Mental Institutions in America: Social Policy to 1875* (New York: Free Press, 1973), pp. 323–336.

14. For a fine discussion of this point in the context of a comparative analysis of Marx and Weber, see Anthony Giddens, *Capitalism and Modern Social Theory: An Analysis of the Writings of Marx, Durkheim and Max Weber* (Cambridge: Cambridge University Press, 1975), p. 235.

15. On Hall see Dorothy Ross, *G. Stanley Hall: The Psychologist as Prophet* (Chicago: University of Chicago Press, 1972). On the history of adolescence in America see Joseph Kett, *Rites of Passage: Adolescence in America, 1790 to the Present* (New York: Basic Books, 1977). On the demographic basis of adolescence see Katz, Doucet, and Stern, *Social Organization*, pp. 242–285.

16. American Federation of Teachers and Houston Federation of Teachers, *The Houston Public Schools: A Study in Violence and Cover-Up*, Report presented to the Executive Council of the Houston Federation of Teachers, Local 2415 AFT/AFL-CIO, May 4, 1977.

17. David B. Tyack, *The One Best System: A History of American Urban Education* (Cambridge, Mass.: Harvard University Press, 1974), pp. 50–56; Carl F. Kaestle, ed., *Joseph Lancaster and the Monitorial School Movement* (New York: Teachers College Press, 1973); Edward Eggleston, *The Hoosier Schoolmaster* (1871; reprint, New York: Hill and Wang, 1957); Paul E. Peterson, *The Politics of School Reform, 1870–1940* (Chicago: University of Chicago Press, 1985), pp. 31–32.

18. For positive views about the potential of citizen and neighborhood movements see Harry Boyte, *The Backyard Revolution: Understanding the New Citizen Movement* (Philadelphia: Temple University Press, 1980); Manuel Castells, *The City and the Grassroots* (Berkeley: University of California Press, 1983); Pierre Clavel, *The Progressive City: Planning and Participation, 1969–1984* (New Brunswick, N.J.: Rutgers University Press, 1986).

19. My argument in this paragraph has been inspired by two sources: Henry Levin, "The Limits of Educational Planning" (Manuscript, April 1977), and, for the concept of mimetic reform, Ira Katznelson, *City Trenches: Urban Politics*

and the Patterning of Class in the United States (New York: Pantheon, 1981). Also stimulating on the relation between social policy and social science is Charles E. Lindblom and David K. Cohen, *Usable Knowledge: Social Science and Social Problem Solving* (New Haven: Yale University Press, 1979).

20. Christopher Lasch, *The Culture of Narcissism: American Life in an Age of Diminishing Expectations* (New York: Norton, 1979), pp. 310, 315. See also Michael Zuckerman, "Dr. Spock: The Confidence Man," in Charles E. Rosenberg, ed., *The Family in History* (Philadelphia: University of Pennsylvania Press, 1975), pp. 179–205.

21. Henry J. Perkinson, *The Imperfect Panacea: American Faith in Education, 1865–1965* (New York: Random House, 1965).

22. Calhoun, *Intelligence of a People*, pp. 70–132.

23. Katz, *Irony*, Part III.

24. Lawrence A. Cremin, *The Transformation of the School: Progressivism in American Education, 1876–1957* (New York: Random House, 1961); Stephen Jay Gould, *The Mismeasure of Man* (New York: Norton, 1971), pp. 146–157; Daniel J. Kevles, *In the Name of Eugenics: Genetics and the Uses of Human Heredity* (New York: Knopf, 1985).

25. Arthur R. Jensen, "How Much Can We Boost IQ and Scholastic Achievement?" *Harvard Educational Review*, 39 (1969), 1–123.

26. See Tyack, *The One Best System*; David Tyack and Elizabeth Hansot, *Managers of Virtue: Public School Leadership in America, 1820–1980* (New York: Basic Books, 1982); Peterson, *Politics of School Reform*, stresses the achievements of educational reform.

27. My interpretation of the effective schools strategy is based on the report of the faculty of the Harvard Graduate School of Education, *Harvard Graduate School of Education Association Bulletin*, 25 (Fall 1980).

28. Cremin, *Transformation*, pp. 348–349.

29. National Commission on Excellence in Education, *A Nation at Risk: The Imperative for Educational Reform* (Washington, D.C.: U.S. Department of Education, 1983).

30. National Commission, *Nation at Risk*, p. 5.

31. For an excellent analysis of the post-Sputnik educational reform movement, see Joel Spring, *The Sorting Machine: National Educational Policy since 1945* (New York: David McKay, 1976).

32. Peterson, *Politics of School Reform*, is very informative about the content of school reform movements.

33. Kett, *Rites of Passage*, pp. 18–20; Theodore R. Sizer, ed., *The Age of the Academies* (New York: Teachers College Press, 1964).

34. Carl F. Kaestle, *The Evolution of an Urban School System: New York City 1750–1850* (Cambridge, Mass.: Harvard University Press, 1973), pp. 51, 89.

35. Carl F. Kaestle and Maris A. Vinovskis, *Education and Social Change in Nineteenth-Century Massachusetts* (Cambridge: Cambridge University Press, 1980), pp. 11–12, 24–26.

36. The best study of a movement to centralize control of education is David Hammack, *Power and Society: Greater New York at the Turn of the Century* (New York: Basic Books, 1982), pp. 259–302.

37. This is one important message of Ira Katznelson and Margaret Weir, *Schooling for All: Class, Race, and the Decline of the Democratic Ideal* (New York: Basic Books, 1985).

5. The Politics of Educational History

1. Carl F. Kaestle and Maris A. Vinovskis, *Education and Social Change in Nineteenth-Century Massachusetts* (Cambridge: Cambridge University Press, 1980), p. 1.

2. Ibid., p. xviii.

3. Thomas L. Haskell, *The Emergence of Professional Social Sciences: The American Social Science Association and the Nineteenth-Century Crisis of Authority* (Urbana: University of Illinois Press, 1977); Kaestle and Vinovskis, *Education and Social Change*, p. 233.

4. Mary O. Furner, *Advocacy and Objectivity: A Crisis in the Professionalization of American Social Science, 1865–1905* (Louisville: University of Kentucky Press, 1975); Kaestle and Vinovskis, *Education and Social Change*, p. 5.

5. Maris A. Vinovskis, *The Origins of Public High Schools: A Reexamination of the Beverly High School Controversy* (Madison: University of Wisconsin Press, 1985).

6. Vinovskis, *Origins*, p. 95.

7. Personal letter to the author.

8. See especially Sean Wilentz, *Chants Democratic: New York City and the Rise of the American Working Class, 1788–1850* (New York: Oxford University Press, 1984).

9. Vinovskis, *Origins*, pp. 77, 107.

10. Ibid., pp. 119–120.

11. Diane Ravitch, *The Revisionists Revised: A Critique of the Radical Attack on the Schools* (New York: Basic Books, 1978).

12. Vinovskis, *Origins*, p. 119.

13. Ravitch, *Revisionists Revised*, p. xi.

14. Ravitch prefaced her discussion by observing that revisionist historians had "encountered very little opposition"; even "scholars who disagreed profoundly chose to look the other way rather than engage in controversy with the radical historians." One "prominent historian" told her that he "agreed" with her argument but "had been afraid to state the same things himself," and a second wrote her that he "now realized that his error in the 1960s was in keeping silent for fear of being shouted down" (*Revisionists Revised*, p. xi). In fact, each of the works Ravitch attacked was criticized in reviews and at professional meetings, and the revisionists hardly formed a powerful group, strong enough to silence criticism within the field. At the time *The Irony of Early School Reform* (Cambridge, Mass.: Harvard University Press, 1968) appeared I was a twenty-

nine-year-old assistant professor; Joel Spring published his first book before he had tenure; and Samuel Bowles suffered professionally for his politics. At the time she wrote, not one major piece of radical educational history had been published by a tenured faculty member at Harvard, Chicago, Stanford, or Columbia, the most powerful and prestigious schools of education. Ravitch's intimation of a conspiracy of radical historians to silence criticism clearly bore little relation to the facts.

15. When I attempted to answer these questions about the sponsorship and distribution of Ravitch's review by the National Academy of Education, I received only vague and unhelpful answers from the then president, Patrick Suppes. In 1980, under the presidency of the late Stephen Bailey, the Academy published a collection of responses to Ravitch.

16. I was a prime target, and Ravitch's treatment of my work is representative of the way she dealt with the work of other scholars she attacked. For example, she argued that in *Irony*, in my analysis of the vote to abolish Beverly High School, I made a simple situation far too complex. She attempted to show that the occupational figures I gave were ambiguous and that the opponents of the school lived far away from it and had no school-age children—in other words, that the opposition lacked structural roots or a class basis, as I contended (pp. 119–122). However, I stated quite clearly that distance from the center of the town and the age of children played important parts in the vote. I also showed that clear differences in wealth, as measured by property value, separated supporters and opponents; that all the laborers, clearly the lowest occupational group on any social or economic ranking, voted against the high school; and that in both central and peripheral districts, occupation and wealth influenced the way people voted (*Irony*, pp. 20–21, 272–279). Ravitch did not cite any of the latter three pieces of evidence, nor did she even mention that I considered wealth or controlled for location.

Elsewhere Ravitch contended that my analysis of bureaucracy was deficient because it merely stressed the relation between organizational structure and class and did not consider the role of objective conditions such as population pressure or administrative chaos (*Revisionists Revised*, p. 50). She did not mention my detailed description of the development of bureaucracy in Boston (see Chapter 3 of this volume), which stressed both objective conditions and process. A condensation of my first account ("The Emergence of Bureaucracy in Urban Education: The Boston Case, 1850–1884," Parts I and II, *History of Education Quarterly*, 8 [1968], 155–188, 319–357) made up roughly one-third (pp. 56–104) of *Class, Bureaucracy, and Schools: The Illusion of Educational Change in America* (New York: Praeger, 1975), the very book she was attacking.

17. Not only did Ravitch omit inconvenient aspects of the work she criticized; she also neglected revisionists' attempts to grapple with critics, refine interpretations, or utilize new historiographic techniques for which she praised others. With regard to my own work, for example, she did not mention my attempt to answer other critics in the epilogue to the expanded edition of *Class, Bureaucracy, and Schools* (pp. 147–149); synthesis of recent scholarship in "The

Origins of Public Education: A Reinterpretation"; or work on family and social structure in *The People of Hamilton, Canada West: Family and Class in a Mid-Nineteenth Century City* (Cambridge, Mass.: Harvard University Press, 1975), as detailed an empirical investigation of social mobility as any she used to support her thesis about the openness of American society.

Ravitch claimed I argued "that the irony of mid-nineteenth-century school reform is that it was not the product of working-class demands but rather that it was imposed" (*Revisionists Revised*, p. 117). That is not the irony. Irony means unintended outcome, and the principal one in my book is the discrepancy between the intention and the results of educational innovation, a point made clearly in the text. She also stated that I implied that "tax funds should be spent only on services used by each segment of the community in proportion to its numbers" (ibid., p. 122), a point I never made or implied. Later she claimed I assumed that "the goals of educational radicals and working-class parents are the same" (ibid., p. 125). In fact I made exactly the opposite point and discussed the dilemma that arises from a contradiction between the two.

Samuel Bowles' and Herbert Gintis' work also suffers from Ravitch's omissions. She did not mention that a substantial portion of their *Schooling in Capitalist America: Educational Reform and the Contradictions of Economic Life* (New York: Basic Books, 1976), rests on a sophisticated multivariate analysis whose nature and conclusions undercut her criticisms (see esp. pp. 102–148 and 201–223). Ravitch presented their thesis as simply one more discovery of the relation between family background and educational achievement (*Revisionists Revised*, p. 149). She failed to mention that their case demonstrates that, with controls for socioeconomic background, IQ has relatively little independent effect upon income inequality. In other words, by its own standards the meritocracy is a failure. To dismiss Bowles' and Gintis' careful and complex analysis of the relations between measured IQ, socioeconomic background, and education and their tightly argued account of the contradictions between socialization and schooling as "nothing more than speculation masquerading as sociology" (ibid., pp. 150–151) was to caricature an important piece of serious, imaginative scholarship.

Ravitch not only omitted; she also distorted and invented. For example, she stated: "A decent respect for the complexity of causation will make the historian reluctant to claim that the activities of an institution in the mid-twentieth century were directly determined by the ideas of a man who was influential in 1850" (ibid., p. 46). Of course, but none of the historians she attacked had argued to the contrary. Nor is there any basis for her assertion that "the radical historian describes the terrible way things turned out and asserts that it must have been intended by policymakers" (ibid., p. 48). I could go on (see, for example, ibid., pp. 58 and 73). The point is that she invented preposterous statements and ascribed them, without evidence, to the historians she attacked, who had never made them.

18. Ibid., p. 154.

19. Bowles and Gintis, *Schooling in Capitalist America*, p. 14. Similarly

outrageous was Ravitch's questioning of Clarence Karier's integrity (*Revisionists Revised*, p. 136). When Ravitch agreed with a point made by the revisionists, she presented it as her own, without acknowledgment. For example, at the end of her book she cautioned against unrealistically expecting schools to solve social and economic problems that "might be more directly and fruitfully attacked in noneducational ways" (ibid., p. 173). An excellent point, which many of those she criticized had been making in print for a decade.

20. See, for example, *Revisionists Revised*, p. 34. A much more sophisticated and responsible celebratory history is Lawrence Cremin, *American Education: The National Experience, 1783–1876* (New York: Harper and Row, 1980). Only with respect to blacks and Indians does Cremin seriously criticize American behavior and attitudes; and even here his treatment is curious. For instance, education during Reconstruction receives only four pages. These stress the black desire for education and northern attempts to spread their educational ideals to the South but omits the acquiescence of northern educators in the establishment of segregated school systems and their collaboration with southern conservatives. Cremin's book gives few hints of the violence, poverty, corruption, and racism of late nineteenth- and early twentieth-century America, let alone an earlier period. He concludes that by 1876 "the nation had been tested in the crucible of civil war and had endured. The dream of the founding fathers was now capable of realization, on a sound national basis; and, as the founding fathers had themselves understood, a new order of education would be at the heart of the achievement" (pp. 510–511).

21. Ravitch, *Revisionists Revised*, p. 126.

22. Jane Addams, *Democracy and Social Ethics* (1902; reprint, Cambridge, Mass.: Harvard University Press, 1964), p. 220.

23. Ravitch, *Revisionists Revised*, p. 168.

24. Ravitch, *Revisionists Revised*, pp. 43–44. The best discussion of class as a concept that I have read is Ira Katznelson, *City Trenches: Urban Politics and the Patterning of Class in the United States* (New York: Pantheon, 1981), pp. 201–207.

25. Ravitch, *Revisionists Revised*, pp. 49–50; Bowles and Gintis, *Schooling in Capitalist America*, p. 81; Anthony Giddens, *Capitalism and Modern Social Theory: An Analysis of the Writings of Marx, Durkheim and Max Weber* (Cambridge: Cambridge University Press, 1971), pp. 232–238.

26. Her assertion that revisionists claim that "only those from high-status families do well in school" was a fabrication, as was the unfounded assertion that they assert the "irrelevance of schooling" to social mobility; Ravitch, *Revisionists Revised*, pp. 73–75.

27. For an example of the way structural factors influence mobility rates, see Richard M. Bernard and John B. Sharpless, "Analyzing Structural Influences on Social History Data," *Historical Methods*, 2 (1978), 112–131.

28. Peter M. Blau and Otis Dudley Duncan, *The American Occupational Structure* (New York: Wiley, 1967), pp. 402–403, 405–406.

29. Ravitch, *Revisionists Revised*, pp. 112–115.

30. U.S. Bureau of the Census, Department of Commerce and Economic Statistics Administration, *The Social and Economic Status of the Black Population in the United States, 1974*, Current Population Reports, Special Studies, Series P–23, No. 54 (Washington, D.C., 1975), pp. 30, 37.

31. Ibid., pp. 123, 126.

32. U.S. Commission on Civil Rights, *Social Indicators of Equality for Minorities and Women: A Report* (Washington, D.C.: U.S. Government Printing Office, 1978).

33. Ibid., pp. 14, 18, 20.

34. Ravitch, *Revisionists Revised*, pp. 11, 171, 115.

35. Ibid., p. x.

36. See, for instance, the totally uncritical review in the *Wall Street Journal* or the long review by Peter Clecak in *The Chronicle [of Higher Education] Review*, 16 October 1978, 14–15. Clecak accepts as accurate all Ravitch's substantive criticisms of the revisionists. His review is accompanied by an interview with Ravitch. The effect is to buttress her image as a fair, objective commentator. Reviewers should compare the accuracy of a criticism against the texts it attacks. The point, though, is that these reviews, like Ravitch's book, are attempts, masked by assertions of objectivity and fairness, to discredit radical scholarship.

37. Diane Ravitch, *The Troubled Crusade: American Education, 1945–1980* (New York: Basic Books, 1984).

38. See, for instance, Frank F. Furstenberg, Jr., Theodore Hershberg, and John Modell, "The Origins of the Female-Headed Black Family: The Impact of the Urban Experience," in Theodore Hershberg, ed., *Philadelphia: Work, Space, Family, and Group Experience in the Nineteenth Century* (New York: Oxford University Press, 1981), pp. 435–454; Clarence J. Karier, Paul C. Violas, and Joel Spring, *Roots of Crisis: American Education in the Twentieth Century* (Chicago: Rand McNally, 1973); Joel Spring, *The Sorting Machine: National Educational Policy since 1945* (New York: David McKay, 1976).

39. Clarence Karier, "Liberal Ideology and the Quest for Orderly Change," in *Roots of Crisis*; Spring, *The Sorting Machine*.

40. Denys Vaughn-Cooke, "The Economic Status of Black America—Is There a Recovery?" in National Urban League, *The State of Black America 1984* (Washington, D.C., 1984), p. 21.

41. Ravitch, *Troubled Crusade*, p. 45.

42. Diane Ravitch, "A Debate on Education: Diane Ravitch Comments, Deborah Meier Replies," *Dissent*, Spring 1984, p. 223.

43. Ibid.

44. Ravitch, *Troubled Crusade*, p. 221.

45. Ibid., p. 303.

46. For example, ibid., pp. 268–269.

47. Ibid., pp. xi–xii.

48. Chester E. Finn, Jr., Diane Ravitch, and Robert T. Fancher, eds., *Against Mediocrity: The Humanities in America's High Schools* (New York: Holmes and Meier, 1984).

49. Deborah Meier, " 'Getting Tough in the Schools,' " *Dissent*, Winter 1984, pp. 61–70, and Ravitch, "A Debate on Education," pp. 225–228. Ravitch objects vigorously to Meier's criticism, which she claims quotes her inaccurately and distorts her meaning. Although Meier did not quote accurately in some places and did leave the impression that Ravitch was more explicit about some of her views than she was, she is right about the thrust of the story.

50. Ravitch, *Troubled Crusade*, p. xii.

51. Ibid., p. 330.

52. Paul E. Peterson, *The Politics of School Reform, 1870–1940* (Chicago: University of Chicago Press, 1985). Peterson stresses the achievements of educational reform and tries to reduce the influence of class. His creation of straw men and obsessive attacks on what he misrepresents as revisionist history, coupled with his strenuous attempts to avoid the role of class in his own data, undercut his useful research and leave him unable to weave his important observations into a coherent and consistent interpretation.

53. Ira Katznelson and Margaret Weir, *Schooling for All: Class, Race, and the Decline of the Democratic Ideal* (New York: Basic Books, 1985).

6. The Moral Crisis of the University

1. Clark Kerr, *The Uses of the University* (Cambridge, Mass.: Harvard University Press, 1963), pp. v–vi.

2. Paul Axelrod, *Scholars and Dollars: Politics, Economics, and the Universities of Ontario, 1945–1980* (Toronto: University of Toronto Press, 1982); Peter N. Ross, "The Establishment of the Ph.D. at Toronto: A Case of American Influence," in Michael B. Katz and Paul N. Mattingly, eds., *Education and Social Change: Themes from Ontario's Past* (New York: New York University Press, 1975), pp. 193–214.

3. Kerr, *Uses of the University*, pp. 18, 20.

4. Ibid., pp. 49–50, 90–91.

5. Ibid., pp. 23, 98–99.

6. Ibid., p. 115.

7. Francis Wayland, *Thoughts on the Present Collegiate System in the United States* (1842), in Richard Hofstadter and Wilson Smith, eds., *American Higher Education: A Documentary History*, vol. 1 (Chicago: University of Chicago Press, 1961), pp. 356–375.

8. "Francis Lieber on the Purposes and Practices of Universities, 1830," in Hofstadter and Smith, *American Higher Education*, pp. 297–300.

9. Edward Slosson, *Great American Universities* (1910), in Hugh Hawkins, ed., *The Emerging University and Industrial America* (Lexington, Mass.: D.C. Heath, 1970), p. 66.

10. Colin B. Burke, *American Collegiate Populations* (New York: New York University Press, 1982), pp. 215–234.

11. Laurence R. Veysey, *The Emergence of the American University* (Chicago: University of Chicago Press, 1965), p. 311.

12. Quoted in ibid., p. 346.

13. Thorstein Veblen, *The Higher Learning in America* (1918; reprint, New York: Hill and Wang, 1957).

14. Veysey, *Emergence*, pp. 350–352.

15. On this theme see David F. Noble, *America by Design: Science, Technology, and the Rise of Corporate Capitalism* (New York: Alfred A. Knopf, 1977).

16. Burke, *American Collegiate Populations*, p. 222.

17. Michael B. Katz, "From Theory to Survey in Graduate Schools of Education," *Journal of Higher Education*, 37 (June 1966), 325–334; Arthur G. Powell, *The Uncertain Profession: Harvard and the Search for Educational Authority* (Cambridge, Mass.: Harvard University Press, 1980).

18. Stephen J. Diner, *A City and Its Universities: Public Policy in Chicago, 1892–1919* (Chapel Hill: University of North Carolina Press, 1980). On the academic freedom cases see Mary Furner, *From Advocacy to Objectivity: A Crisis in the Professionalization of American Social Science* (Lexington: University of Kentucky Press, 1975).

19. See Furner, *From Advocacy to Objectivity*.

20. Walter P. Metzger, *Academic Freedom in the Age of the University* (New York: Columbia University Press, 1955), pp. 194–216.

21. Furner, *From Advocacy to Objectivity*, p. 8.

22. Veysey, *Emergence*, p. 353.

23. Carol S. Gruber, *Mars and Minerva: World War I and the Uses of the Higher Learning in America* (Baton Rouge: Louisiana State University Press, 1975).

24. Axelrod, *Scholars and Dollars*, passim; Joel Novek, "University-Industry Interaction: Graduates and Jobs," *Social Sciences in Canada*, 11 (December 1983), 8–9.

25. Frederick Rudolph, *The American College and University: A History* (New York: Alfred A. Knopf, 1962), pp. 455–461, 479–485; Daniel Bell, *The Reforming of General Education: The Columbia College Experience in Its National Setting* (New York: Columbia University Press, 1966).

26. Robert Paul Wolff, *The Ideal of the University* (Boston: Beacon Press, 1969), pp. 36–42.

27. Ibid., p. 127.

28. Regina Austin, Jean Crockett, Michael B. Katz, and Robert E. A. Palmer, "Report to the Senate Executive Committee from the Committee to Review the Administrative Actions Pertaining to the ATO Incident," (University of Pennsylvania) *Almanac*, 30 (December 13, 1983), 3–6.

Index

Academic freedom, 169–171, 179
Academies, 22, 38, 39, 40, 41, 133
Adams, Brooks, 84, 88, 104, 105
Adams, Charles Francis, Jr., 85, 87
Adams, Henry Carter, 169
Addams, Jane, 147
Adolescence, and institutionalized dependence, 120–121
American Association of University Professors, 170
American Federation of Teachers, 121
Apologist case for American education, 146, 151
Axelrod, Paul, 161, 172

Barnard, Henry, 43, 44, 45
Bates, Joshua, 92
Behavior regulation, and bureaucratization, 70–71
Bemis, Edward W., 169
Beverly high school, 141, 142, 143
Bicknell, Thomas, 70, 98, 99
Bilingualism, 47
Blau, Peter M., 148
Boston: incipient bureaucracy in, 58–110; English High School, 60; Latin School, 60; Prince School, 102–103
Boston Masters' Association, 91
Boston Primary School Committee, 47, 48, 53, 60, 66
Boutwell, George, 41
Bowles, Samuel, 146, 148

Brace, Charles Loring, 9
Braverman, Harry, 15
Brownson, Orestes, 33, 37, 56
Bureaucratization of education, 118, 120, 126; incipient bureaucracy, 8, 41–56, 58, 71; in Boston, 58–110; criticism of early Boston system, 72–91; in universities, 165–166; and democratic procedures, 175–176
Burke, Colin, 165

Calhoun, Daniel, 124
Capitalism, 20, 21–22; and schooling, 12–15; and universities, 167
Carnegie Corporation: Study of the Education of Educators, 112
Centralization of education, 126, 127; and incipient bureaucracy, 44–45, 53; and bureaucratization, 59, 60, 70, 74, 87, 109; in universities, 182
Class analysis, 6, 7, 14–15, 127–128, 141–142, 147–148
Class bias: and free schools, 31; and incipient bureaucracy, 46–47
Class size, 121
Class Structure in the Social Consciousness, 116
Clinton, DeWitt, 28
Commons, John R., 170
Competence, social implications of, 131
Complexity of administration, and bureaucratization, 66–68, 71, 79

Compulsory education, 50–53, 119

Conservative educational agenda, legitimation of, 152–159

Control of education, 25, 134; and paternalistic voluntarism, 26–27, 55; and democratic localism, 32–33, 55; and corporate voluntarism, 39–40, 55; and bureaucratization, 59–60, 109; in universities, 162–163, 169, 171

Corporate voluntarism, 37–41, 54–55, 164

Cremin, Lawrence, 129

Crime, as moral problem, 17, 19, 52, 95

Crisis in the Classroom, 112–114

Cultural diversity, 17–19, 47–48; and paternalistic voluntarism, 29

Democratic localism, 32–37, 41–43, 54–55

Democratic politics, 6–7; and schooling, 15–16; and paternalistic voluntarism, 28–29; and bureaucratic forms, 175–176

Dewey, John, 147, 166

Dialectical conception of social policy, 118–124

Differentiation of function, and bureaucratization, 59–61, 68

Discretion, and bureaucratization, 59, 65

Discrimination, elimination of, 118

Dobb, Maurice, 12

Domesticity, 11–12

Dreeben, Robert, 115–116

Duncan, Otis Dudley, 148

Economic develoment, promotion of, 6, 130

Effective school movement, 126–129

Eggleston, Edward, 122

Eliot, Samuel, 84, 90, 99

Ely, Richard, 169

Enrollment statistics, 138

Equality of opportunity, 117–118

Etzioni, Amitai, 109

Eugenics movement, 125

Excellence, social implications of, 129–132

Expertise in performance, and bureaucratization, 59, 64

Family: redefinition of, 7, 9–12; decline in size of, 11

Finance of education, 25, 127; and paternalistic voluntarism, 27, 55; and corporate voluntarism, 39, 54–55; and incipient bureaucracy, 50–51, 55; and democratic localism, 55; and bureaucratization, 72–73; federal support of universities, 162, 171; responsibility-based budgeting, 177

Fitzgerald, John E., 74–75

Ford Foundation, 145

Free schools, 12, 25, 26, 31, 55

Friedrich, Carl, 59

Furner, Mary, 170–171

Gaffield, Thomas, 103, 104

General education movement, 171–172

Gintis, Herbert, 146, 148

Gould, Stephen Jay, 125

Grading of schools, 45, 61

Great School Wars, The, 147

Gruber, Carol, 171

Gulliver, J. P., 38–39

Hall, G. Stanley, 121

Hamilton, Gail, 73, 85, 86, 87

Harris, William Torrey, 96

Haskell, Thomas, 140

Hereditarian theories, 124–125, 151

Hierarchy of teaching positions, and bureaucratization, 61, 64, 68–69, 87, 90

Higher Learning in America, The, 166

Hinsdale, Burke A., 65, 73, 85, 86, 87

Historical realism, 5

Historical scholarship, 5, 6, 10, 23, 111, 134, 136–137, 171–172; statistical techniques, 137–144; critical history, 144–152; conservative educational history, 152–159

Hitchcock, Edward, 39–40

Hoosier schoolmaster, myth of, 36–37, 122

Hyde, George, 84, 93

Ideal of the University, The, 178

Immigration, 7, 12, 17, 18

Incipient bureaucracy, 8, 41–56, 71

Industrialization, 6, 7, 10, 12, 20

Inequality, legitimation of, 116–118

Intelligence of a People, The, 124

Isbell, Lydia A., 103–104

Jensen, Arthur, 125
Jones, David Lamar, 14
Junior high schools, failure of, 112–113

Kaestle, Carl, 12, 15, 137–140
Katznelson, Ira, 15–16, 159
Kerr, Clark, 161–163, 165, 171, 178

Lasch, Christopher, 15, 123
Laslett, Peter, 10
Learning problems, 124

Managerial class, 119–120
Mann, Horace, 32, 42, 46, 49, 50, 96
Marketplace, influences of, 163–164,
    166–167, 170, 171, 176–178, 180
Massachusetts: democratic localism in,
    32–35; State Board of Education, 32–
    33, 50, 138; incipient bureaucracy in,
    45, 51; compulsory education in, 51–
    52; corporate voluntarism in, 54
Meier, Deborah, 157
Meritocracies, 131
Mindlessness, as cause of educational fail-
    ure, 113–114
Minority sensibilities, and incipient bu-
    reaucracy, 46
Monitorial system, 16, 28, 121
Multiversity, 171, 178; origins of, 161–
    169

Nation at Risk, A, 156
National Academy of Education, 145, 151
National Commission on Educational Ex-
    cellence, 130–132
National Council of Education, 70, 98
New York Free School Society, 12, 25,
    26, 42
New York Public School Society, 12, 25–
    30, 32
Normal schools, 33, 54
Norwich (Conn.) Free Academy, 38–39

Objectivity, and bureaucratization, 59, 64
Occupational mobility, 148
Ontario Institute for Studies in Education,
    174–176
On What Is Learned in Schools, 115
Open classrooms, 122
Organizations, professional, 98, 99, 170,
    176
Ossowski, Stanislaw, 116

Parker, Francis, 58, 71, 81, 101–105
Paternalistic voluntarism, 25–32, 49, 53,
    55, 56
Payne, William H., 67, 69
Pedagogy: and incipient bureaucracy, 49–
    50; and bureaucratization, 85–86; au-
    thoritarian, 123–124
Pennsylvania: free schools in, 31; demo-
    cratic localism in, 35; incipient bureau-
    cracy in, 45; compulsory education in,
    51–52
Permissive innovations, 122–123
Peterson, Paul, 159
Philanthropic associations, 8
Philbrick, John Dudley, 60, 67, 76–77,
    79–83, 91–93, 109
Politics: and bureaucratization, 69–70, 71,
    75; and educational excellence, 132. *See
    also* Democratic politics
Poverty, as moral problem, 17, 19, 95
Precision and continuity, in bureaucratiza-
    tion, 59, 64
Professionalism, 25, 98–99, 126; and pa-
    ternalistic voluntarism, 27, 55; and
    democratic localism, 33, 54–55; and in-
    cipient bureaucracy, 45–46, 55; and
    corporate voluntarism, 55; and bureau-
    cratization, 60, 70; and university fac-
    ulty, 171
Progressivism, 125, 126, 144
Publications, professional, 98–99
Public educational systems: formation of,
    6–7, 14–15, 21; purposes of early sys-
    tems, 16–23; and corporate voluntar-
    ism, 41; criticism of early Boston public
    schools, 72–91; results of, 115–118;
    failure of, 124–126, 128; redefinition
    of, 132–135

Qualification for office, and bureaucrati-
    zation, 59, 64
Quincy public schools, 101

Racial issues, 148–150
Ravitch, Diane, 144–150, 152–158
Reform schools, 51, 54
Religiosity: evangelical Protestantism, 15,
    50; and paternalistic voluntarism, 29–
    30; and incipient bureaucracy, 46
Revisionists Revised, The, 144–145
Rickoff, Andrew, 93, 94

Rigid formalism, and bureaucratization, 85–86, 89, 93, 118
Ross, Edward R., 170

Scale of organizations, 25; and paternalistic voluntarism, 30; and corporate voluntarism, 54–55; and democratic localism, 54–55
School attendance, 138
School boards, locally elected, 54, 74, 75, 78, 80, 83, 132
Schooling for All, 159
School-leaving statistics, 138–139
Seaver, Edwin, 100, 106, 107
Secondary education, 130; and corporate voluntarism, 37–38; in Boston, 60–61
Semiautonomy of children, 10
Silberman, Charles, 112–114, 123
Slosson, Edward, 165
Social conflict, 127–128
Socialization function: of schools, 6, 16, 19, 22–23, 43–44, 46–47, 55–56, 96, 115; of families, 10–12; and paternalistic voluntarism, 27–28
Social mobility, 21–22, 148
Social order, maintenance of, 6, 14, 16, 17, 28, 52, 96, 122
Social policy, 118–124
Social research, 127
Social welfare: state responsibility for, 6–7, 8, 12, 14, 52; institutions, 7–9, 12
Socioeconomic groups, and school-leaving, 139
Specialization: of institutions, 10–11, 14; and bureaucratization, 68, 89; promoted by universities, 167, 172
Spencer, John C., 32
Stevens, Thaddeus, 31, 52
Student behavior, 70–71, 180–182; revolts during 1960s, 171
Supervision: and incipient bureaucracy, 45; and bureaucratization, 59–60, 67, 69, 76–77, 79, 80, 89, 92, 106–109; of student behavior, 180
Systems of public education. *See* Public educational systems

Teachers: feminization of teaching, 12; appointment and promotion of, 59, 64; hierarchy of teaching positions, 61, 64, 68–69, 87, 90; salaries of, 61, 121, 130, 167; training of, 112, 167–168

Tenure system, 64, 170, 171, 179, 180
Tetlow, John, 78
Thompson, E. P., 19
Troubled Crusade, The, 152–153, 157
Tyack, David, 46

Unionization of university faculty, 176–177
Universities: multiversity, 161–169, 171, 178; federal financing of, 162, 171; marketplace influences on, 163–164, 166–167, 170–171, 176–178, 180; bureaucratization of, 165–166; enrollment in, 165; specialization promoted by, 167, 172; teacher training departments, 167–168; and public service, 168–169; academic freedom, 169–171, 179; tenure system, 170–171, 179–180; core curriculum, 171; fragmentation of, 172; unionization of faculty, 176–177; moral crisis of, 177–183; responsibility-based budgeting, 177; as communities of learning, 178–179; as decentralized institutions, 182; justice within, 182
Urbanization, 6–7, 12, 17, 20; and democratic localism, 42–43; and incipient bureaucracy, 48; and bureaucratization, 65–66

Veblen, Thorstein, 166
Veysey, Laurence, 165, 166, 171
Vinovskis, Maris, 137–143
Violence in schools, 121–122, 160, 180–181
Voluntarism: paternalistic, 25–32, 49, 53, 55, 56; corporate, 37–41, 54–55, 164

Wayland, Francis, 164
Weir, Margaret, 15, 16, 159
Westboro reform school, 51
White, Hayden, 5
White, Richard Grant, 73, 87, 94, 95
Wickersham, J. P., 95
Wolff, Robert Paul, 178
Women: cult of true womanhood, 11–12; feminization of teaching, 12; unequal pay for, 12
Working class, formation of, 6–7, 14–15

Zelizer, Viviana, 11